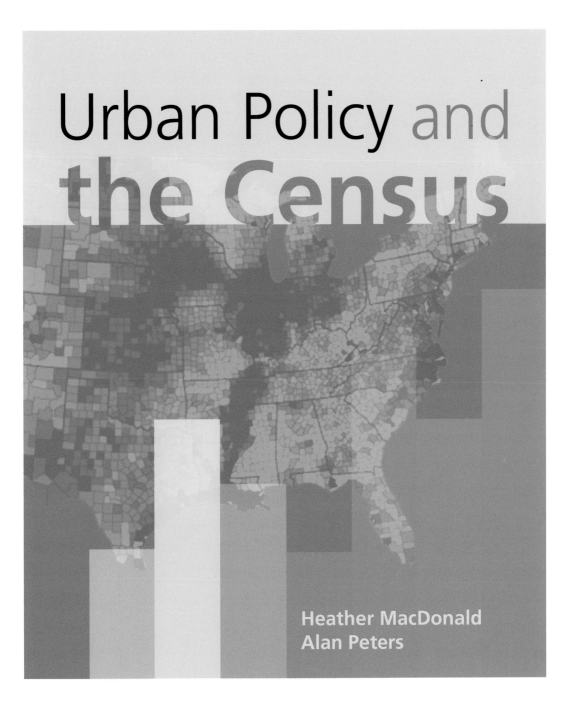

Urban Policy and
the Census

Heather MacDonald
Alan Peters

Esri Press
REDLANDS|CALIFORNIA

Esri Press, 380 New York Street, Redlands, California 92373-8100

Printed in the United States of America

Library of Congress Cataloging-in-Publication Data
MacDonald, Heather I. (Heather Isabella), 1960-
    Urban policy and the census / Heather MacDonald, Alan Peters. -- 1st ed.
        p. cm.
    Includes bibliographical references and index.
    ISBN 978-1-58948-222-7 (pbk. : alk. paper)
    1. Urban policy--United States. 2. American community survey. 3. United States--Census. I. Peters, Alan H. II. Title.
    HT123.M13 2011
    307.760973--dc2   2011002644

Ask for Esri Press titles at your local bookstore or order by calling 800-447-9778, or shop online at www.esri.com/esripress. Outside the United States, contact your local Esri distributor or shop online at www.eurospanbookstore.com/esri.

Esri Press titles are distributed to the trade by the following:

In North America:
Ingram Publisher Services
Toll-free telephone: 800-648-3104
Toll-free fax: 800-838-1149
E-mail: customerservice@ingrampublisherservices.com

In the United Kingdom, Europe, Middle East and Africa, Asia, and Australia:
Eurospan Group
3 Henrietta Street
London WC2E 8LU
United Kingdom
Telephone: 44(0) 1767 604972
Fax: 44(0) 1767 601640
E-mail: eurospan@turpin-distribution.com

Contents

List of figures and tables   vii

Preface   xi

Acknowledgments   xiii

Chapter 1   Introduction to the U.S. Census   1

Chapter 2   Mapping continuous measures: The American Community Survey   15

Chapter 3   Interpretation and communication   33

Chapter 4   Analyzing demographic and social data   53

Chapter 5   Analyzing housing data   71

Chapter 6   Analyzing economic data   97

Chapter 7   Analyzing transportation data   121

Chapter 8   Making sense of the data   139

References   163

About the authors   173

Index   175

List of figures and tables

Figure 1.1   Children in households headed by grandparent, Lake Co., Indiana, 2000   2
Figure 1.2   Hierarchy of census geography   11

Figure 2.1   Family poverty rates, Pittsburgh, Pennsylvania, 2000 and 2007   19
Figure 2.2   Carpooling, Flathead, Montana, 2000–05   20
Figure 2.3   Commuting mode confidence intervals, Flathead, Montana, 2005   21
Figure 2.4   Commuting mode confidence interval comparison, Flathead, Montana, 2005   22
Figure 2.5   Bus ridership, Denver, Colorado, 1990–2000   22
Figure 2.6   Bus ridership confidence intervals, Denver, Colorado, 1990–2000   22
Figure 2.7   Carpooling confidence intervals, Flathead, Montana, 2000–05   24
Figure 2.8   Carpooling range estimates, Flathead, Montana, 2000–05   26
Figure 2.9   Carpooling geographic confidence intervals, Flathead, Montana, 2000–05   28

Figure 3.1   Election results by state, population, and Electoral College, 2008   35
Figure 3.2   Election results at county level, 2008   36
Figure 3.3   Election results at county level, party split, 2008   36
Figure 3.4   Linguistically isolated non-English-speaking households, Hennepin Co., Minnesota, 2000   40
Figure 3.5   Linguistic isolation by language group, Hennepin Co., Minnesota, 2000   42
Figure 3.6   Language and linguistic isolation census question   43
Figure 3.7   Imputed responses for English ability, Hennepin Co., Minnesota, 2000   46
Figure 3.8a   Households that speak a foreign language   48
Figure 3.8b   Linguistically isolated households that speak a foreign language   48
Figure 3.9a   Foreign-language speakers, quantiles, Hennepin Co., Minnesota, 2000   50
Figure 3.9b   Foreign-language speakers, equal intervals, Hennepin Co., Minnesota, 2000   50
Figure 3.10   Eugene Turner's Life in Los Angeles   52

Figure 4.1   Households and families   56
Figure 4.2   African American racial change, Houston, Texas, 2000 to 2005–07   58
Figure 4.3   "Some other race," San Diego, California, 2000   60
Figure 4.4   Hispanic "some other race," San Diego, California, 2000   62
Figure 4.5   In-migrants living in different metropolitan area last year, Houston, Texas 2005–07 average   64
Figure 4.6a   Disability census question, 2000 and 2005   65
Figure 4.6b   Disability question reworded for ACS, 2005   65
Figure 4.7   ACS subjects, PUMS   66
Figure 4.8   Super-PUMAs, Montana and New Jersey   68

Figure 5.1   Homeownership rate changes, Florida, 2005–07   74
Figure 5.2a   Overcrowded renter households, San Diego, California, 2000   80
Figure 5.2b   Severely overcrowded renter households, San Diego, California, 2000   80
Figure 5.3a   Homes without complete plumbing, Alaska, 2000   82
Figure 5.3b   Homes without complete plumbing, Missouri, 2000   82
Figure 5.4   Median gross rent, San Diego, California, 2000   84
Figure 5.5   Cost-burdened renters, Massachusetts, 2005–07   86
Figure 5.6a   Cost-burdened owners with mortgages, Massachusetts, 2005–07   88
Figure 5.6b   Cost-burdened owners without mortgages, Massachusetts, 2005–07   88
Figure 5.7   Building permits, starts, completions, 2004–09   92
Figure 5.8   Residential vacancy rates, Gary, Indiana, first quarter, 2009   94

Figure 6.1   Poverty rates among school-age children, unified school districts, Arizona, 2007   102
Figure 6.2   Near-poverty, uninsured population, Missouri, 2006   104
Figure 6.3   Measures of employment, Rhode Island, 2007   106
Figure 6.4a   Workers in professional, scientific, technical services industries, Boulder, Colorado, 2000   108
Figure 6.4b   Workers in professional occupations, Boulder, Colorado, 2000   108
Figure 6.5   Grocery stores and liquor stores, Maryland, 2002   114
Figure 6.6   Construction firms, Florida, 2005–07   116
Figure 6.7a   Employment concentrations, Portland, Oregon   118
Figure 6.7b   Labor sheds, Portland, Oregon   118

Figure 7.1   Reverse commuters, Hennepin Co., Minnesota, 2000   124
Figure 7.2a   Work trips by public transport (residence), New Jersey, 2005–07   126
Figure 7.2b   Work trips by public transport (workplace), New Jersey, 2005–07   126
Figure 7.3a   Change in work trips by public transport, New Jersey, 2000 to 2005–07   128
Figure 7.3b   Change in work trips by public transport, Missouri, 2000 to 2005–07   128
Figure 7.4a   Change in work trips (less than 15 minutes), Portland, Oregon, 2000 to 2005–07   130
Figure 7.4b   Change in work trips (more than 45 minutes), Portland, Oregon, 2000 to 2005–07   130

Figure 7.5   Change in retail industry workers driving alone to work, Rhode Island, 2000 to 2005–07   132

Figure 7.6   Low-income female workers, Austin, Texas, 2000   134

Figure 7.7   Work destinations, Allegheny and Montgomery Cos., Maryland   135

Figure 8.1   Chinese American population, New York City's Chinatown   140

Figure 8.2   Sample frame for survey of housing conditions, selected for census tract in Scott Co., Iowa   148

Table 1.1   Children in households headed by grandparent, Lake Co., Indiana, 2000   3

Table 1.2   American Community Survey release schedule by area population   6

Table 2.1   Midyear estimates for travel time, Bronx, New York (minutes)   26

Table 2.2   Differences between ACS and Census 2000 estimates   30

Table 2.3   Household self-response and nonresponse rates, 2000   31

Table 5.1   Imputation rates for tenure, units, year, Massachusetts, 2000   78

Table 5.2   Imputation rates for housing cost variables, Massachusetts, 2009   90

Table 6.1   Poverty thresholds, 2007   100

Table 6.2   Recreation-, arts-, entertainment-sector classification schemes   110

Table 6.3   Geographic coverage for establishment-based economic data   113

Table 8.1   Spatial aggregation of administrative data used by NNIP partners   158

Preface

Local governments face increasingly complex decisions on how to maintain or regain economic prosperity, ensure social stability, and pursue improvements in quality of life for all residents. An array of federal and state-level incentives, regulations, and subsidies provides some tools toward these ends, but to be effective these tools must be carefully calibrated to local circumstances and integrated with local resources. Community advocates, elected officials, and public servants who make these policy and program design decisions often have limited analytic resources. Facts and data are abundant, but turning data into relevant and usable information requires time, skill, and wise judgment.

Recent changes to the structure of the U.S. Census, with the introduction of the American Community Survey (ACS) in 2005, have increased the potential and the pitfalls of the most widely used of these data sources. In particular, using spatially detailed information as a basis for spatially targeted decision making is more complex with the advent of continuous survey methodologies that improve timeliness but reduce precision. Methodological questions about sample error, confidence intervals, and comparability over time and between places have assumed greater importance; they are crucial questions if public debates and decisions are to be based on sound evidence. GIS analysis offers useful ways to interpret and communicate meaningful information, but to do so analysts need to consider the broader context of how that information is produced and the technical limitations of that information.

Urban Policy and the Census is intended to prepare private and public policymakers, researchers and analysts, and college students and academics for the new complexities and to use the new opportunities offered by a restructured census information infrastructure. Our focus is on spatial analysis for decision making, but the book also provides a broader perspective on the methodological challenges posed by the ACS and the decennial census. Chapter 1 introduces the census and the ACS to provide a basis for understanding the methodological issues that researchers and decision makers face. Chapter 2 explains the ACS in more detail, focusing on the challenges it poses for thinking spatially. Chapter 3 offers a more theoretical discussion of how information becomes evidence and outlines a series of considerations when using and interpreting spatial data. Chapters 4 through 7 explore census and ACS information in four substantive areas of urban policy: demographic and social characteristics, housing markets, the local economy, and transportation issues. The chapters investigate the meaning of variables, links among related data sources, and emerging strategies to address new methodological challenges. The final chapter develops a series of hypothetical study designs to illustrate how the multifaceted methodological issues can be addressed within the constraints of the available data and concludes by outlining a series of lessons for spatial analysis of census and ACS data.

This book evolved out of a decade of applied policy research projects aimed at providing sound evidence for public debates about urban policy at the federal, state, city, and county levels. During this time the use of GIS as a policy analysis tool expanded rapidly. Both authors were involved in a range of projects in a number of different roles—as analysts, academic reviewers, critics, and advisors to decision makers. Over the course of this involvement, we developed the strong sense that traditional discussions of methodology missed an important element of the challenge: very few proposed in much detail how one should make sense of the data and why an integrated understanding of how data was produced, disseminated, and used should be the starting point for spatial and other sorts of analyses. The cliché of "garbage in, garbage out" undermined much of the potential value of often-expensive and time-consuming studies that paid minimal attention to the gap between the question posed and the evidence used to answer it. We also understood the difficulty of providing carefully hedged analyses larded with complex statistical caveats to policymakers who wanted simple, easily communicable answers. This was one of the major dilemmas we faced in designing and conducting research that would have some measurable impact on peoples' lives: how to make sense of the data without making nonsense of it.

Our aim with this book is to help others resolve similar dilemmas. We have attempted to explain the technical and the epistemological challenges involved in using this new generation of census data to answer policy questions. Because census analysis is very often undertaken within a spatial or historical environment, the focus is on the difficulties of geographic and cross-time comparisons. But because many of the technical issues here turn out to be as much art as science, we have tried to show where the role of good judgment is crucial and also where and how the census needs to be supplemented by other data if analysis is to provide reasonable answers to policy questions.

Acknowledgments

It is impossible to name and acknowledge everyone who contributed to this book. Almost everyone we worked with on a wide range of applied research projects over many years did so. However, Michael Tramontina, Bret Mills, Loyd Ogle, Carla Pope, Mickey Carlson, and Rick Schloemer deserve special thanks. During the past two decades we have also been deeply involved in the institutionalization of GIS in local government and in the education of urban planners and policy analysts. An extensive network of GIS professionals helped us over this period, but Rick Havel and Jim Giglierano warrant special mention.

We owe a debt to our colleagues, especially Peter Fisher, John Fuller, and Richard Funderberg, and to several generations of wonderful students at the University of Iowa and more recently at the University of Sydney, University of Western Sydney, and University of Technology, Sydney. Some of the students deserve particular mention because of their contributions to the research projects we drew on in writing this book: Tracy Glaesseman, Li Zhang, Carrie Marsh, Ann Russett, Malynne Simeon, Christine Ralston, and Christina Kuecker. We are also very grateful for the support and assistance those institutions provided during the writing of this book, which coincided with a period of considerable professional (and geographic) upheaval in our lives.

Finally, we are grateful for the assistance Esri Press provided. Mark Henry edited the text and guided it to production. Thanks also to Peter Adams, Dave Boyles, Claudia Naber, and Judy Hawkins on the editorial team; Brian Harris in permissions; Riley Peake in cartography; and the entire production team. We are also grateful to the anonymous referees who helped us hone the book's focus.

Heather MacDonald and Alan Peters

Urban Policy and
the Census

Chapter 1

Introduction to the U.S. Census

The special value of the decennial U.S. Census is not only that it charts important social trends over time but that it does so consistently and fairly reliably for particular places. Local policymakers—school district staff, agencies providing services to senior citizens, city planners, electoral candidates, and neighborhood advocates—need not only reliable estimates of overall trends, but also spatially specific estimates that enable comparisons with neighboring communities, the state, and the nation. Without reliable, consistent, and spatially comparable census data, our ability to invent creative solutions to complex urban challenges would be far more limited. Census data is part of a national information infrastructure, and GIS plays a key role in enabling access to that infrastructure.

This book aims to help many different sorts of census users navigate this information infrastructure and understand the full potential of spatial analysis to inform urban policy. Public and private policymakers, researchers and analysts, and college students and academics should all benefit from learning about and making use of the restructured census information. Spatially refined census data offers answers to many questions local policymakers, citizens, government agencies, and nonprofit organizations all face. Access to data has become easier and less costly with continuing advances in computing capacity and GIS technology. Presenting analyses in maps rather than tables offers a far more powerful and graphic communication strategy, one that can engage decision makers and the public in new sorts of debates about spatial inequality or patterns of growth and decline that would be difficult to grasp if results were presented only in tables. For example, compare table 1.1, with all its columns and numbers, to the visual power and simplicity of figure 1.1.

As the comparison shows, mapping data makes it far easier to detect relationships and associations that we might otherwise miss. It can help us explore whether patterns in family structure are associated with other characteristics, such as the age and configuration of homes, the ethnic background of residents, or labor force participation and unemployment rates. GIS technology offers an increasingly simple and streamlined way to access and organize census data and to investigate relationships among variables and with other sorts of data.

Figure 1.1   Children in households headed by grandparent, Lake Co., Indiana, 2000

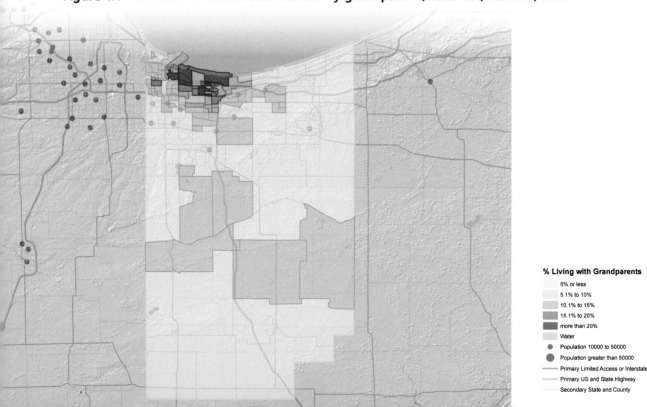

% Living with Grandparents

- 5% or less
- 5.1% to 10%
- 10.1% to 15%
- 15.1% to 20%
- more than 20%
- Water
- Population 10000 to 50000
- Population greater than 50000
- Primary Limited Access or Interstate
- Primary US and State Highway
- Secondary State and County

Table 1.1   Children in households headed by grandparent, Lake Co., Indiana, 2000

Census Tract FIPS Code	Percentage Children	Census Tract FIPS Code	Percentage Children
18089010100	9.66	18089030800	11.53
18089010201	11.22	18089030900	14.24
18089010202	22.70	18089031000	6.74
18089010203	13.70	18089040100	5.36
18089010301	24.09	18089040200	5.20
18089010302	18.96	18089040300	4.93
18089010400	18.01	18089040401	3.26
18089010500	19.44	18089040402	1.63
18089010600	19.71	18089040403	2.34
18089010700	21.76	18089040500	5.53
18089030400	9.41	18089043401	4.22
18089030500	9.55	18089043403	3.18
18089030600	6.02	18089043404	9.25
18089030700	20.80	18089043405	5.55

Source: Census of Population and Housing 2000, SF1

It is now easier than ever to think spatially about the complex structure of our society, incorporating spatial analysis into the fabric of urban policy decisions and program design at every level: from estimating the proportion of adults without a high school diploma and their likelihood of employment by county to estimating the gap between the demand for and supply of affordably priced rentals in neighborhoods close to job concentrations. Policy decisions about the need for re-skilling programs and strategies to reduce urban sprawl are enriched by the spatially consistent and comparable information available through a variety of Census Bureau data sources (and, increasingly, standardized local administrative data sources). The restructuring of part of the decennial Census of Population and Housing into a continuous survey (the American Community Survey, or ACS)—thus providing annual estimates of social, economic, and housing stock characteristics—offers new possibilities for improving the quality and timeliness of evidence on which we base many sorts of policy decisions and program evaluations. But the ACS introduces new complexities into the more detailed spatial analyses on which urban policymakers are likely to rely. For instance, because the survey is based on a much smaller sample of the population than previous decennial census surveys, ACS-based estimates for small geographic areas are less precise than those based on the 2000 census.

The U.S. Census and the American Community Survey

The word *census* came to us from the Latin *censere*, and referred to the enumeration and registration of people and property, often for the purpose of taxation. In its more modern sense (which entered the English language only in the middle eighteenth century), a census is usually understood to be an enumeration, or a count of everybody or everything. A census is a socially constructed process: decisions about whom we count (all residents, or just citizens?) and what we measure (religion, or income?) are made based on a common understanding of social structure. The political, cultural, legislative, and technological context in which each national census evolves helps explain why we have the sort of census we do today and why the U.S. Census is different than Canada's or Mexico's. This context helps explain the methodological challenges encountered in any attempt to count the population.

One of the most important of these challenges is the differential undercount of some groups of people. The undercount is a significant issue for urban policy because census estimates of local populations and their demographic and economic characteristics are the basis for distributing federal funds and for political representation. Cities with a higher proportion of the groups likely to be undercounted (compare Detroit, Michigan, which has a large and undercounted African American population, with Des Moines, Iowa, which has a small but also undercounted African American population) have a strong incentive to challenge the census count, even taking those challenges to court if necessary (Cantwell, Hogan, and Styles 2003).

People are missed for many different reasons. If people do not have permanent addresses, or the permanent addresses are not on the master address file (MAF) used to distribute surveys, they will not receive a survey form. If they are only periodic or occasional members of a household, the respondent may not list them as being part of that household or they may be counted twice. Historically, African Americans are more likely to be missed than other racial groups. Men (white or African American) are more likely to be missed than women; some researchers have argued that men are more likely to be temporary members of households (Anderson and Feinberg 1999). The age pattern of the undercount for African American males is particularly interesting. In 2000, black males ten to seventeen years of age were slightly overcounted (-1.9 percent undercount). The undercount shoots up, however, for eighteen to twenty-nine-year-olds (5.7 percent), and is even greater for thirty- to forty-nine-year-olds (9.9 percent).

Demographic analysis and special postcensus surveys can be used to estimate the size of the undercount. Demographic analysis uses records of births, deaths, migration, Medicare enrollment, estimates of emigration, and undocumented immigration to estimate how many persons (by age, sex, and race) should have been counted in the census. The method is entirely separate from the census count itself and thus provides an independent evaluation of the completeness of census coverage. To be useful, the method relies on accurate and complete administrative records. Unfortunately, emigration is poorly recorded in the United States, and undocumented immigration has increased over the past few decades, so demographic analysis may not be a good basis for evaluating the census count. However, demographic analysis can be helpful in developing assumptions about undercounts based on sex ratios. If women are less likely to be missed than men, it is possible to adjust estimates of the male population based on the female population (Anderson and Feinberg 1999).

Postcensus surveys offer a statistical alternative to administrative data sources, akin to the tagging (or capture-recapture) techniques often used to estimate animal populations in the wild. Essentially, an independent sample is drawn and each person is interviewed to determine whether the individual or the household was included or missed on the census. Statistical methods allow the success rate of these attempts to be converted into an estimate of the total population. Evaluations suggest that the undercount has declined significantly during the past sixty years, from 5.4 percent in 1940 to 1.2 percent in 1970, up slightly in 1990 to 1.8 percent followed by a sharp drop in 2000 to 0.1 percent (no estimates of the accuracy and coverage of the 2010 census are available as this book goes to press). For smaller groups, such as Native Americans and Hawaiian and Pacific Islanders, the undercount estimate was not statistically significant in 2000. But the differential undercount between owners and renters has worsened since 1990, as has the undercount of adult males younger than fifty. Unsurprisingly, the net undercount also varies by state.

The effort to reduce the undercount and the increasing difficulty of counting an ever more diverse population greatly increased the cost of the census. The 1950 census cost the equivalent of $2.50 per capita (in 1980 dollars). The 1980 census cost nearly twice that, at $4.85 per person counted. Costs increased again in 1990, and Congress became less receptive to arguments for increased funding (GAO 2004). The Census Bureau was one of the agencies targeted for elimination after the Republican landslide in the 1994 elections. Clearly, a dramatic strategy would be needed to satisfy critics on both sides: the quality of the population estimates had to improve, and costs had to be managed better (MacDonald 2006). The Census Bureau proposed moving to a sample survey as the basis for estimating the total population. Many statisticians agreed that sampling could produce a higher quality result than enumeration, because it could manage the problem of the differential undercount. It would also help contain costs,

substituting statistically defensible estimation techniques for more costly efforts to identify the housing units and people missed by conventional approaches (Prewitt 2003). However, in January 1999, the Supreme Court ruled that Section 195 of Title 13 of the U.S. Code (the census-enabling legislation) precludes the use of statistical sampling to produce congressional apportionment counts. Sampling is legal for other (nonapportionment) purposes, including redistricting.

The bureau had few alternatives, and the 2000 census went ahead with a short-form enumeration and a one-in-six sample of households for the long form (Prewitt 2003). It cost $16 per capita (a further increase from the equivalent $10.14 it cost to count each person in 1980, in 2000 dollars). Rather than an undercount, the 2000 census resulted in a slight overcount, but the accuracy differential persisted. African American men, recent immigrants, and others were still undercounted, but college students and elderly people were probably overcounted (Robinson and Adlakha 2002). Other countries faced similar problems, but solved them differently. In 2001, Britain released a One Number Census. A Census Coverage Survey was used to estimate the number and characteristics of people missed by the census, and final 2001 results were amended to reflect those missed. Statistical methods were used to estimate the undercount in areas where the Census Coverage Survey was not conducted. The Office for National Statistics estimates that the 2001 census was Britain's most accurate ever, coming within 0.2 percent of the true population (2006).

In 2010, the United States moved away from the short-form enumeration/long-form sample survey structure used from 1940 to 2000 to an initial short enumeration accompanied by a survey of social, economic, and housing characteristics in a continuous assessment to take place throughout the decade. First rolled out in 2005, the ACS was introduced to resolve several shortcomings in the traditional census: the increased costs, decreased response rates, and dated results. Other countries have resolved the same problems through other strategies: adjusting statistics, conducting a census every five years, and relying on administrative data instead of survey data. The United States decided to resolve these problems with a continuous measurement survey rather than other methods.

By all standards, the 2010 U.S. Census was a historic turning point in the decennial enumeration. For the first time since 1940, no long form was distributed. Instead, data equivalent to that gathered on the long form in 2000 has been collected and measured continuously through a new monthly survey. This approach offers far more timely data, with averages released each year for each level of census geography down to census tracts (the release schedule is shown in table 1.2). The ACS released the first five-year averages of small geographic areas (fewer than 20,000 people) in late 2010.

The annual sample size of about 3 million addresses equates to a 2.5 percent sample (12.5 percent during a five-year cycle). This is substantially smaller than the 17 percent sample for the 2000 long form, so sample error is approximately 1.3 times larger for the ACS than for the

2000 census. However, a permanent and professional staff and better quality control may result in lower rates of nonsample error (U.S. Census Bureau 2002b). The ACS changes several procedures. Only one in three nonrespondents will be followed up by phone and then by in-person visits. The characteristics of other nonrespondents will be imputed. Interviews may only be completed with a household member, not with neighbors or other informants (U.S. Census Bureau 2002b).

The annual release of ACS results provides far more current data than previous censuses. The 2000 long form data was released from August to October 2002, by which time many of its estimates were outdated. Another argument in favor of separating the count of people and basic household characteristics from the more detailed information in the long form is that doing so may boost return rates for the short form, thus improving the quality of the count. Chapter 2 discusses the ACS in far more detail, exploring its implications for census-based spatial analyses.

Sources of error

Beyond the basic problems with counting a fluid and diverse population, census enumerations and surveys are never an absolute representation of the world. Surveys, such as the ACS, encounter

Table 1.2   American Community Survey release schedule by area population

Data Product	Population	2006	2007	2008	2009	2010
1-year estimates	65,000+	2005	2006	2007	2008	2009
3-year estimates	20,000+			2005–07	2006–08	2007–0'
5-year estimates	all areas*					2005–0
* 5-year estimates will be available for areas as small as census tracts and block groups						

Source: U.S. Census Bureau, *Release Schedule for ACS Data*, http://www.census.gov/acs/www/data_documentation/data_main

both sampling error (the chance that the people randomly chosen for the sample do not represent the population being generalized) and nonsampling error (the chance that the information generalizations are based on is inaccurate). Enumerations are not based on samples, but are vulnerable to nonsampling error.

Sampling error

In principle, we could survey every resident of every state to gather data on all the questions on the ACS. In practice, the cost would be prohibitive, not just in dollar terms, but also in terms of the responses we would lose as the costs in time to individuals rise. The 2000 census long form sampled one in six housing units on average. In other words, a single household was answering questions (hypothetically) on behalf of five other households. In the case of the ACS data reported in 2010, a single household may provide data for between seven (in the case of five-year averages) or as many as thirty-nine other households (in the case of the one-year averages released for larger places). The accuracy of these estimates depends in part on how typical the people within the sampled housing units are to others within the geographic area.

Understandably, the population characteristics we estimate based on sample responses will not be identical to those we would obtain from an enumeration of characteristics. However, as long as they are close enough, less precision may be a worthwhile trade-off against exorbitant costs and lower response rates. In statistical terms, we care about the extent of sampling error.

Fortunately, we can estimate the size of sampling error reasonably well and calculate a margin of error (or confidence interval) around our survey results. A one-in-ten sample from a town with a population of 100 will have larger errors than a one-in-ten sample from a town with a population of 30,000. Two identical-size samples from identical-size populations may also have quite different sampling errors. One community may be far more diverse than another, so the chance that each randomly chosen household can be assumed to look roughly like five other households is smaller in the more diverse community. We estimate sampling error based on the size of the sample relative to the population and the extent of variability within that population.

In previous censuses, users would calculate sampling errors and confidence intervals based on formulas provided in the technical documentation (U.S. Census Bureau 2007a). The technical definition of a confidence interval is the range of values within which we could expect a certain percentage of all possible means from an infinite number of similar sized surveys of the population to fall. In other words, were we to take an infinite number of surveys of the number of children under age five living in families, the 90 percent confidence interval would be the range of values that included 90 percent of survey results. Calculating confidence intervals around estimates mattered in previous censuses if one was concerned with small estimates or small places. However, sampling error has become a much more central concern with the introduction of the ACS because the survey data is based on a much smaller sample. To make it easier

2011	2012	2013
2010	2011	2012
2008–10	2009–11	2010–12
2006–10	2007–11	2008–12

to consider the effect of error, all ACS estimates are published with their confidence intervals.

Sample surveys are not only less expensive and less annoying to respondents. They may also be more accurate, or at least no less accurate, than enumerations. Consider again the issue of the undercount. If our enumeration is likely to miss particular groups of people (because they are less willing to speak to government officials or are only loosely attached to households), our estimates of population characteristics will be biased (Prewitt 2003). Statistical adjustments can correct for this error, which results not from sampling the population, but from the social context in which we try to count people.

Nonsampling error

Better quality control, such as training and overseeing interviewers more thoroughly and checking data entry processes in more ways, could eliminate other random but nevertheless damaging sources of error. More careful pilot testing of responses could narrow the conceptual gap between the question researchers think they're asking and the question respondents think they're answering. These are all examples of nonsampling errors. They apply to enumerations just as much as to sample surveys, and they may be more difficult to estimate and thus control. One of the Census Bureau's arguments for the ACS is that continuous surveying will allow for a permanent, skilled interviewing staff, and that this will help reduce some nonsampling errors (Alexander 2001).

Some sources of nonsampling error are almost impossible to reduce or eliminate. People answer questions incorrectly. They lie about their age or the value of their home (a nonrandom source of error). They round off estimates instead of reporting the precise value (for instance, they round the

length of their work trip to the nearest five-minute interval) (U.S. Census Bureau 2002b). The line between accurate and inaccurate answers is a fine one.

An important subset of nonsampling errors is an incomplete or inaccurate sample frame or universe. For most urban households, the universe is defined by the master address file (MAF). The MAF begins with the U.S. Postal Service delivery sequence file. This is then checked and updated by the relevant local government in the Local Update of Census Addresses (LUCA) program. Building, demolition, conversion permits, street construction, and renaming all help to update the postal files (U.S. Census Bureau GD 2006a). About 80 percent of U.S. households receive census questionnaires in the mail.

Households living in areas without city-style street addresses (much of the rural United States) have their questionnaires delivered to their homes. Again, local governments play a key role in ensuring that all rural residents are included, but in some places this is far more difficult to guarantee. In sparsely settled and rugged countryside, some Native American reservations, and unorganized county subdivisions, the sample frame may not be as complete as in ex-urban Kansas City or Philadelphia (Van Auken et al. 2004). Densely settled city neighborhoods pose other sorts of challenges. Single-family homes may have been converted informally into multiple units. Where people live in overcrowded conditions (the case for many recent immigrants), a household may be difficult to define (de la Puenta 1995). As of mid-April 2010, census participation rates in 124 New York City census tracts were less than 40 percent, compared with rates of 72 percent for the nation as a whole, in part because of the difficulty of identifying dwelling units (Virella 2010).

Ethnographic research investigating why coverage varies among different ethnic groups suggests that incomplete address lists may be partly to blame (in addition to factors such as not wanting to have anything to do with the government). Illegally divided and unmarked apartments, complex households of migrant workers where day-shift workers share beds with night-shift workers, and informal housing alternatives such as tents or cars do not show up on U.S. Postal Service delivery routes or on local government administrative records (de la Puenta 1995). Counting the homeless population is incredibly difficult, and attempts to do so in the 1990 and 2000 censuses failed (GAO 2003).

In preparation for the 2010 census, tests and dress rehearsals were conducted in several locations that posed enumeration challenges: the San Joaquin Valley, California; the Fayetteville, North Carolina, region; Travis County, Texas (part of the Austin metropolitan area); the Cheyenne River Reservation, South Dakota; Queens County, New York; and rural southwestern Georgia. Handheld computers and GPS devices were tested as a strategy to improve the census address list and to improve directions to enumerators (U.S. Census Bureau GD 2006b). The LUCA program, established in 1994, involves local governments in improving the MAF. But participation in LUCA does not guarantee that the complex residential structures of high poverty neighborhoods will be mapped accurately. Although improvements in local GIS systems promise to increase accuracy through the LUCA program, they will not eliminate all errors. Some households and individuals will remain too difficult to count.

Nonresponse rates are another type of nonsampling error. After the 2010 census, census enumerators telephoned or visited households that did not complete the form. A total of 74 percent of households completed the 2010 census questionnaire. The law requires people to respond to the census, but many people could (or would) not be contacted. Interviewers could ask neighbors about the missing respondents, but neighbors were usually unable to answer many of the more detailed questions. In these cases, the Census Bureau imputes the missing answers. In other words, the household is assigned the characteristics of a nearby household, or one of similar ethnic origin, age, or some other relevant attribute (U.S. Census Bureau 2007a). Imputation processes are discussed in more detail in chapter 3. Imputation methods are often debatable, with no clearly agreed best way to provide some kinds of missing data.

Counting the U.S. population is a daunting task. The 2000 census encountered methodological problems with the census count, with demographic analysis, and with the Accuracy and Coverage Evaluations (ACE) that estimated census coverage (U.S. Census Bureau 2003b; Robinson 2001; Robinson and Adlakha 2002). As this book goes to press, the Census Bureau faces a new set of challenges in evaluating the results of the 2010 census. Did the improvements to the MAF enable a more complete enumeration? How did economic turmoil alter response rates and the validity of the address file? Were some groups under- or overcounted in 2010?

Conceptual census framework

Data is not a random collection of facts: its usefulness depends on how it is organized, summarized, and accessed. Census data is organized according to population and geographic categories. In this section, we introduce the conceptual framework that underpins what we might think of as a giant filing system.

The population framework

The census divides the population into two categories:

- population in households, which are defined as people who share living quarters. They are further divided into
  - ✓ family households (made up of people related by blood or marriage)
  - ✓ nonfamily households (made up of single people, roommates, or other unrelated people). Although the census identifies unmarried-partner households, they are classified as one type of nonfamily household.
- group quarters population, which includes everyone not living in households. People living in group quarters are further divided into
  - ✓ the institutionalized population (in places such as prisons or mental health facilities). As a rough guide, people are institutionalized if they are not free to leave the institution (a prison warden living within a prison would be part of the group quarters population, but would not be counted as institutionalized)
  - ✓ the noninstitutionalized population (in places such as college dormitories, homeless shelters, or migrant worker hostels). Noninstitutionalized residents are free to leave the residence

The census aims to count everyone living in the United States, regardless of whether they are citizens, temporary residents, or undocumented migrants. In practice, because the census is address-based, it has been difficult for previous censuses to count people who are homeless. However, U.S. citizens living outside the country at census time also are not counted. The state of Utah sued the U.S. Census Bureau after the 2000 census, arguing that population estimates were deflated because many Utah residents living abroad as missionaries for the Mormon Church were not counted. Utah lost the case because the census is intended to count residents rather than voters (Cantwell, Hogan, and Styles 2003). This has been a continuing source of dissension: children, and legal and undocumented migrants are included in census population estimates for apportionment, but registered voters living abroad are not.

The geographic framework

Census data is spatially aggregated for several reasons:

- to protect confidentiality for individual responses (by aggregating the characteristics of every respondent in an area, it is impossible to identify the characteristics of individuals)
- to provide reasonably reliable statistical estimates of the characteristics of people living in a particular place (such as a city, neighborhood, or block)
- to provide summaries (i.e., tables at various summary levels) in a form useful for local decision making

Local areas are defined according to two overlapping classification schemes:

- Political boundaries, such as counties, cities, parishes, congressional districts, and Native American trust lands. This system seems straightforward but gets complicated once we consider that cities can cross county (but not state) lines, and that states differ in how they define local jurisdictions (Louisiana, Hawaii, Alaska, Puerto Rico, and all states in New England have quite different categories of *places*).
- Boundaries that are used mainly for statistical and data-reporting purposes (census blocks,

tracts, and metropolitan or micropolitan areas). In practice, these artificial concepts have acquired real meanings. Neighborhoods are often defined for planning purposes by census tracts, because such a division streamlines data availability. Statistical boundaries coincide with county boundaries, but not necessarily with city and state boundaries.

Figure 1.2 summarizes the hierarchy of statistical entities and shows how they can overlap with political entities.

Census blocks are the basis from which larger statistical units are created; to enhance comparability over time, they are redefined as little as possible. Local governments help define census tracts, which in principle are meant to be relatively homogenous areas with easily identified physical boundaries (in practice, this can be quite difficult, and census tract definitions rarely reflect residents' views of their neighborhoods). Census tracts are often split or amalgamated to reflect population growth or decline over the previous decade, and GIS is an invaluable tool for developing a historically comparable geographic framework. Using GIS, you can combine or split tracts to create a consistent unit of comparison over several different censuses. For instance, if a particular 2010 tract represented 42 percent of a 2000 tract, you can use the blocks that made up the tract-equivalent in 2000 to create a 2010 definition tract that has 2000 census characteristics. GIS simplifies what would otherwise be a very tedious operation. Counties change their boundaries far less often, although it does happen. After the 2000 census, Colorado acquired a new county, Broomfield (contiguous with the boundaries of Broomfield City), made up of parts of Adams, Boulder, Jefferson, and Weld counties. State boundary changes are even less common and tend to be minor realignments.

Figure 1.2   Hierarchy of census geography

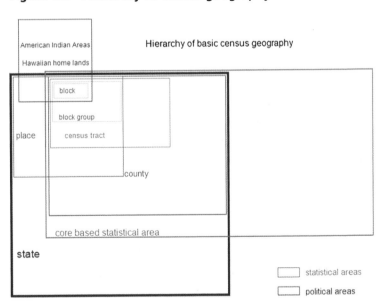

Counties are grouped or classified according to their degree of urbanization and their economic interactions. Metropolitan statistical areas (MSAs) are defined based on urbanized population and the degree of commuting between adjacent counties. MSAs may be made up of one or several counties. A set of adjacent primary MSAs with some interaction (such as Gary, Indiana, and Chicago-Joliet-Naperville, Illinois) make up a consolidated MSA (such as Chicago). Metropolitan areas provide a useful way to visualize many sorts of concepts: regional job market trends, transportation systems and their environmental impacts, and future demands for water supply infrastructure. They allow us to understand trends across several different cities, counties, and even adjacent regions of different states. But while it makes sense to think about some problems at a metropolitan level, the fragmentation of political authority makes it difficult to take action at that scale (although collaborative efforts have developed in a few metro areas).

Micropolitan areas were a new classification introduced after the 2000 census to distinguish cities smaller than metropolitan areas from their more sparsely populated hinterlands. The old distinction between metropolitan and nonmetropolitan has been replaced by a more fine-grained distinction between core-based statistical areas (CBSAs, which include micropolitan and metropolitan areas) and areas outside CBSAs. Confusingly, this is not equivalent to our common-sense distinction between urban and rural areas. In practice, urban includes densely settled locations with a population greater than 2,500, and rural includes places with fewer than 2,500 people (along with agricultural land and open country). Counties included in metropolitan areas can include substantial rural populations, and many urban places exist outside CBSAs.

The hierarchical structure of census geography is far more complex than the basic classification scheme described here; it is defined in detail on the Census Bureau's Web site and in a useful reference publication (U.S. Census Bureau GD 2009a). In addition to the basic classification schemes summarized above, census data is tabulated for several other kinds of districts (school districts, a variety of voting and legislative districts, ZIP codes, and traffic analysis zones). The structure of census geography is the basis for the system of unique identifiers assigned to each geographic entity—the American National Standards Institute (ANSI) codes, which replaced FIPS (Federal Information Processing Standards) codes (U.S. Census Bureau GD 2009b).

Census product formats

Census data is released in several formats for use in different ways. The key issues that govern decisions about census data publication formats are confidentiality and statistical validity. Title 13 of the U.S. Code requires the census to protect the confidentiality of respondents. Census workers must take an oath to protect the privacy of respondents, and security is ensured for the actual surveys. Most important, various techniques are used to prevent the use of census results to identify individuals. Summarizing responses at various levels of spatial detail is one strategy to ensure confidentiality. Because they are based on a minimum sample size, spatial summaries also ensure that estimates are precise enough to be meaningful. Thus, ACS data, like sample data from previous censuses, is not released at the census block level (the lowest level of census geography) because the confidence intervals around the estimates would be so wide that the data would be meaningless.

Census products offer a range of formats to meet different user needs.

Summary files are available at various summary levels, corresponding with the geographic hierarchy. Data is cross-tabulated by the Census Bureau. For example, published tables show median household income by age of householder, poverty status by race, and number of bedrooms by gross rent. Tables are listed in the technical documentation available for each census data product. Not all tables are available at all summary levels. It is important to consider the universe from which the table is drawn: Does it include all people, only workers in the labor force, or only those over the age of 65? Is it for all housing units or only occupied units? Are housing values presented for all owner- occupied housing units, all single-family detached units, or all mobile homes? Cross-sectional data provides spatial detail useful for presenting profiles and comparisons of geographic areas, but is rigid. One cannot analyze relationships among variables that are not cross-tabulated (for instance, level of educational attainment and disability status).

Public use microdata sample (PUMS) data is a sample of a sample and is released in the form of individual records, not summary tables. PUMS data enables us to design our own cross-tabulations and to perform analyses that are not possible on the cross-sectional data in the summary files. In each row of a PUMS database, we find a single individual's (or household's) characteristics: their age, whether they are disabled, their highest level of education, the income they earned in the previous year, and so on. Thus we can investigate the relationship between educational attainment and disability status and test whether or not this is associated with income, for example. Because such detailed data would obviously violate privacy if it were released at a detailed geography, PUMS data

is released only at the level of public use microdata areas (PUMAs). PUMAs include about 100,000 people; thus, at best, we can perform our own analyses only for subareas of a large metropolitan area. In more sparsely settled places, PUMAs might include several counties. PUMS data is discussed in more detail in chapter 4.

Census transportation planning package (CTPP) data is cross tabulated by traffic analysis zones (TAZs), for work-trip origins and destinations. The data is available in three files. The first two summarize worker characteristics by place of residence and place of work. The third file shows work-trip flows between pairs of TAZs. CTPP data is discussed in more detail in chapter 7.

Census reports are also published in a variety of formats. Brief profiles of economic, demographic, housing, and social characteristics provide a convenient quick reference format. Special reports on topics such as the work-life earnings of people with different levels of education, population mobility, or trends in fertility, often present analyses based on cross tabulations that are not available to the public because they might endanger individual confidentiality.

Conclusions

Spatial analyses can offer new insights into the social, economic, and other trends charted in various census products. The U.S. Census has evolved over a full cycle, from a minimalist enumeration in 1790 to a detailed survey on a range of characteristics during the twentieth century, and back to a minimalist enumeration in 2010. The ongoing tensions among cost, coverage, and accuracy continue to shape debates over the role of the census. More detailed economic, demographic, social, and housing data are now provided through annual releases of the ACS estimates. Although ACS estimates are more up to date, they are less precise than the estimates of previous censuses, which affects the sorts of spatial analyses that are possible. The census's methodological challenges fall into two categories: sampling error and nonsampling error. Both affect how users should approach the data. Sampling error can be estimated and controlled (at least in principle) through choices about sample size. Nonsampling error is more diverse and more difficult to control. The conceptual structure of the U.S. Census establishes the categories of people and places for data reporting. The geographic framework defines a hierarchy of political and statistical units, which constitute the summary levels at which data is released. The spatial boundaries of some of those units may change over time as the population and economic activity change. The next chapter examines the implications of the methodological changes the ACS makes in how we gather and interpret social, economic, and other data.

Chapter 2

Mapping continuous measures: The American Community Survey

The ACS promises to transform the way we measure and thus understand our society, culture, and economy. Continuous measurement, the Census Bureau tells us, offers a "video" rather than a "snapshot" (Alexander 2002, 2). But what does that metaphor really mean, and in particular, what does it mean for those of us mapping the data? In this chapter, we discuss four important reasons continuous measurement transforms our analytic framework:

- The ACS redefines who makes up a community: it offers an abstract compilation of the year-round population, rather than a point-in-time picture.
- Averaged data smooths out variability that point-in-time snapshots may capture.

- Sampling households continuously rather than once a decade enables the Census Bureau to keep a permanent professional staff, thus improving data quality.
- Cost-control decisions have dictated a smaller sample of addresses, and consequently a higher sample error in ACS than in the 2000 Census of Population and Housing (CPH 2000).

The first section of this chapter examines each of these themes in more detail.

Two ACS characteristics pose new challenges for spatial presentations of census analysis. First, higher sample errors make it more difficult to present data in ways that are meaningful but not misleading, especially given the range of sample errors for different variables. Because one-year estimates are released only for larger places, big cities will have data that is far more current than that for smaller cities, which will make geographic comparisons more complex. We discuss the implications of these challenges in the second section of this chapter, and outline the choices analysts must make to address them.

The third section of the chapter summarizes a wealth of research on the differences between the ACS, the 2000 Census of Population and Housing (referred to here as Census 2000), and the Supplementary Survey carried out simultaneous with the census in 2000 (referred to here as C2SS). C2SS was designed to test the ACS methodology and provide a benchmark for comparison. This section of the chapter highlights key comparisons between the 2000 census and 2010 data releases from the decennial census and the ACS. Later chapters provide more detailed discussions of how specific variables have changed.

Continuous versus point-in-time measurement

When casual data users look up a community's unemployment rate or median income on the American FactFinder page on the Census Bureau Web site, they are unlikely to think much about how the data is constructed from raw survey responses. But data is constructed through several choices: about spatial scale and the continuity or discontinuity of that scale over time; about the categories used to distinguish people in different parts of the employment continuum (employment, unemployment, out of the labor force); and about what counts as income (only wage earnings and investment income, or other sources such as alimony).

Continuous measurement produces different sorts of data than point-in-time measurement does, because it is collected differently, it deals with time and space differently, and it enables us to define new sorts of categories (such as part-year residence), and makes others (such as residence on a particular date) irrelevant. In this section, we discuss two logical differences (dictated by the structure of continuous rather than point-in-time surveys) and two contingent differences (which are not logically necessary, but a result of choices made in a particular economic and social context). It is helpful to discuss each separately, but in practice they are linked.

First, continuous measurement offers an abstract picture of community residents averaged over the course of a year (or several years), rather than a specific representation of residents as they are on one particular day. Thus, just as artist George Braque's still life of apples showed us perspectives we would not see staring at even the most artful arrangement of apples, the ACS shows us at least glimpses of the population—the vacationers, retirees, people displaced by economic disruption, and migrant farm workers—we may not see if we visit a community on April 1.

To offer this abstract schematic, the Census Bureau must use several intervening adjustments if the data is to be accessible to the general public. Household income, for instance, is both averaged (with peaks and troughs within the reporting period smoothed over), and also indexed to current dollars. The information we have on income from the ACS is not directly comparable to the information we had on income in 1999 (as reported in Census 2000). It is mediated by several other methodological choices (such as the choice of index), as well as reflecting fourteen definitions of the previous year (the twelve survey cycles plus two months of follow-up). This is a necessary rather than a contingent feature. Although the data must be manipulated to be meaningful to a general audience, there is nothing inevitable about the precise methodological choices made.

Third, the ACS sample households are surveyed gradually over time, rather than simultaneously on a census day. Thus, for any given sample size, the Census Bureau can use a much smaller but permanent staff. A permanent professional staff enables higher-quality follow-up on surveys—and consequently in principle—higher-quality data (U.S. Census Bureau 2004). It is a practical rather than necessary outcome of using continuous surveys.

Finally, the ACS five-year sample size (the period for which averaged census tract-level data is reported) is roughly 12.5 percent of addresses in the master address file (MAF), smaller than the 17 percent sample used for the 2000 CPH. Thus, sample error is substantially higher in ACS census

tract data releases than in 2000 CPH releases (U.S. Census Bureau 2004; Salvo et al. 2007). For some variables with small numbers of respondents (such as people who walk to work in suburban Orange County, California), sample errors will be much higher than for variables with many respondents (those who drive alone to work in Orange County). Thus, there are likely to be gaps in what we can say about different population attributes. Higher sample error is a result of budget choices rather than a necessary feature of continuous measurement (MacDonald 2006).

Implications of necessary differences

Are fluid definitions of how a community looks on average over the year a more accurate schematic picture than point-in-time snapshots, offering a better basis for decisions about health-care services, traffic congestion, or housing needs? They may be, because they can capture needs that may not be explicit at any one time, such as the need for Spanish-language health-care workers to serve Spanish-speaking farm workers. But because continuous measurement averages out the picture, it also introduces significant blurring and smooths down peak demand—in practice, temporary housing demand isn't driven by average numbers but by peak flows (of students, tourists, or farm workers). However, in many cases those needs were not reflected in our point-in-time snapshots. The ACS does not estimate the actual numbers of population groups—these are reported, but numbers are benchmarked to the Population Estimates Program (to which ACS estimates also contribute), the appropriate source of intercensal estimates of population by age, race, and ethnicity (discussed further in chapter 4).

More important, continuous measurement also averages out attributes that may differ substantially across groups of residents. Household income measures based on the April 1 population would be very different than income measures reflecting the migrant farm workers of summer, or the retiree snowbirds of winter. Comparing trends in income, educational attainment, and the characteristics of the occupied housing stock from 2000 to 2010 requires careful consideration of whether we are seeing real changes in community attributes rather than the effects of including a different, more diverse set of residents in our sample. For instance, including seasonal residents in two retirement-destination Wisconsin counties (Oneida and Vilas) changed community profiles in several ways (Van Auken et al. 2004). The composition of household income was substantially different in parts of the two counties, with much higher proportions of households in some tracts earning retirement income. Vacancy rates were lower, and home ownership rates and median home values were higher. Over time this difficulty will diminish as we move further away from point-in-time comparisons, but it poses some challenges during the next few years.

Reported averages are based on different periods for different sizes of communities, as we explained in chapter 1. Thus, one-, three-, and five-year averages will be reported for metropolitan places and large counties; three- and five-year average data will be reported for micropolitan places and medium-sized counties; and five-year average data will be reported for nonmetropolitan places, smaller counties, and census tracts. The averaging periods are driven by cumulative sample sizes. This has several implications for analysts.

First, five-year samples for large places will be much larger than five-year samples for small places,

and so precision will be greater for estimates at the city rather than census tract level, for instance. Second, averages over different lengths of time will be centered on different midyear estimates (MYEs). A three-year average reported in 2010 would be based on 2007, 2008, and 2009, and the mid-point of this estimate would refer to 2008. A five-year average reported in 2010 would refer to 2005, 2006, 2007, 2008, and 2009; the MYE would refer to 2007. Although the Census Bureau emphasizes the need to compare apples with apples and use the averaging period appropriate for the smallest place in a comparison, this may be politically difficult to ensure in all cases (we discuss this problem in more detail below).

Implications of contingent differences

One argument for moving from a point-in-time to continuous measurement approach to detailed census data was the rising cost of the traditional census (GAO 2004). In the political debate over whether the ACS should go forward, the Census Bureau argued that it offered a way to slow cost increases in the future (U.S. Congress 2003). Finally, the bureau had to accept a scaled-back ACS program to manage costs. Instead of the 5 percent annual sample proposed in 1997, which would have enabled shorter averaging periods for most geographies and sample errors comparable to those of decennial censuses, the final ACS legislation provided for a sample size that equated to approximately 2.5 percent of the nation's 2005 addresses. The differences related to sample errors result from policy choices that could change rather than any inherent differences between point-in-time and continuous data.

The Census Bureau argues that although sample error is higher for the ACS, nonsample errors (in particular, the error resulting from non-response, miscoding, inexperienced temporary staff, and inadequate quality control) are lower. Evaluations of the ACS test program concluded that because nonresponse rates were lower than in Census 2000, the nonsample error introduced through imputation and allocation was lower in the ACS (U.S. Census Bureau 2004, 4–5). But even if nonsample error is reduced, it cannot be eliminated. Being alert to nonsample error is still important in assessing ACS results, especially those indicating dramatic swings in community characteristics.

No matter how far nonsample error is reduced, higher sample error constrains what we can reasonably conclude from ACS estimates. Sample error varies: it is higher for some groups, and in some places. Figure 2.1 compares the 90 percent confidence intervals around 2000 census estimates with those around 2007 ACS estimates, for the city of Pittsburgh. Although estimated 2007 poverty rates for most sorts of families appeared to be higher than in 2000, once we consider sample error, clear conclusions about trends in poverty rates are difficult to draw.

Although we can conclude poverty rates increased in Pittsburgh between 2000 and 2007, we cannot say much about how they might have changed for the families most likely to be in poverty—single-mother families with young children. Because far fewer Pittsburgh families are headed by single females than by couples, the ACS survey would have to oversample this group to maintain a comparable margin of error around estimates of their characteristics. Although the ACS sample has been adjusted in some places to oversample minority households, widespread adjustments for many different sorts of groups (if we oversample families headed by single females, why not elderly Asian-American households?) would result in the uncontrolled growth of sample size, and thus, costs. It is ironic that the groups most in need of targeted resources often may be the most difficult to "measure" in meaningful ways. We might draw better conclusions about poverty-rate trends among families headed by single females citywide based

Figure 2.1 Family poverty rates, Pittsburgh, Pennsylvania, 2000 and 2007

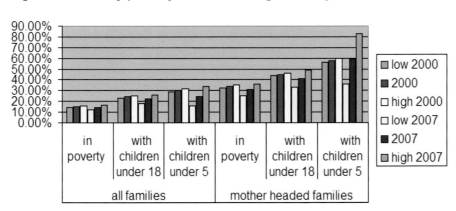

Source: Census of Population and Housing 2000, SF3; ACS 2007

on five-year averages, but the data would be less current.

However, it would be more difficult to draw conclusions about this group at the census tract level. Figure 2.2 uses five-year average data to demonstrate another dimension of sample error: it varies not just across groups but also across places. Confidence intervals around estimates of Flathead, Montana, residents carpooling to work are proportionately much wider than those around estimates of people driving alone. But the relative width of confidence intervals also varies across census tracts.

In absolute terms, the confidence interval around drive-alone estimates is larger than around carpool estimates (figure 2.3). But when we consider the proportional size of the sample error, we see that it is proportionately larger around the carpool category, and that it is wider in smaller tracts with fewer commuters (figure 2.4).

Are transit planners facing a major crisis as data they rely on for policy assessments and recommendations effectively disappears? The problem of wider sample errors around some group estimates is not unique to the ACS: it existed in the decennial censuses too, but most users ignored it. Because transit riders have constituted such a small share of commuters (at least since the Census Bureau started collecting data on them in the 1960 census), estimating trends in ridership at detailed spatial scales has always been a risky business. The following two figures demonstrate the shaky nature of conclusions based on tract level bus ridership as reported in the 1990 and 2000 censuses.

Figure 2.2   Carpooling, Flathead, Montana, 2000–05

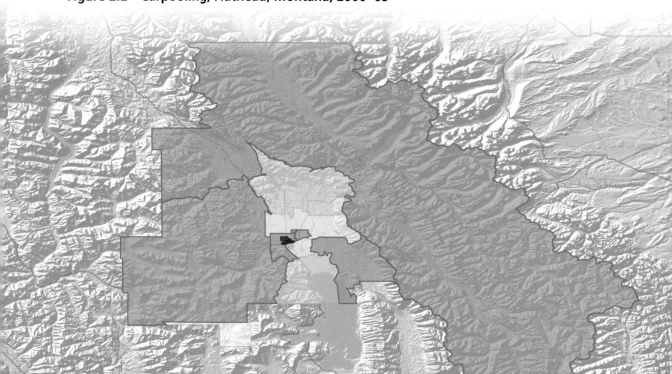

Figure 2.5 uses decennial data from the 1990 and 2000 censuses to analyze whether bus ridership increased or decreased in an arbitrary selection of census tracts from Denver, Colorado, during the 1990s. There appear to be several substantial differences in ridership trends over the decade, from a decline of 44 percent in one tract, to a gain of 111 percent in another. Evidence seems to indicate that commuting by bus has changed in many tracts during the decade.

However, bus riders make up a fairly small percentage of commuters in each tract. A closer look at the sample errors around these estimates (figure 2.6) demonstrates that our evidence may be much less conclusive than we first thought. In the tract with the largest decline (501), where the percent of commuters riding the bus declined from 9 percent

to 5.03 percent, once we consider the confidence intervals around those two estimates (from a low estimate of 5.22 percent in 1990 to an upper estimate of 7.46 percent in 2000), it is not clear that ridership has declined. In only two tracts (401 and 402) is it reasonable to argue that bus ridership changed significantly during the decade. Although the ACS exacerbates the problem and makes it more difficult to ignore, wide margins of error were a problem for decennial census-based analyses too: we were just more likely to ignore them.

Increased sample error is probably the major negative of the ACS compared to the decennial census. As argued, this resulted from a particular set of political and financial choices made when Congress passed the ACS legislation in 2004. Perhaps this reflects the ambivalence of our social

% Work trips by carpool

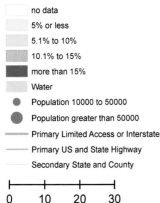

- no data
- 5% or less
- 5.1% to 10%
- 10.1% to 15%
- more than 15%
- Water
- ● Population 10000 to 50000
- ● Population greater than 50000
- —— Primary Limited Access or Interstate
- —— Primary US and State Highway
- —— Secondary State and County

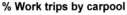

0   10   20   30
Miles

Figure 2.3 Commuting mode confidence intervals, Flathead, Montana, 2005

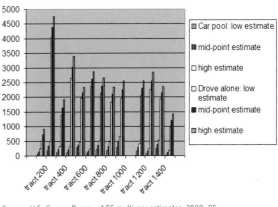

Source: U.S. Census Bureau, ACS multiyear estimates, 2000–05

Figure 2.4 Commuting mode confidence interval comparison, Flathead, Montana, 2005

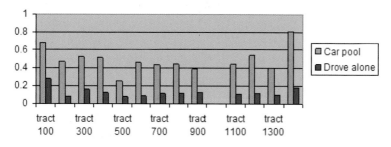

Source: U.S. Census Bureau, ACS multiyear estimates, 2000–05

Figure 2.5 Bus ridership, Denver, Colorado, 1990–2000

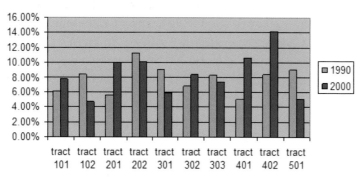

Source: Census of Population and Housing 2000, SF 3; 1990, STF 3.

Figure 2.6 Bus ridership confidence intervals, Denver, Colorado, 1990–2000

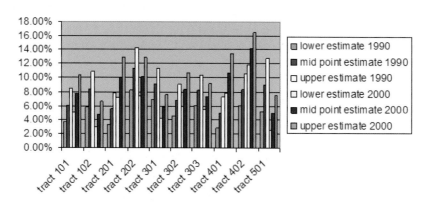

Source: Authors' calculation based on Census of Population and Housing 2000, SF 3; Census of Population and Housing 1990, STF 3.

commitment to high-quality data. Remember also that the choice was not necessarily one between the ACS and a 2010 census identical to its 2000 counterpart. We might have seen significant reductions in sample size in a 2010 census to control rising costs, without the benefits of timeliness or the improvements in scope and data quality the ACS offers.

Solving ACS mapping challenges

Given that estimates have become much less precise, especially at finer spatial scales, we cannot expect the ACS to provide the same basis for analysis as previous decennial censuses. The ACS offers new sorts of capabilities: mid-census estimates, more timely updates for larger areas, and new information about year-round communities. But it brings with these capabilities new limitations: discontinuities in trends because variable definitions or collection methods have changed, and some loss of precision, especially for smaller places. This new set of constraints and opportunities raises three issues for the analysis and presentation of spatial data from the ACS:

- How do we decide whether spatial analyses are justified?
- When we decide to use ACS data for spatial analyses, how should we convey confidence intervals?
- How do we address geographically uneven data?

This section outlines the practical and often ethical choices to be made in answering these questions.

When are spatial analyses justified?

In some cases, ACS data will not be precise enough to serve as a basis for meaningful geographic comparisons. For some variables (among them public transit ridership and poverty rates for mother-only households), the groups of interest are too small to enable us to draw any precise spatial comparisons based on ACS data alone. It will still be possible to talk about small groups at the metropolitan, county- or in some cases city-wide level, but census tract-level comparisons are probably not valid.

This is not an easy stance to take. Too often, research clients are less concerned with the provenance and validity of evidence than they are with its existence; in the view of some, any numbers are better than no numbers. Evidence *is* often used as window dressing for entrenched positions rather than as an objective basis for deciding among many options (Starr 1987; Skerry 2000; Innes 1990). If spatial comparisons will help argue for the client's preferred position, why not present them despite their statistical imprecision?

This is a complex choice. On the one hand, using fuzzy but recent data may be argued to be no worse than what we've been doing for decades—using somewhat more precise but older data that is updated using questionable methods. At least the small print about sample error defines the extent of inaccuracy with the ACS. On the other hand, meaningless data undermines the power of all evidence and gradually erodes everyone's trust in the idea that some places or people really are worse off than others, and are in greater need of help. If we don't have any concept of facts to refer to, why not make policy decisions purely on the basis of political expediency, tribal ties, or some other affiliation? At a more practical level, weak evidence used as a basis for bad advice is unlikely to build the long-term reputation of any professional researcher, and the ethical choices posed by drawing conclusions based on inconclusive data should be carefully considered.

But fuzzy data is not always and inevitably bad data. If it is intended as a way to educate elected officials or the public about broad spatial trends rather than serving as the basis for firm programming commitments with hard costs, even fuzzy data may have a role to play. If it is supported by other evidence (for instance, bus ridership rates by route, or school-level participation in free lunch programs), even fuzzy data may gain some legitimacy. In reality, "it all depends" may be a more appropriate answer to a question than yes or no. The choice then may be framed around a series of smaller questions:

- What sort of variable or subgroup are we interested in, and at what spatial level? Are there ways to recategorize the groups or spatial levels to improve precision?

- What is the purpose of this analysis? How important is precision in the context of what is being asked of the analysis?
- Could corroborating data be used to strengthen the validity of the ACS estimates?

Our argument is that analysts need to be fully aware of the limitations posed by ACS and other data if they are to understand how to address those limitations. Communicating those limitations to the audience is the next issue we consider.

Conveying differences in data precision

Once we decide whether data is reasonably useful for spatial analyses, our next responsibility is to clearly convey data limitations to our audience. But full disclosure needs to be balanced against

Figure 2.7 Carpooling confidence intervals, Flathead, Montana, 2000–05

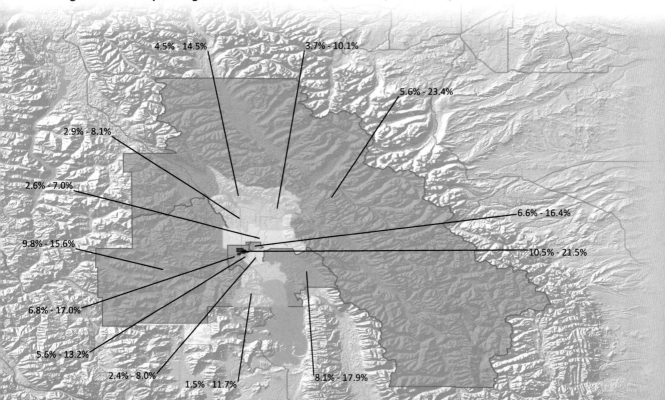

confusion. How can maps—two-dimensional spatial representations—convey ACS estimates and the interval around those estimates? Essentially, we need to add a third dimension to each map, conveying the width of the confidence interval as an overlay on the primary theme. A variety of ways can show the precision of data on an overlay. Figure 2.7 uses labels to indicate the range defined by a confidence interval.

Although straightforward, this method doesn't work well for the small tracts clustered around the urban center. It also isn't a particularly visual method of presenting the range: one has to read this map, rather than being able to grasp its point at a glance.

Figure 2.8 presents the same information using graphs. This is a more visual approach, but it suffers from the same problem labels do: too much information is clustered in the smaller tracts.

Figure 2.9 offers an alternative approach: identifying geographic areas with narrower and wider confidence intervals. If we were investigating change over time, we could use a similar method to indicate where changes are statistically significant, based on confidence intervals around estimates from each period.

Addressing geographically uneven data

Some sorts of imprecision result from the nature of the variables we focus on, others from the nature of the locations we are comparing. Ideally, ACS data would be infinitely flexible, so we could split up and recombine spatial categories to approximate similar levels of precision. This is not yet possible.

An alternate approach would be to use the shortest averaging period available for all the geographies we wish to compare but present the data at the finest available spatial scale. A statewide comparison at the census tract level would thus avoid some of the sharp disparities between larger and smaller counties and places, although more densely populated geographies would have far more detail. A regional comparison might use three-year averages at the county level. A similar graphic approach to that presented in figure 2.9 could distinguish variations in precision by place.

Tucker McElroy (2007) presents a creative solution to the dilemma that the averages reported for different-sized places differ in age. Rather than using an older one-year average to be consistent with the midyear estimate of a three-year (MYE3) or five-year (MYE5) average, he proposes constructing a trend filter to update the MYE3 or MYE5 value to one compatible with the most current one-year average. Essentially, time-series analysis is used to

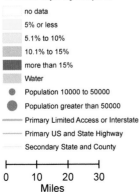

% Work trips by carpool

no data
5% or less
5.1% to 10%
10.1% to 15%
more than 15%
Water
● Population 10000 to 50000
● Population greater than 50000
— Primary Limited Access or Interstate
— Primary US and State Highway
— Secondary State and County

0   10   20   30
Miles

Table 2.1   Midyear estimates for travel time, Bronx, New York (minutes)

Year	One	Three	Five
1999	40.05		
2000	40.00		
2001	41.00	40.00	
2002	41.80	41.00	
2003	40.80	41.20	40.70
2004	40.60	41.00	40.80
2005	41.70	41.10	41.20
2006	42.04	41.28	41.45

Source: McElroy 2007, 11

backdate and forecast values for smaller places to develop comparable estimates.

Time-series analysis uses a linear regression model to smooth out the effects of seasonal fluctuations and random variation, in order to identify longer-term trends. McElroy (2007) provides more detail on the trend filter model.

Comparing the ACS with Census 2000

A key challenge the Census Bureau faced in introducing the ACS was ensuring continuity with the 2000 census. Two separate data collection efforts aimed to provide the basis for comparisons.

Figure 2.8   Carpooling range estimates, Flathead, Montana, 2000–05

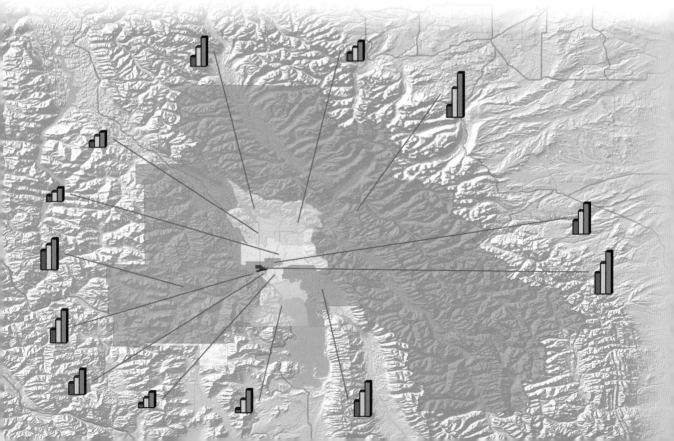

The first was the Census 2000 Supplementary Survey, which used the same operational and data collection methods as the ACS but was conducted during the same time frame as the 2000 census. C2SS information was collected from the thirty-six ACS first-wave test counties, plus an additional 1,203 counties (which were added to subsequent waves of ACS tests leading up to full-scale implementation in 2005). Although the C2SS used similar methods to the ACS, it was also a point-in-time study. The second point of comparison was the three-year average of ACS data collection in the thirty-six initial test counties, from 1999 to 2001 (U.S. Census Bureau 2004). This provided two dimensions of comparison:

- how averages centered on the 2000 census period would compare with the census long form (where methods, key definitions, and time period differed), and
- how averages would compare with data collected using similar methods and definitions but a different time period.

To ensure that comparisons were as valid as possible, ACS sample sizes were increased during the 1999 to 2001 period to be roughly equivalent to samples collected during a five-year period. This ensured that (in most cases) data could be analyzed and compared at the small-county and census-tract levels.

National comparisons of the ACS and Census 2000 concluded that the ACS operational approach was at least as good as, and may produce better quality data than, Census 2000 (U.S. Census Bureau 2004). Census 2000 respondents were more likely to mail their surveys back than ACS respondents (as expected, given the greater marketing effort devoted to the 2000 census). However, overall ACS nonresponse rates were lower than Census 2000 because of more effective follow-up with households that did not mail their forms back. ACS surveys from occupied units were likely to have more completed items, resulting in lower rates of imputation for missing items (U.S. Census Bureau 2004).

Some of the differences in substantive results for Census 2000 and the ACS and C2SS are attributed to these quality differences. Table 2.2 shows the consistency between Census 2000 and the ACS on most variables; many of the statistically significant differences detected are small (less than 1 percent) and thus not meaningful. However, the results differed both significantly and substantially on three topics: race, disability status, and vacant housing units.

% Work trips by carpool

- no data
- 5% or less
- 5.1% to 10%
- 10.1% to 15%
- more than 15%

12

- Lower
- Middle
- Upper

- Water
- Population 10000 to 50000
- Population greater than 50000
- Primary Limited Access or Interstate
- Primary US and State Highway
- Secondary State and County

0   10   20   30
Miles

Overall, the ACS (and C2SS) produced higher estimates of people who were one race only and who were white and lower estimates of those who were "some other race" or "two or more races" than Census 2000. Claudette Bennett and Deborah Griffin (2002) show that this is attributable to people who identify as Hispanics self-reporting they belonged to "some other race" or "two or more races" in Census 2000. In the ACS and C2SS follow-up with nonrespondents, skilled interviewers addressed the confusion between questions about race and ethnicity, and far more Hispanic respondents were reported as identifying with "one race" and "white" responses (this raises interesting questions about the census's underlying reliance on self-identification for both racial and ethnic categories, a point discussed further in

chapter 4). Disparities are likely to persist between the responses of self-reporting households and those who are interviewed.

Far fewer ACS respondents reported that they had a disability compared to Census 2000 respondents. Census 2000 estimates of people with disabilities were also strikingly higher than those for Census 1990. Sharon Stern (2003) argues that the wording of the question on both the census and ACS mail-back form and on the census follow-up instrument could be interpreted to mean "is this person over sixteen?" instead of serving as a filter to the question about whether a disability prevents the person working outside the home (see chapter 4 and figure 4.6 for the wording of the question and further discussion). The ACS follow-up interviews are computer-assisted

Figure 2.9   Carpooling geographic confidence intervals, Flathead, Montana, 2000–05

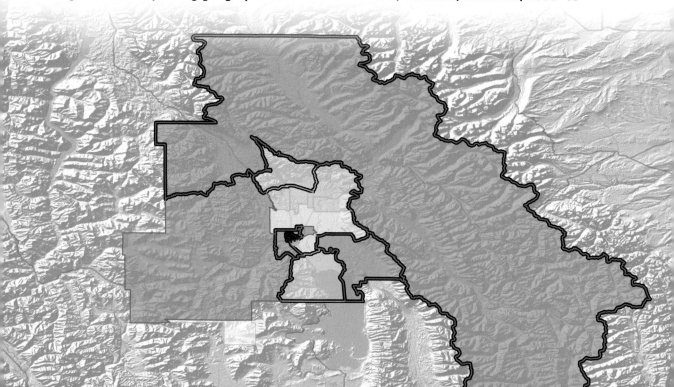

and screen out people under the age of sixteen, eliminating the filter question and thus the inappropriate responses. Again, because a higher proportion of ACS responses were obtained through direct interviews rather than self-responses, ACS estimates of people with disabilities are likely more accurate than Census 2000 estimates. The ACS mail forms were corrected once this problem was identified, and thus more recent ACS estimates of people with disabilities are likely to be reasonably accurate. Nevertheless, this issue will complicate drawing comparisons between numbers of people with disabilities in 2000 and 2010.

ACS procedures may systematically undercount vacant units compared to enumerations. The difference lies in the ACS's more limited follow-up procedures. Although every nonresponding

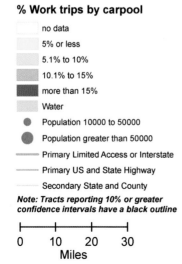

% Work trips by carpool

no data
5% or less
5.1% to 10%
10.1% to 15%
more than 15%
Water
● Population 10000 to 50000
● Population greater than 50000
—— Primary Limited Access or Interstate
—— Primary US and State Highway
—— Secondary State and County
Note: Tracts reporting 10% or greater confidence intervals have a black outline

0   10   20   30
Miles

address was contacted in the follow-up to the 2010 census, with most of the follow-up efforts occurring soon after the census day, only one in three nonresponding addresses are contacted in ACS procedures, over the two months following the survey mailing. Vacant units would only be identified through the in-person visits in the third month after the address was sampled. By that time, a vacant for-rent or for-sale unit might well have been rented or sold and may be counted as occupied by the time follow-up occurs (ORC Macro 2002; U.S. Census Bureau 2004).

School enrollment, people in the labor force, and number of rooms also showed substantial and significant differences, but these may not have important impacts on comparisons between Census 2000 and ACS 2010 estimates, as Greg Diffendahl, Rita Petroni, and Andre Williams (2004) explain. Several other variables, sixteen in all, showed statistically significant differences between ACS and Census 2000 data for the test counties, but most of these differences were small and are unlikely to materially affect the continuity required for comparisons over time.

A second series of evaluations looked in detail at ACS and Census 2000 differences in individual counties. External data sources (such as administrative records) were used to evaluate the estimates derived from each survey. These are far more revealing of potential discontinuities that may occur in particular places, even if their effects are difficult to detect at the aggregate scale of national comparisons. The evaluations highlighted an important issue: in places where response rates were very low (see table 2.3), the problem of larger sample errors was compounded.

Table 2.3 shows substantial variation among the test counties examined. But in all except one (Flathead, Montana), nonresponse rates were lower for the ACS than for the 2000 census.

Table 2.2 Differences between ACS and Census 2000 estimates

Variable	Counties with Significant Differences	Variable	Counties with Significant Differences
Sex	Few	Industry	Few
Age	Moderate	Class of worker	Moderate
Race	Many	Household income	Moderate
Hispanic	Many	Income type	Many
Relationship	Many	Family income	Few
Household type	Many	Poverty	Few
Housing occupancy	Many	Units in structure	Many
Tenure	Moderate	Year structure built	Many
School enrolment	Moderate	Number of rooms	Many
Educational attainment	Moderate	Year householder moved into unit	Few
Marital status	Moderate	Number of vehicles	Moderate
Grandparents as caregivers and veteran status	Few	House heating fuel	Moderate
Disability	Many	Selected housing characteristics	Many
Nativity and place of birth	Moderate	Occupants per room	Many
Region of birth of foreign-born	Few	Housing value	Moderate
Language spoken at home	Many	Mortgage status and selected owner costs	Few
Ancestry	Many	Selected monthly costs as percentage of household income	Moderate
Employment status	Many	Gross rent	Moderate
Commuting to work	Moderate	Gross rent as percentage of household income	Many
Occupation	Few		

Source: Diffendahl, Petroni, and Williams 2004, xviii–xviv

Table 2.3   Household self-response and nonresponse rates, 2000

County	Self-Response		Occupied Unit Nonresponse	
	ACS	Census	ACS	Census
Multnomah, Oregon	65.0	70.4	3.8	5.1
Tulare, California	50.1	63.4	3.9	10.1
San Francisco, California	57.9	65.7	6.4	12.0
The Bronx, New York	36.0	53.0	11	21
Oneida, Wisconsin	71.6	78.0	5.94	12.18
Vilas, Wisconsin	56.6	NA	10.73	14.18
Flathead, Montana	60.1	72.9	4.41	4.35
Lake, Montana	52.4	74.5	7.7	9.24
Note: Self-response rates are the proportion of households that returned the survey by mail. Occupied unit nonresponse rates are the proportion of households (occupied units) that neither mailed back the survey nor responded to follow up by enumerators.				

Source: Authors' compilation based on Hough and Swanson 2004; Gage 2004; Salvo, Lobo, and Calabrese 2004; Van Auken et al. 2004

Compensating for high nonresponse rates requires larger samples in difficult-to-survey places, which will entail corresponding reductions in sample size elsewhere. Actual five-year samples in particular places vary between 8.5 percent and 50 percent (Waite and Reist 2005), reflecting differences in population size, diversity, and survey barriers in particular locations.

Overall, evaluations of ACS methods compared to Census 2000 methods suggest that continuity is reasonably assured in aggregate, but that specific places may face greater challenges in comparing estimates over time. Places where population is more fluid, either seasonally or because of fluctuations in permanent migration, will face more challenges, because Census 2000 captured much less of that fluidity than the ACS. Over time, this discontinuity will dissipate, especially given the continuous comparisons the ACS will enable with rolling averages available annually at every geographic level (U.S. Census Bureau 2006).

But some of the disparities and discontinuities are less resolvable: some populations are simply more difficult to measure than others. Ensuring a complete and accurate master address file and gathering responses from all members of ill-defined and nebulous households can be far more difficult in some cultural (and spatial) settings than in others, as we have discussed. High rates of nonresponses and limited follow-up in the ACS will also affect comparability, despite the Census Bureau's efforts to compensate through larger sample ratios in some places.

Planners and policymakers may be able to minimize these problems and make it more likely for the ACS to provide higher-quality data. Local data quality will be determined in part by the quality of the local sample frame, and in principle at least planners and local policymakers should be able to improve that. Comprehensive and accurate GIS updates of both new development and residential conversions will help. Better developed rural data systems are an obvious area for improvement in some locations. But not all MAF updates will be feasible. When conversions have occurred under the radar of the building permit or rental inspection system, the employees of the agency with oversight responsibility may have difficulty obtaining accurate unit information. Similar barriers could face official efforts to ensure full and accurate surveys of members of marginalized households that may violate other legal or regulatory codes, such as employment authorization, public housing occupancy rules, or restrictions on residents per room. These problems are not unique to the ACS, but have an increasing impact on any attempt to measure our increasingly complex society, and are particularly important in light of the ACS's smaller sample sizes and larger sample errors.

The transformation of the census into a more up-to-date but less precise continuous measurement framework offers opportunities and challenges. Later chapters explore some of the interesting questions this raises, such as whether administrative data could be better tied to ACS estimates, and whether so-called synthetic data could provide a substitute for spatial precision.

Conclusion

The ACS will transform the analytic framework we use for census data, for several reasons. It reports data far more frequently, eliminating the need to update aged census data. The concept of residence is redefined, offering a composite "video" of the year-round population rather than a point-in-time "snapshot" of the community. Consequently, the data collected over the course of each year is averaged, inevitably smoothing out some variability. The ACS's reduced sample size will increase sample error over that of the 2000 census, decreasing the precision of its estimates. However, because the ACS enables the Census Bureau to employ a permanent, skilled professional staff, this may reduce nonsample error.

These new constraints and opportunities change our approach to analyzing and presenting spatially detailed census data. Higher sample errors make it more difficult to present data in ways that are meaningful but not misleading, especially given the variability in sample errors for different variables. The data release schedule varies based on size (urban places will have data that is far more current than rural places, for example), which will make geographic comparability more complex. Careful consideration should be given to the question of whether spatial analyses are justified for specific variables and places. If they are, it will be more important than ever to provide data-quality assessments. Ideally comparability should be maintained by using the same averaging periods for each locality. Statistical adjustments, however, could be used to maintain compatibility yet use the most up-to-date data available.

Overall, comparisons of the ACS and Census 2000 suggest that reductions in nonsample error at least partly offset the increases in sample error. More professional ACS interviewing and follow-up procedures explain the differences in results on race and disability status. However, more limited ACS follow-up explains the other major difference—on housing vacancy status—where the ACS probably provides inferior data to the decennial census.

Chapter 3

Interpretation and communication

In the darkest days of the Great Depression, city planners were paralyzed by the lack of basic information about trends in state-to-state migration, business closures, and unemployment: "In the eighth year of the severest industrial depression this country has ever experienced, the actual number of workers unemployed was still a matter of conjecture" (Neufeld 1938). How could this be? The 1930 census included questions on unemployment; President Hoover had put substantial effort into developing more sophisticated economic statistics during the 1920s. But the Census Bureau's release of early estimates in May 1930 that between 2.3 and 2.5 million people were unemployed set off a storm of protest in the news media from those who argued that the figure was in fact somewhere between 4 and 6.6 million (Anderson 1988). The intense debate over the estimates reveals the significance of the social and political context in which we define, measure, and report basic information about our society and economy. This context defines the meanings we attach to concepts such as unemployment, worker, and employer.

Social historian Margo Anderson's summary of one of many battles over unemployment statistics and the real magnitude of unemployment illustrates the impossibility of disentangling facts from how we produce them:

> *The ensuing public discussions revealed that the [Census] officials had no clear conception of how to count the unemployed when they planned the census. They thus intended to cast as wide a net as possible—ultimately providing seven measures of the number of unemployed. When Steuart [Census Bureau director] agreed to publish preliminary hand counts directly from the unemployment schedules, he chose the most conservative count possible. The administration data initially included neither the number of workers with a job but who were laid off nor new workers who were looking for jobs but had not yet found them. (Anderson 1988)*

Facts are defined by wider agreement on two underlying premises. First is what to measure: the temporarily laid off as well as those literally without a job, volunteer and family workers as well, or only those who earn wages? Second is how to measure: by asking people whether they were at work in the previous week, whether they were looking for work, or how many weeks they had been unemployed in the previous year? This story demonstrated little agreement on what should be measured or how. The Committee on Statistics of the Unemployed, set up by Hoover in 1921, had disbanded without reaching agreement on how to define the phenomenon of unemployment. Public dissension and competing claims about unemployment rates (for instance, from state governors such as Franklin D. Roosevelt of New York) both

undermined the validity of the official estimates and provided Hoover with a rationale for inaction, citing the lack of sound evidence on the extent and nature of unemployment (Anderson 1988).

Ignoring the social context in which facts are constructed limits our ability to interpret, present, and make sense of data. Policy decisions based on (or justified by) misunderstood data are especially vulnerable to attacks that may undermine perfectly sound decisions. We need to understand the production of information at both the macro level (for instance, what social phenomenon a particular indicator sets out to measure, and why it is measured in a particular way) and at the micro level (for instance, how the sample for that particular variable is composed, how the question was constructed, what the question response rates were, and the size of the sample error).

Spatial analyses raise additional considerations. During the last several U.S. elections, much has been made about the split between Red states (voting predominately Republican) and Blue states (voting predominately Democratic). Political analysts hold forth on the differences between the two camps, backed by the striking graphic of a bicolored map of the United States. Demography, history, race and ethnicity, and economic structure provide partial (but often contradictory) explanations of the divide. E-jokes circulate about the "two Americas."

The dichotomy is not strictly wrong, but it is misleading: more detailed analyses reveal a far more complex picture. Differences between large urban places (with populations of more than 500,000) and smaller suburban and rural places were much sharper than differences between whole states in the 2008 presidential election. Once we factor in the effect of the actual percentage of voters in each place that supported Democrats and Republicans and the relative size of populations in those places, the simplistic red and blue map becomes a quite different picture of regional political affiliations. Mark Newman, of the Center for the Study of Complex Systems at the University of Michigan, uses cartograms to show how the 2008 election results really looked without the distorting effects of the land area.

Figure 3.2 removes the distorting effects of land area, but the picture that remains is still of a highly polarized nation. The map also assumes that all voters within each state voted the same way—clearly not an accurate representation of the political landscape.

Newman's next set of maps breaks down results by county to show the relative weight of different counties. He goes further still, representing counties in a range of colors based on the proportion of

Republican versus Democratic voters, rather than merely red or blue. The resulting map looks anything but polarized.

These two stories about estimating unemployment and understanding election results illustrate the centrality of two sorts of challenges: of interpretation and of communication. How we solve those challenges relies on a range of methodological, technical, epistemological, and ethical considerations that shape our understanding of information and our expectations of how information shapes decisions. There are no rules defining how spatial (or other) data should be analyzed, but analyses can demonstrate better or poorer judgment, just as our understanding of data can. Rather than offering specific guidelines for good judgment, this chapter outlines the questions we should ask ourselves as we try to make sense of

Figure 3.1   Election results by state, population, and Electoral College, 2008

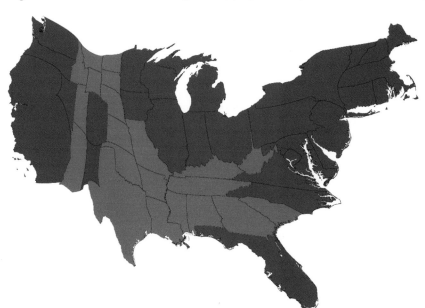

Source: Mark Newman, "Maps of the 2008 U.S. Presidential Election Race," http://www-personal.umich.edu/~mejn/election/2008/

Figure 3.2 Election results at county level, 2008

Source: Mark Newman, "Maps of the 2008 U.S. Presidential Election Race," http://www-personal.umich.edu/~mejn/election/2008/

Figure 3.3 Election results at county level, party split, 2008

Source: Mark Newman, "Maps of the 2008 U.S. Presidential Election Race," http://www-personal.umich.edu/~mejn/election/2008/

secondary data and explore its spatial dimensions, so that we can develop meaningful evidence that can inform policy. Our goal should be to become better informed and more self-critical users of census and other data sources; if we do not recognize and anticipate the flaws in our own interpretations and conclusions, others are very likely to do so.

The chapter begins by discussing how information is produced and the different ways it is used to inform and shape public policy. We discuss the nature of the evidence needed for different sorts of policy questions and review some of the key limitations faced in using census and American Community Survey data. In the next section, using an example related to local education policy, we outline five questions to guide spatial analysis of census (and similar) data. The discussion of each question addresses the methodological, technical, epistemological, and ethical considerations that should inform evidence-based policy decisions.

Information, evidence, and policymaking

The information economy has rewritten our social, cultural, and economic lives. Stock market news, sports results, weather forecasts, Internet dating sites, and restaurant reviews are instantly accessible on our mobile phones. Political campaigns are customized based on fine-grained distinctions among voter concerns. Supermarkets stock their shelves based on sophisticated spatial analyses of customer clusters and spending patterns. It is difficult to overstate the role the internet has played in our growing dependence on information. The effect is self-reinforcing: we expect an ever-wider range of information to be available electronically, and information that isn't is usually ignored. A

growing array of data, including annual releases of American Community Survey data, is available at the sort of detailed spatial scale for which GIS analyses are ideal. Public debates and decisions are now potentially enriched with a depth and quality of evidence unimagined only two decades ago.

But more information is not always equivalent to better evidence. Rather than being enriched by more information, we are often deafened by it. Furthermore, the questionable provenance, relevance, or quality of some evidence in the public realm can lead audiences to devalue all evidence, dismissing it as the product of yet another narrowly defined interest group. The significant changes to the census, the most standard of official social data sources, highlight questions about reliability and validity. Urban policy decisions will be improved if we think more critically about how information is constructed, and how it contributes to our spatial policy, planning, and other decisions.

How evidence informs policy

Evidence informs policy in four ways. First, the rational model of policymaking implies that information is used to identify new problems, to track how they differ among communities or populations, and to develop solutions. In this view, information provides objective evidence about the nature of a problem, and possible solutions. In practice, studies of the role of information in policymaking suggest that the process rarely works precisely this way (Starr 1987; Nathan 1987).

Second, policy decisions are made and then evidence is gathered to help implement policy. Instead of information and analysis defining policy, it is much more likely that policy issues will be defined in the political realm first. Often, no information exists about new problems, so policy solutions are crafted based on argument rather than evidence. Competing interest groups use available data, or collect new data, to frame positions. Once new policies are in place, new data is collected to track policy impacts and guide program targeting (Skerry 2000).

Third, evidence educates decision makers rather than informing specific policies. Social scientists argue that information is used to expand policymakers' understanding of broad concerns and the context of current problems. Judith Innes (1990) points out that policymakers value this educational role, even if they do not use data to identify specific problems or propose solutions. Rather, it forms a context for creative problem solving.

Last, evidence improves the quality of public debate. Evidence-based policy research can change the political environment by educating voters, community residents, and the general public about broader social and economic concerns. It can improve the quality of public discourse about problems and policy solutions. Evidence can help to depoliticize contentious decisions by demonstrating the basis for those decisions and empowering critics of decisions (Kingsley and Pettit 2008).

Although these models of the relationship between evidence and policymaking differ, collectively they suggest a few broad conclusions. One is that information is only collected if we have a use for it. Each question on the decennial census, the ACS, the Current Population Survey, and the economic censuses, must be justified to the Office of Management and Budget by reference to a specific policy need enshrined in legislation. Although local administrative data may have somewhat looser threshold requirements, it too is unlikely to be collected without a clear purpose. Thus, the purposes for which any specific piece of information is designed may or may not fit with the uses

to which we want to put that information. Second, the validity and provenance of information matters as much as what it tells us. Innovative data gathered and analyzed by an advocacy group may have disappointingly limited impacts on policy change. Unofficial evidence may be dismissed as biased, of questionable quality, or as too locally specific to serve as a basis for policy change. Thus, despite the clear limitations of some secondary data, we are often compelled to use it for analyses precisely because it is deemed official (Starr 1987).

The Census Bureau is an important source of relatively high-quality data, despite the methodological caveats discussed in chapter 1. But just because data is sound does not mean it will always be used appropriately, responsibly, or effectively. This is particularly so when we are dealing with fine levels of spatial detail. If we are to become more sophisticated consumers of evidence and use it to inform sound decisions, we need a more detailed understanding of what each data element means and what we may or may not say based on it.

Understanding the limitations of census data

The generalized information offered by the various census products has many advantages: it is free and easily accessible, it is widely accepted as reliable, and it is usually comparable over time and across places. However, it is rarely available in precisely the form, or for the scale and period, in which we are interested. Administrative data can often supplement census data, but it may not be comparable with other places or periods, and it may raise confidentiality or quality concerns. Gathering precisely the data we need is expensive and time consuming, and justifying such an investment will be easier if we have a clear grasp of the limitations of the available secondary data.

In chapter 1, we identified four significant limitations to be considered when designing spatial analyses. First, census data has always entailed a trade-off between timeliness and precision. Proposals to introduce a five-year census failed in the 1930s and again in the 1970s. Although the ACS promises to address the timeliness issues, it does so at the cost of precision, and that precision diminishes as spatial detail increases. Chapter 2 discussed these issues in detail.

Second, census data can only be released in forms that protect the confidentiality of respondents. Consequently, data may not be aggregated at the spatial scale (or by the combination of variables) of most interest to us. GIS tools can help construct new aggregations (for instance, to track trends over time within a changing census tract geography) but those constructions will be arbitrary. In some cases, administrative data can supplement this gap (for instance, property tax assessments can update and supplement census reports on median home value).

Third, census data reports on characteristics that are easily measured, and these are not necessarily the same as the items we are interested in from a policy point of view. For example, high school completion rates are often used as indicators of social disintegration and juvenile disadvantage. But if we stop to think about the variables that might cause high school completion rates to differ, this link becomes more questionable. Ethnicity, age, national origin, and local employment sectors may be more important explanations of variations in high school completion rates than social disintegration, juvenile disadvantage, or school quality. Although there is often no good alternative to using simplifying proxies, we should be aware

of the interpretive limitations imposed by what is actually measured.

Finally, quality control is never perfect. Census data is probably as reliable as it can be within the constraints of funding, staffing, and legislation, but as the Census Bureau freely admits, it is not without flaws. As we explained in chapter 1, missing survey responses are filled in by asking neighbors or imputing characteristics from nearby or otherwise similar responses. Nonresponses are not randomly distributed; people with less stable lives and homes that are vacant are much more likely to have characteristics imputed to them. Interviewer error is another important source of discrepancies. Although the Census Bureau devotes significant effort to interviewer training and quality control, no system is perfect.

Five questions

How is the novice (or even experienced) analyst to negotiate the pitfalls that can undermine any research project? Researchers need to recognize limitations and focus on how they can be dealt with or minimized. We offer five questions for analysts to consider, using the example of one census topic—linguistic isolation. We do not aim to undermine the concept of linguistic isolation but to draw attention to the complex issues that underlie any effort to measure and communicate social phenomena. We use data from the 2000 Census of Population and Housing, because more recent census tract-level data was not available as this book went to press.

What sort of information is needed?

What sort of information is needed for the decision or policy issue at hand? Expectations for the precision of information will vary depending on how it is expected to contribute to the policymaking process. For instance, information intended to educate the public and elected officials about the diversity of languages spoken within the community and extent of linguistic isolation meets different expectations than information designed to serve as the basis for establishing dual-language instruction programs at specific elementary schools.

Figure 3.4 shows the percent of linguistically isolated households by census tract in Hennepin County, Minnesota. The map shows some clustering around the downtown, but overall the problem appears to be quite widespread, with most of the denser tracts reporting linguistic isolation rates of more than 15 percent.

Figure 3.5 shows the percent of linguistically isolated households within two language groups: Spanish, and Asian and Pacific Islander (API) languages. This set of maps tells a different story: linguistically isolated households speaking API languages are found in a much larger number of tracts than Spanish-speaking linguistically isolated households. The wide distribution of linguistically isolated households shown in figure 3.4 reflects the distribution of API households rather than Spanish-speaking households.

Is this information presented at the appropriate level of detail? For general background purposes, much more detail—such as a consideration of imputation rates and the confidence intervals around estimates of Spanish versus Asian and Pacific Islander language-group speakers at the

Figure 3.4   Linguistically isolated non-English-speaking households, Hennepin Co., Minnesota, 2000

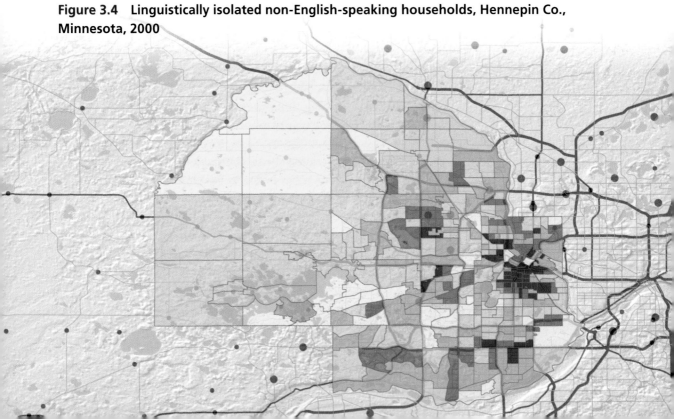

census tract level—would be overkill. But we should have different expectations if this information was being used as evidence to meet the need of a specific program, policy, or other action. A clear sense of how much precision and spatial detail is needed should be the starting point of defining a project.

What does the data measure?

What does the available data actually measure? Does the available secondary data answer the question being asked? Two related questions are likely to concern us: how is the data defined (that is, what concepts does it measure), and are the data available at the cross tabulations needed? Continuing with our linguistic isolation example, we would need

to understand precisely how linguistically isolated households are defined. Even the most common sense concepts may be measured in ways we do not expect. First, what counts as speaking another language at home? The concept of a mother tongue was used in every census between 1910 and 1970 (with the exception of the 1950 census). In censuses since 1980, mother tongue has been replaced with a less metaphorical concept, "language spoken at home." Figure 3.6 shows how the question was worded in 2000 and subsequent ACS surveys.

The technical documentation for the 2000 census (U.S. Census Bureau 2007a) provides a more detailed explanation of how the reported characteristics are derived from the answers people give to these questions. First, the data is collected only from people five years of age or older, but because it is reported at the household rather than individual level, this is no great loss. Second, question 11a is inevitably crude: it does not differentiate between households who use a foreign language at home occasionally and those who use it exclusively. If more than one language is named in 11b, only the first language named is coded. The question clearly doesn't ask whether the person is a native speaker of a foreign language, or merely an enthusiastic student of a foreign language.

Coding and classifying the write-in responses to 11b raises another set of choices. Reported languages are classified into one of four major groups (Spanish, other Indo-European, API, and Other) and into a more detailed set of thirty-nine classes (e.g., differentiating Hindi from Urdu and Mandarin within the API group). Other household members are assigned to the same language group as the first respondent that reports speaking another language, in a complex order of relationship. Thus, if a householder's parent reports speaking a language other the English at home, the siblings or children of the householder (but

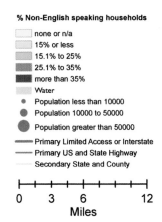

% Non-English speaking households

- none or n/a
- 15% or less
- 15.1% to 25%
- 25.1% to 35%
- more than 35%
- Water
- • Population less than 10000
- • Population 10000 to 50000
- ● Population greater than 50000
- Primary Limited Access or Interstate
- Primary US and State Highway
- Secondary State and County

0   3   6   12
Miles

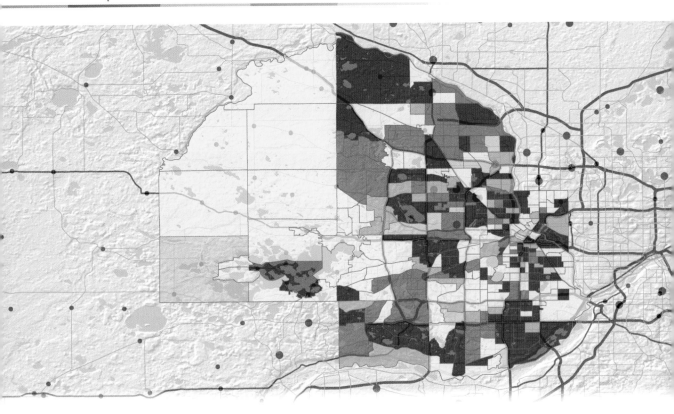

Figure 3.5   Linguistic isolation by language group, Hennepin Co., Minnesota, 2000

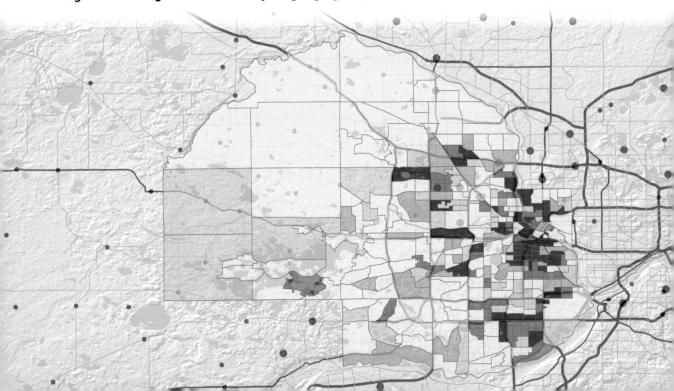

Figure 3.6   Language and linguistic isolation census question

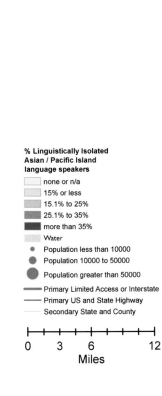

**% Linguistically Isolated
Asian / Pacific Island
language speakers**

- none or n/a
- 15% or less
- 15.1% to 25%
- 25.1% to 35%
- more than 35%
- Water
- Population less than 10000
- Population 10000 to 50000
- Population greater than 50000

— Primary Limited Access or Interstate
— Primary US and State Highway
— Secondary State and County

0   3   6   12
Miles

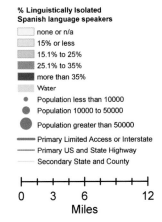

**% Linguistically Isolated
Spanish language speakers**

- none or n/a
- 15% or less
- 15.1% to 25%
- 25.1% to 35%
- more than 35%
- Water
- Population less than 10000
- Population 10000 to 50000
- Population greater than 50000

— Primary Limited Access or Interstate
— Primary US and State Highway
— Secondary State and County

0   3   6   12
Miles

11 **a. Does this person speak a language other than English at home?**

☐ Yes
☐ No → *Skip to 12*

b. What is this language?

(For example: Korean, Italian, Spanish, Vietnamese)

c. How well does this person speak English?

☐ Very well
☐ Well
☐ Not well
☐ Not at all

Source: U.S. Census Bureau 2000, Census of Population and Housing, Questionnaires, http://www.census.gov/dmd/www/pdf/d02p.pdf

not the householder) are classified as speaking that language, although clearly they may not. Thus we may easily overestimate the number of children speaking a language other than English at home. Households are assigned to one of three language density categories: no members speak a foreign language, some speak it, or all speak it.

Question 11c adds to the complexity, in part because it relies on perceptions not just of one's own English-speaking ability, but that of other family members'. This question forms the basis for the definition of linguistically isolated households. A household in which all members aged fourteen or older speak a language other than English at home and who speak English less than "very well," is defined as linguistically isolated. Children younger than fourteen who may speak only English would nevertheless be classified as linguistically isolated along with other household members. Some of these distinctions may seem overly fine, but they should be carefully considered to decide what questions the data can answer.

By now, we might have some reservations about the appropriateness of the data for our purposes. Rather than directly reporting the English-speaking ability of children five and older, the tables report on the linguistic isolation of households. Tables do not report linguistically isolated households by household size or structure, so we have no way of knowing whether isolated households are exclusively elderly or whether they include families with children. It also would be helpful to know something about the future distribution of young children among language groups and by language status: Are there differences in fertility or immigration rates by language group? Do children from some language groups move to different schools more often than others, or are they more likely to attend religious rather than public

schools? Although this information is also gathered in the census questionnaire, it is not cross-tabulated with language indicators.

Yet all is not lost. Individual record-level information that can answer these more detailed questions about correlation is available in the PUMS files. However, to protect confidentiality, PUMS data includes only a small sample (1 or 5 percent, depending on the precise product used) released at a macro-scale. (PUMAs have a population of around 100,000 and are explained in greater detail in the next chapter.) PUMS data could be used to model the relationships among age, English-speaking ability, fertility and immigration rates, and school enrollment and retention rates. Region-wide averages could be used to develop defensible estimates of how many future students in each school catchment district may come from linguistically isolated households, and who may benefit from dual-language instruction programs.

Carefully considering how the available data differs from the data needed is thus not necessarily a basis for abandoning the analysis. It can be a starting point for refining the analysis to compensate for the inevitable limitations. In some cases, of course, the preliminary assessment may conclude that administrative sources (for instance, the number of children scoring below a threshold level on language competency tests) or primary data collection (designing and conducting a survey) are the only ways to answer the questions posed.

How accurate is the measure?

How accurately does the data measure the phenomenon? Once you have decided what data will be assembled to provide the evidence you need, the next step would be to consider the quality limitations that may affect your conclusions. Census and ACS response rates vary widely around the United States. Response rates are affected by the type and extent of outreach in different communities, the quality of the address file (the universe from which the sample was drawn), and the skill and effort of individual census workers responsible for follow up. The availability of assistance and follow up in minority languages vary widely in the census (for the ACS, it is more extensive). One of the major sources of so-called nonsample error is variation in completed questionnaire rates, partly captured by the extent to which missing answers are imputed.

Imputation procedures provide a consistent way for the Census Bureau to complete incomplete questionnaires. Many of the imputations are fairly unobjectionable: for instance, if some people within a household are reported as speaking a language other than English at home, but they did not write in the language they said they spoke on the form, they are assigned to the same language reported for other household members. When this isn't possible, language might be imputed based on the language spoken by a person reporting the same racial and Spanish-origin characteristics from the nearby area, or based on the language reported by someone with the same place of birth or ancestry. At the scale of major language groups, imputation is unlikely to introduce major inaccuracies.

Imputing English competence is more problematic. English competence is already a subjective measure based on the respondents' perceptions of themselves and others. Where information about the ability to speak English is missing, the Census Bureau assigns the individual the same level of English competence reported by a randomly assigned individual of the same age, place of birth, year of entry to the United States, language group, and Spanish origin. Random assignment avoids the problem of assuming all household members have similar abilities, and thus avoids artificially inflating estimates of linguistic isolation. However, it is also possible that the pool of respondents with completed questionnaires may include a disproportionate number of people who are competent English speakers, in which case imputation may systematically over estimate the proportion of nonrespondents who speak English well. This conundrum has no good solution, but imputation rates should be considered before drawing firm conclusions about linguistic isolation.

Figure 3.7 shows the imputation rates for ability to speak English across the same Hennepin County tracts. Imputation rates are fairly high in the larger suburban tracts to the west and northwest of the county, where no linguistically isolated households were reported. This raises an interesting question: were response rates to the question about ability to speak English reduced because suburban non-English-speaking households were less likely to receive assistance with completing the census questionnaire than households in more densely settled inner city tracts, where community assistance might have been better organized? How much weight should we place on estimates that report no linguistically isolated households in those places, when in many cases more than one in four non-English-speakers did not answer the question about English-speaking ability?

How will the information be used?

How will your audience use the information you present? This question is related to the one we began with, but has a slightly different set of implications. Is this analysis the basis for a zero-sum outcome (only one language group will be served)? In that case, small differences in estimates of the size of different groups may precipitate hard-fought battles over statistics. What sort of participation is expected from parents, teachers, and community residents? Are English-only activists likely to protest any public consideration of the issue? What sort of access do people need to the evidence on which policy decisions will be based? Will they be encouraged to critique or challenge that evidence, and are there ways to help them do that constructively? In other words, how contentious will the issue be, and what sort of precision will be needed to come to a solution?

All of these questions help determine how to present the analysis, how much detail people will need to interpret the findings, and whether they will need to learn new concepts (such as confidence intervals) to feel comfortable with disputing the results. An interactive mapping site might serve younger, educated households effectively; poster boards and static public displays may be needed for those without a home Internet connection. How will people ask questions about the analysis? Designing the presentation to maximize access and minimize confusion and frustration could alter the way people respond to a contentious issue.

How will the information be presented and interpreted?

How do the spatial, temporal, or other categories used to analyze and present the information affect how it will be interpreted? Earlier, we showed how

Figure 3.7   Imputed responses for English ability, Hennepin Co., Minnesota, 2000

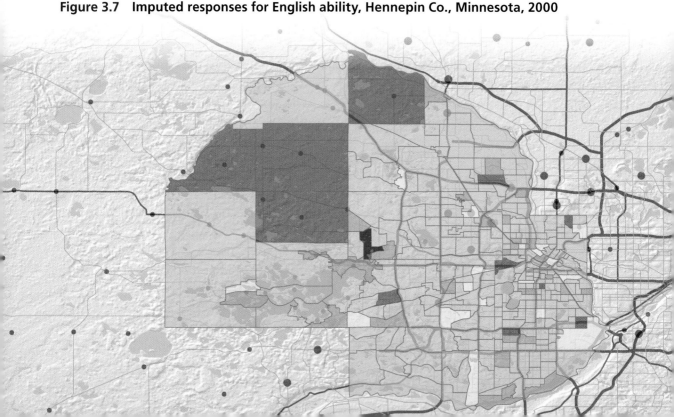

the spatial scale at which information is analyzed and presented (in that case, election results) can fundamentally transform the information we convey. Communicating effectively with maps is like writing well. The basic rules of clear writing are good starting places in thinking about the basic rules of mapmaking. In a passage from "Politics of the English Language" (1946), George Orwell gets to the heart of writing:

> A scrupulous writer, in every sentence that he writes, will ask himself at least four questions, thus: What am I trying to say? What words will express it? What image or idiom will make it clearer? Is this image fresh enough to have an effect? And he will probably ask himself two more: Could I put it more shortly? Have I said anything that is avoidably ugly?

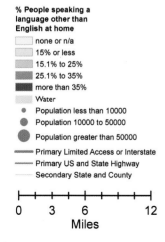

% People speaking a
language other than
English at home

☐ none or n/a
☐ 15% or less
☐ 15.1% to 25%
▨ 25.1% to 35%
■ more than 35%
☐ Water

• Population less than 10000
⬤ Population 10000 to 50000
⬤ Population greater than 50000

━━ Primary Limited Access or Interstate
━━ Primary US and State Highway
━━ Secondary State and County

0　3　6　　　12
Miles

To communicate effectively with maps, we need a thorough understanding of the information we're mapping (and its weaknesses or limitations), a clear sense of the meaning we want to convey in the map, and a grasp of how color, symbol, scale bars, legends, and other elements can communicate that meaning economically and elegantly. Helpful guidance is offered in several books devoted to the topic of mapmaking. Cynthia Brewer's *Designing Better Maps* (2005) and Mark Monmonier's *How to Lie with Maps* (1996) are classics (dealing with different aspects of mapmaking). Four key mapmaking guidelines are highlighted in the section that follows.

Choose an appropriate number format

Most census and ACS data are reported in one of three formats: absolute numbers (number of people with a disability that limits their employment), medians (the median age of homes in the tract), or aggregates (total value of all earnings from social security). Sometimes, it is appropriate to map absolute numbers (estimated homes for monthly rent at $750 or less, or numbers of adults without a high school diploma), because that is what we care about (how many rentals would be available to households below a certain income, or the likely demand for GED programs).

More often, though, we are interested in how the incidence of a particular characteristic varies geographically. In general, comparisons are facilitated by using percentages or rates rather than absolute numbers when we're trying to work out the relative impact of a characteristic on a neighborhood, city, or county. Using percentages raises another issue: who is the base population? Figure 3.8 compares the interpretive impact of just two alternative methods of presenting percentages. If we use all households as the base (as in figure 3.8a), we would draw different conclusions about the spatial

Figure 3.8a   Households that speak a foreign language

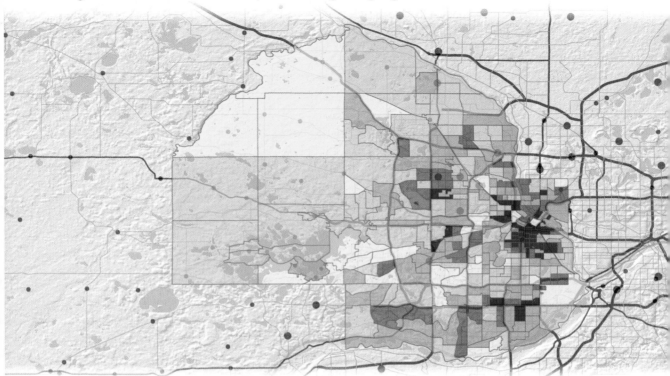

Figure 3.8b   Linguistically isolated households that speak a foreign language

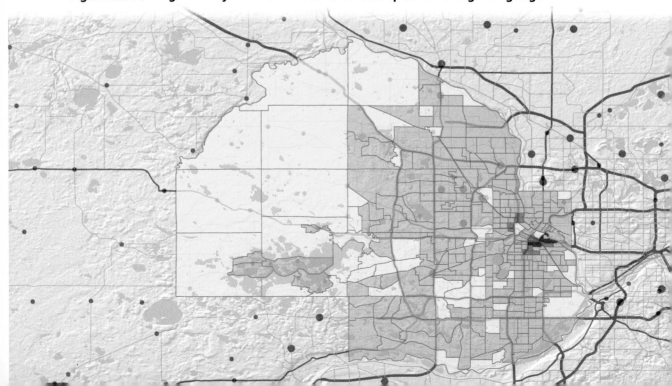

distribution of linguistically isolated households than if we used only non-English-speaking households as our base (as in figure 3.8b).

Alternatively, we may be more interested in the rate of change over time. In this case, is it best to calculate the rate of change in absolute numbers (for instance, of numbers of linguistically isolated households), or the change in the percentage of households that are linguistically isolated? What should we use as the base year? Is one base year enough? Sometimes, apparently sharp changes merely reverse short-term trends and fit with the overall long-term trajectory of change.

Define intervals thoughtfully

Because census data is summarized by polygons of some sort, choropleth maps are the format we usually default to in presenting spatial information. But choropleth maps are notoriously vulnerable to manipulation (Monmonier 1996). A common criticism is that the intervals chosen can have a dramatic effect on the apparent scale of change. Figures 3.9a and 3.9b illustrate two alternative approaches to categorizing the data we show in figure 3.4. Using equal intervals for categories (dividing the distance between the highest and lowest values into five equal categories) has a very different interpretive impact than using quintiles (dividing the cases into five equal categories). In figure 3.4, intervals were chosen manually, to reflect the authors' judgment about meaningful categorical differences. In comparison to the equal interval method, figure 3.4 could be seen as overemphasizing the extent of the problem and biasing perceptions of its importance upwards. But in comparison to the quintile method, figure 3.4 downplays the problem and may be accused of biasing perceptions of its priority downwards.

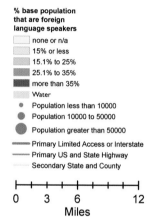

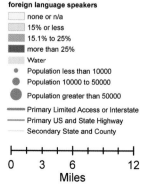

Figure 3.9a   Foreign-language speakers, quantiles, Hennepin Co., Minnesota, 2000

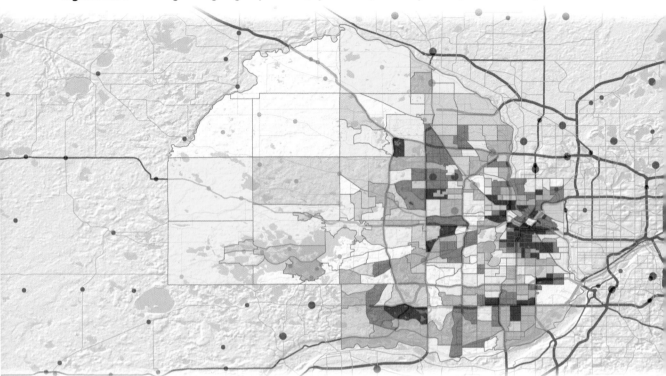

Figure 3.9b   Foreign-language speakers, equal intervals, Hennepin Co., Minnesota, 2000

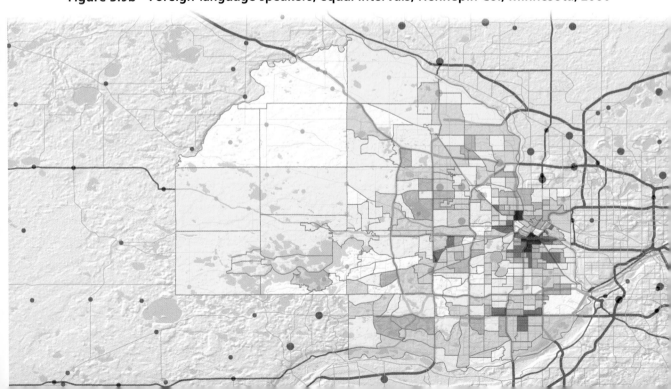

Examining the distribution of values (in a histogram) is the best place to start. In any series of maps, using consistent categories enables simple graphic comparisons. Critical self-evaluation has no substitute; if this is lacking while preparing the analysis and presentation, it may be imposed later, when opponents rework data and maps to undermine the validity of conclusions. The key question may be whether the choice of one approach over alternative ones can be justified.

Choose an appropriate spatial scale

Newman's maps of red and blue states make it clear that large geographic areas do not always have large populations. This is particularly so with census tracts, where the area is usually inversely related to the size of its population. A map showing large areas (such as of sparsely populated suburban census tracts) with a high proportion of homes built in the previous five years can lead readers to overestimate the extent of new construction. Compensatory distortions of surface area are striking but can attract suspicion. Inserting another frame showing the detail for smaller tracts (such as those clustered around the central business district) may be a less contentious way to deal with this.

Provide supporting information

Most of this chapter has focused on the limitations and caveats that apply to census and ACS data. The most important of these are the margins of error around survey-based estimates, but others such as imputation rates or subtle changes in definitions may matter as well. The audience needs to know how those limitations should affect their interpretation of the evidence presented. However, it is also true that too much information can confuse people. "Life in Los Angeles" (figure 3.10) is a cartographic classic for its ability to convey a lot of information with little verbiage.

% Foreign language speakers
Using Quantiles

- 9% or less
- 9.1% to 16%
- 16.1% to 23%
- 23.1% to 33%
- more than 33%
- none or n/a
- Water
- Population less than 10000
- Population 10000 to 50000
- Population greater than 50000
- Primary Limited Access or Interstate
- Primary US and State Highway
- Secondary State and County

```
0     3     6          12
              Miles
```

% Foreign language speakers
Using Equal Intervals

- 14% or less
- 14.1% to 27%
- 27.1% to 39%
- 39.1% to 52%
- more than 52%
- none or n/a
- Water
- Population less than 10000
- Population 10000 to 50000
- Population greater than 50000
- Primary Limited Access or Interstate
- Primary US and State Highway
- Secondary State and County

```
0     3     6          12
              Miles
```

Figure 3.10   Eugene Turner's Life in Los Angeles

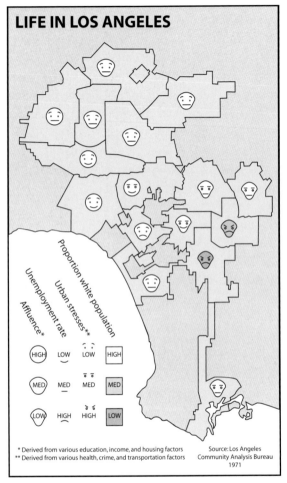

Source: Eugene Turner, 1977. http://www.csun.edu/~hfgeg005/eturner/
gallery/lifeinla.GIF

Visual cues can be more effective than notes alone, though some critics have argued that the basis for the indicators is unclear. The previous chapter presented several strategies to deal with the varying precision of ACS estimates. The accessibility of information is a further consideration. Relying on attractively colored maps that become meaningless when printed or copied in black and white is a common problem. The possibilities of interactive maps can distract us from the need to convey spatial information in a way that will work with or without a computer. Cynthia Brewer (2005) provides invaluable design guidelines that consider access alongside aesthetics.

Conclusions

Not all important policy questions can be answered with easily available secondary data. If the purpose is to investigate whether introducing dual-language programs in elementary schools could substantially improve the social integration, earning capacity, and life opportunities of children from non-English-speaking homes, census data is not well suited to answering the question. This is a longitudinal question, assuming a causal relationship, and requiring the researcher to control for multiple dimensions of differences. It requires entirely different sorts of information than standardized community-wide surveys can provide.

Despite their limitations, the ACS and decennial census provide a uniquely consistent resource of social and economic information, enabling us to compare variables over time and across places. We know so much about the data limitations precisely because of the rigorous quality control and evaluation programs that probe for weaknesses. The next four chapters investigate the substance of the demographic, housing, economic and transportation data that underpin many sorts of urban policy decisions. Chapter 8 returns to the issues discussed in this chapter, developing a variety of hypothetical research designs that consider the methodological, technical, epistemological, and ethical dimensions of census-based spatial analyses for policy decisions.

Chapter 4

Analyzing demographic and social data

Unlike premodern censuses (such as the *Domesday Book*, which recorded the land and property survey William the Conqueror commissioned in Britain in 1086) aimed at estimating the tax-raising and military potential of a population, modern censuses are aimed (at least in part) at understanding changing social structures, often as a basis for distributing services: How many elderly single-person households may need in-home care? From which major language groups will the next generation of preschoolers be drawn? How many veterans with disabilities should the Veterans Administration budget for in its health-care spending projections?

This chapter examines the changing ways we measure several demographic and social characteristics of current public concern and discusses the complex choices that process involves. In the first section, we describe the demographic and social measurement concepts used in the 2010 census and the ACS, and the major formats in which the data is published. Two other important census datasets, the Population Estimates program and the Current Population Survey, are examined in the second section.

The census' focus on people is sometimes interpreted in political terms, and some oppose the census for a variety of reasons, including criticism that it is an instrument of surveillance (Starr 1987; Prewitt 2003). For example, in 2004, news reports revealed that the Census Bureau had provided the Department of Homeland Security with reports on Arab American populations by city and ZIP code. The data was in fact part of a summary report planned to present the results of the 2000 census (before the September 11, 2001, attack on the United States) and was freely available on the Census Bureau's Web site. Homeland Security officials had requested the data subsequently to determine which airports should post Arabic language signs. But the bureau's director understood that the mere perception that the Census Bureau may have violated privacy under political pressure—as it had done in 1942, when Japanese Americans were identified based on census returns—was a serious threat to its legitimacy (Lipton 2004).

Census Bureau marketing campaigns emphasize the statutory requirement for confidentiality and explain that individual information is never shared with other agencies such as Homeland Security or the Internal Revenue Service. In preparation for the 2010 census, the Census Bureau provided detailed justifications for each question on the 2010 census and the ACS, listing the major federal statutory requirements for the information, and the community benefits that rely on this information (U.S. Census Bureau 2008).

Understanding demographic and social data

Census concepts must evolve to reflect our changing social priorities, but they must also remain consistent so we can track changes over time. This is a constant tension.

Defining "residence"

Chapter 2 discussed the broad framework of the ACS and assessed the implications of moving from a point-in-time survey, like previous decennial censuses, to a continuous measurement survey. In this section, we explain how the ACS's approach will alter the measurement concepts used in past censuses.

Residence

Different definitions of residence distinguish the 2010 census and the ACS: the census gathers information on a different statistical universe of people than the universe of people the ACS samples. (*Universe* is a specific statistical term referring to the entire group that is enumerated or sampled). In the case of the 2010 census, the universe is everyone who lived in the United States on April 1, 2010, whereas for the ACS for 2010, it is everyone who lived in the country during the entire year. The 2010 census defines residents as those living in the housing unit where they were surveyed on April 1 that year, unless they were on a short vacation. This definition is consistent with those of previous censuses. In the ACS, people who expect to live in a housing unit for at least two months at the time they are surveyed are counted as residents of that unit (unless they have no other permanent home) (U.S. Census Bureau 2009a). People are surveyed year round; a snapshot of residents on April 1 may be quite different than one of residents in January, June, or October. The concept of residence defines who can be interviewed and who counts as living in a particular place (or, in other words, as belonging to a particular universe). The ACS's minimum two-month residency rule has three exceptions:

- Children away at boarding school (but not college) are always counted as residents of their parents' home.
- Children living under joint custody arrangements are counted as living in whichever parent's home they are staying when surveyed.
- People who have a place to stay near their work but return regularly to their family home are counted as residents of the family home.

Group quarters residence

Everyone staying in a group quarters facility when it is surveyed is counted as a resident of that facility and is included in the sample universe from which ACS interviewees are chosen. Group quarters are explained in more detail in chapter 5. They include facilities where residence is voluntary—such as student dormitories, hospitals, homeless shelters—and those where it is not—such as prisons, detention facilities for undocumented immigrants.

In 2005, the first year the ACS was conducted nationwide, the group quarters population was not surveyed. In the heated debate over whether the ACS should go ahead, congressional appropriations were cut to the point that the Census Bureau could not afford to survey the group quarters population. Congress restored the shortfall

the following year, and the 2006 ACS surveyed the group quarters population as well as people living in households.

Basic demographic measures

Information on basic demographics was collected for every person in the 2010 and all previous censuses and for every member of households sampled (or sampled group quarters residents) in the ACS survey.

Age and sex

Age is used as a filter for several sample questions on the ACS, such as educational attainment, which is only asked of people age twenty-five and older. Although age seems the most straightforward of information to collect, it is not. Analysis of the 1990 census suggested that many people round their age up to their next birthday, or the next birthday ending in a zero or five, so age may be overstated. Since the 2000 census, age has been calculated based on the person's reported date of birth.

Like age, information on sex or gender has been collected in every census, as it was originally the basis of voting eligibility. People are asked whether they are male or female, and a sex ratio is reported, dividing the total number of males by females. Ratios over 100 indicate more males than females. Sex is another dimension along which many other variables, such as employment and income, are reported.

Household and family structure

In a rather circuitous way, households are defined as all the people occupying a housing unit, whereas housing units (discussed in chapter 5) are defined as the separate living quarters of a household.

Figure 4.1 Households and families

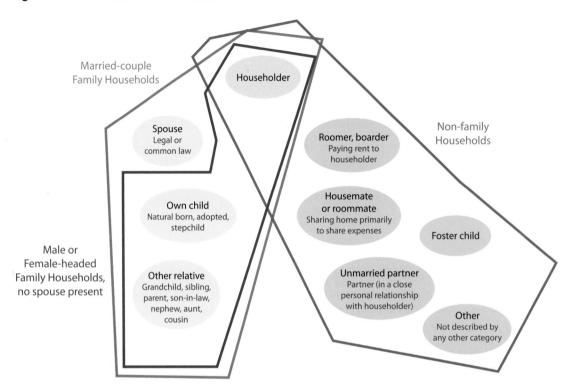

Households are not the same as families. Families are a group of individuals related to the householder by blood, marriage, or adoption. Nonfamily households include single people living alone and groups of unrelated people living together as roommates or as unmarried partners. Figure 4.1 summarizes how households and families are defined.

The householder is the person who answers the survey, and every other member of the household is defined in relation to the householder (e.g., parent, spouse, or unrelated). The householder is usually one of the people in whose name the home is owned or rented. But this definition is arbitrary, and its arbitrariness means that the same combinations of individuals could be defined in different ways, depending on who is designated as the householder. Consider the case of two women, one of whom has a child, living together and renting a home jointly. If the childless woman responds as the householder, this would be a household of unrelated individuals because neither the other woman nor her child are related to the householder. If the woman with a child responds as the householder, this same group would be described as a family household (the woman and her child) with one nonrelative (the other woman) also in the household.

The term *own children* refers to the householder's children by birth, marriage, or adoption, who are unmarried and under the age of eighteen. *Related children* are under the age of eighteen but may be related to the householder in many ways—for instance, as nephews, cousins, grandchildren, or daughters-in-law. They may be married or unmarried but would never be the spouse of the householder, even if they were younger than eighteen.

Because families are defined based on their relationship to the householder, each household contains only one family by definition. Subfamilies, such as an adult child of the householder with her own child, or the householder's brother and his wife and children, are not counted as separate families. However, subfamilies and the numbers of households with subfamilies are reported separately.

Race and Hispanic origin

Defining race is not an easy task. Biological or anthropological definitions are no longer acceptable. Some countries, such as Canada, avoid the question altogether and ask merely about national origin and the cultural group with which the respondent identifies. Given the continuing legacy of racial inequality in many parts of the United States, race and Hispanic origin continue to be important concepts for social policy. The Census Bureau asks respondents for the race (or races), cultural group, or national origin with which they identify most closely (U.S. Census Bureau 2009a). Thus race is an amalgam of national or ethnic origin concepts that are socially rather than anthropologically or biologically defined.

Racial change may be a key indicator of local community change, whether in response to policy (e.g., neighborhood desegregation efforts) or other forces. The Houston metropolitan area was one of many where refugees from Hurricane Katrina resettled. Figure 4.2 shows the counties where the African American population increased fastest between 2000 and 2005–07 and the African American share of county populations in 2000. The most rapid growth in African American populations occurred in counties that had relative small proportions of African Americans in 2000.

The fluid concept of race is often confused with the concept of Hispanic origin. It is inaccurate to report Hispanic origin as just another racial category. People of Hispanic origin may be of any race. However, many people of Hispanic origin describe themselves as some other race, such as Mexican or Cuban. Hispanic origin is a purely cultural variable, defined by language or heritage (U.S. Census Bureau 2009a). People from Portuguese- or French-speaking countries in Latin America and the Caribbean are not Hispanic. Europeans from Spain, Asians from the Philippines, and Native Americans from Mexico may all describe themselves as Hispanic. Figures 4.3 and 4.4 compare the proportion of all San Diego residents reporting they were some other race and the proportion of residents of Hispanic origin reporting they were some other race.

In 2000, the census definition of race was brought into line with the definition the Office of Management and Budget adopted in 1997. Because of this change, it is difficult to compare racial change from periods earlier than 2000, but it is simple to compare racial change between 2000 and later periods. People can choose to identify with two or more race categories to reflect mixed parentage, though they still have the choice of "some other race alone." Write-in responses are also accepted, but an automated coding system classifies write-ins into one of five racial categories: white, black or African American, American Indian or Alaska Native, Asian, Native Hawaiian or Pacific Islander. For people reporting more than one race, fifty-seven combinations of races are possible.

Fifty-seven racial categories make cross-tabulations cumbersome. In some cases, cross-tabulations summarize responses from all people who reported each race category (e.g., "Asian alone or in combination with one or more other races" would include everyone who reported being Asian or part Asian).

This solves one of the practical problems resulting from multiracial identities, but people may be counted twice or more (results do not sum to 100 percent). In other cases however, cross-tabulations are based on people who reported belonging to one racial group only. This would exclude people reporting more than one race: in 2000, people in this category accounted for 2.6 percent of the national population.

Sample demographic characteristics

Information on the following characteristics is collected for every member of households sampled in the ACS. In 2000, these questions were

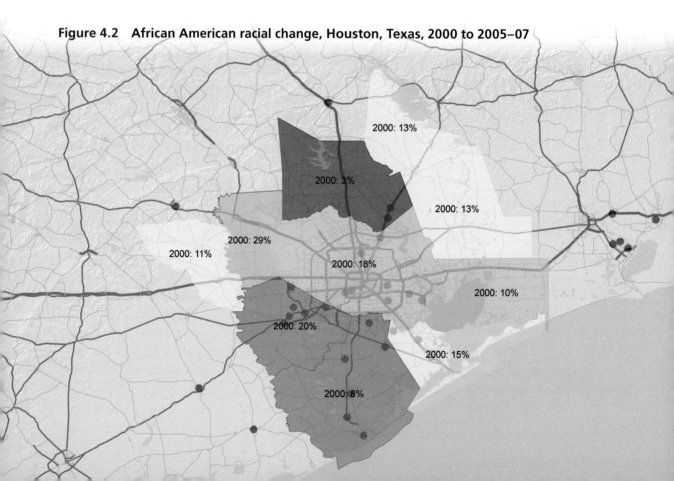

Figure 4.2   African American racial change, Houston, Texas, 2000 to 2005–07

asked on the long form, which sampled one in six housing units.

Marital status and history

Marital status is a sample question asked for all members of the household over the age of fifteen, not just the householder. Because subfamilies are not counted as families, there are more married couples than married couple family households. People who are now married include a subcategory of those who are separated. Legally separated couples, those living apart and intending to divorce, and couples living apart because of marital discord are in this subcategory. People with an absent spouse are not necessarily separated. A spouse may live away from home because of employment, service in the military, or being institutionalized (such as in a health-care facility or prison). Thus the numbers of married men and women in a place are not always equal—reporting differences, absent spouses, and sample weighting procedures account for these differences.

Marital status is defined by the respondents, not by their legal status. Unmarried partners are different than roommates—they are considered to be in a close personal relationship with the householder. In contrast to people who consider themselves to be in common-law marriages, unmarried partners are nonfamily households. Unmarried partners, unlike a couple in a common-law marriage, may be of the same or opposite sexes.

The ACS added a new measure, marital history, in 2008. For each household member for whom marital status is asked, respondents are also asked whether the person was married, widowed, or divorced in the previous twelve months, how many times they have been married, and the date of their most recent marriage. In an era of increasing concern with government intrusion, gathering new data on the history of an individual's marital status appears incongruous. However, the data was required by new legislation adding the Healthy Marriage Initiative to the Temporary Assistance to Needy Families (TANF) program in the Deficit Reduction Act of 2005. An explicit social policy focus on influencing marriage and divorce rates requires benchmark data to assess its achievements (U.S. Census Bureau 2008).

Fertility

A new question was added to the ACS in 2008, asking whether each female listed in the survey had given birth to any children in the past twelve

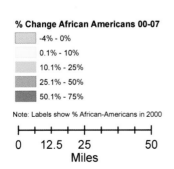

% Change African Americans 00-07

- -4% - 0%
- 0.1% - 10%
- 10.1% - 25%
- 25.1% - 50%
- 50.1% - 75%

Note: Labels show % African-Americans in 2000

0   12.5   25   50
Miles

months. Fertility rates are important for constructing population projections and for planning for social and health services related to pregnancy and birth.

Grandparents as caregivers

This question was first asked in the 2000 census. For each household member, respondents are asked whether the person has any grandchildren living in the household and if so whether and for how long they have been responsible for caring for most of the child's basic needs. Welfare reform legislation establishing the TANF program required the Census Bureau to gather this information, as grandparents form an increasingly large share of caregivers for children covered under the program.

Place of birth and ancestry

Place of birth is a fairly straightforward question, but ancestry is an even muddier concept than race. Respondents are asked for the state, territory, or foreign country of their birth, using current political divisions. In contrast, the question about ancestry could be interpreted to refer to the person's parents' place of birth, or the cultural or ethnic group or groups with which the person identifies. Would people born in Australia of Italian parents describe themselves as Australian or Italian? Would people born in the United States with three American grandparents and one Turkish grandparent and a Turkish surname describe themselves as having American or Turkish ancestry? Individuals with identical ancestry may describe themselves in quite different ways or differently over time.

Figure 4.3 "Some other race," San Diego, California, 2000

A further complication is that the ancestry question is designed to supplement the questions on race and Hispanic origin. Not all ancestry categories are associated with a country—some refer to a cross-national region (Basque) or sub-region (Acadian/Cajun). But although regions may be the basis for ancestry, religion is usually not. For example, responses such as Sephardic, Jewish, or Sunni Muslim would be classified as "not reported." However, Hindu would be coded as "East Indian."

Language

Householders are asked whether household members aged five and older sometimes or always speak a language other than English at home. The language spoken most often, or learned first, is recorded.

Write-in answers are coded into 380 detailed language categories, which are classified into thirty-nine language groups, and then summarized into four main groups: Spanish, other Indo-European, Asian and Pacific Island, and all other languages. Clearly, these groups do not reflect actual linguistic relationships. In households where at least one person speaks a language other than English at home, all household members are assigned to that language group, even if they speak only English. Language density shows how many household members speak another language at home (none, some, or all).

People who speak a language other than English at home are asked how well they and other household members speak English: very well, well, not well, or not at all. There are no guidelines for how to interpret this very subjective question. A household where no one older than age fourteen speaks English only or very well is classified as linguistically isolated. Chapter 3 explored the concept of linguistic isolation in detail.

Citizenship, year of entry, and migration

Citizens are defined as people born in the United States or its territories, those born abroad of parents at least one of whom is a U.S. citizen, and foreign-born people who have naturalized. All other residents of the United States are noncitizens, but the census does not distinguish among permanent residents, legal temporary residents (such as students or refugees), and undocumented immigrants. Nevertheless, we know that undocumented noncitizens are undercounted.

The year of entry to the United States is reported for all noncitizens and naturalized citizens. Many other characteristics, such as linguistic isolation and the likelihood of home ownership, are related to the cohort of immigration. ACS information on the foreign-born population is used to estimate the

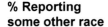

**% Reporting
some other race**

	0% - 5%
	6% - 10%
	11% - 25%
	26% - 50%
	51% - 75%

0   5   10   20
Miles

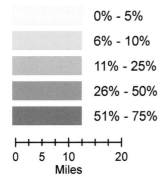

migration component of population estimates, as we describe below.

In addition to foreign immigration, the ACS and previous censuses report on population shifts within the United States. The ACS asks people where they lived one year ago. In 2000 and prior censuses, respondents were asked where they lived five years ago. Figure 4.5 shows the proportion of households in the Houston metropolitan area that reported living in a different metropolitan area the previous year.

Comparing this with figure 4.2, we can see that the county with the largest proportion of in-migrants (people who moved from one metropolitan area to another) was also the county with the fastest growth of African American residents.

Educational attainment

Respondents are asked for the highest level of education completed by each household member age twenty-five and older. High school graduates are those who received a diploma, not all those who completed the twelfth grade. Those who have completed some college but not graduated are shown in two categories: some college credit (less than one year), and one or more years of college (no degree). Professional graduate degrees (in medicine, law, and theology) are classified separately from master's degrees. Courses at trade schools or company training are not included in the definition of educational level unless they are accepted for credit toward a degree at a university or college.

Figure 4.4 Hispanic "some other race," San Diego, California, 2000

Educational attainment is an important indicator of peoples' employment prospects and human capital. Adults who have not graduated from high school and those who have not completed a college degree usually have much weaker employment and earnings prospects than those with at least a bachelor's degree. In 2009, high school graduates earned about $27,000 less than college graduates, on average (U.S. Census Bureau 2010a).

School enrollment

The question of school enrollment is asked for all people age three and older. Enrolled people attended a public or private school or college (including nursery school or preschool) during the academic year in which the survey is completed.

Enrollment in a trade or business school, company training, or tutoring, would not count unless the education is accepted for credit at a university or college. Public schools and colleges (supported and controlled by federal, state, or local government, including tribal governments) are distinguished from private ones. For people ages sixteen to nineteen, school enrollment (and high school graduation) is cross-tabulated with employment or military service.

Disability

Identifying people with disabilities is important for planning supportive services. Different types of services are needed for people with a self-care disability compared to a disability that prevents them from holding a job. Census 2000 made significant changes to the definition of disability to improve the data's usefulness for service providers, such as sheltered employment programs, adult daycare agencies and organizations providing in-home care (U.S. Census Bureau 2008). More precise information was collected on the nature of the person's disability for all people age five and older.

Householders are asked whether household members age five years and older have long-term sensory disabilities (blindness, deafness, or severe vision or hearing impairments), or movement disabilities (substantial limits on walking, reaching, lifting, or carrying). A second question asks whether the person has a physical, mental, or emotional condition lasting six months or more that substantially limits any of four categories of activity:

- mental activity
- self-care (such as bathing, eating or dressing)
- going outside the home alone
- employment

Age determines whether a limitation constitutes a disability. People are defined as disabled if they are age five and older and have a sensory, physical,

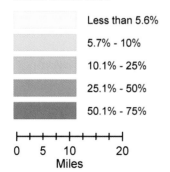

% Hispanic reporting some other race

	Less than 5.6%
	5.7% - 10%
	10.1% - 25%
	25.1% - 50%
	50.1% - 75%

0   5   10   20
Miles

mental, or self-care disability; age sixteen and older and have a "going outside the home" disability; or between the ages of sixteen and sixty-four and have an employment disability (U.S. Census Bureau 2009a).

An unanticipated confusion occurred on the mail-back questionnaires in 2000: some respondents misread the question about employment disability and thought they were being asked whether they were age sixteen or older. The question was intended to filter responses so that the question about employment disability was only asked of people age sixteen and older (i.e., of working age). A sharp increase in the number of people reported having a disability that prevented them working compared to 1990. Closer inspection revealed that many people identified as having an employment

disability also reported being employed (Stern 2003). The ACS survey reworded the question to eliminate the confusion, but it makes comparisons with 2000 reported disability rates very difficult. Figure 4.6 shows the original (Census 2000) and the reworded (ACS 2005) question.

Veteran status and period of military service

Information is gathered on whether a person has ever served on active duty in any branch of the military service and the periods they served. A new question now asks whether the person has a Veterans Administration (VA) service-connected disability rating, and if so, what that rating is. This question helps the VA measure veterans' entitlement to compensation for disabilities incurred as a result of active service, as a basis for estimating the

Figure 4.5   In-migrants living in different metropolitan area last year, Houston, Texas, 2005–07 average

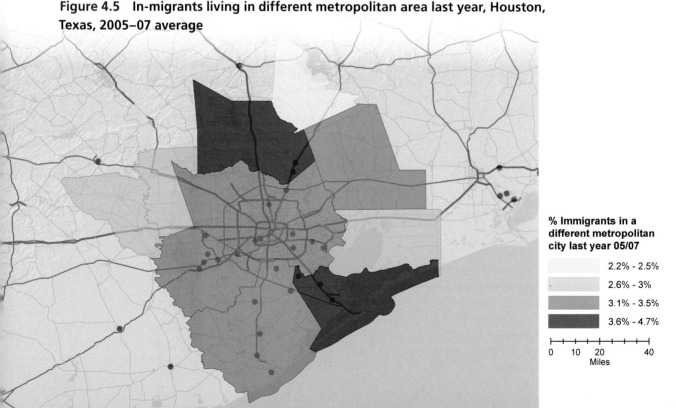

% Immigrants in a different metropolitan city last year 05/07

- 2.2% - 2.5%
- 2.6% - 3%
- 3.1% - 3.5%
- 3.6% - 4.7%

0   10   20   40
Miles

Figure 4.6a Disability census question, 2000 and 2005

17 **a. Is this person deaf or does he/she have serious difficulty hearing?**

☐ Yes
☐ No

b. Is this person blind or does he/she have serious difficulty seeing even when wearing glasses?

☐ Yes
☐ No

G *Answer question 18a – c if this person is 5 years old or over. Otherwise, SKIP to the questions for Person 2 on page 12.*

18 **a. Because of a physical, mental, or emotional condition, does this person have serious difficulty concentrating, remembering, or making decisions?**

☐ Yes
☐ No

b. Does this person have serious difficulty walking or climbing stairs?

☐ Yes
☐ No

c. Does this person have difficulty dressing or bathing?

☐ Yes
☐ No

19 **Because of a physical, mental, or emotional condition, does this person have difficulty doing errands alone such as visiting a doctor's office or shopping?**

☐ Yes
☐ No

Source: U.S. Census Bureau 2000, http://www.census.gov/dmd/www/pdf/d02p.pdf

Figure 4.6b Disability question reworded for ACS, 2005

16 **Does this person have any of the following long-lasting conditions:**

	Yes	No
a. Blindness, deafness, or a severe vision or hearing impairment?	☐	☐
b. A condition that substantially limits one or more basic physical activities such as walking, climbing stairs, reaching, lifting, or carrying?	☐	☐

17 **Because of a physical, mental, or emotional condition lasting 6 months or more, does this person have any difficulty in doing any of the following activities:**

	Yes	No
a. Learning, remembering, or concentrating?	☐	☐
b. Dressing, bathing, or getting around inside the home?	☐	☐
c. (Answer if this person is 16 YEARS OLD OR OVER.) Going outside the home alone to shop or visit a doctor's office?	☐	☐
d. (Answer if this person is 16 YEARS OLD OR OVER.) Working at a job or business?	☐	☐

Source: U.S. Census Bureau 2008

appropriations needed to cover the VA's health-care budget (U.S. Census Bureau 2008).

Data formats

The preliminary results of each census must be released to Congress by December 31 of the census year, but usually the full data is not available until some months later. Release schedules for ACS data are finalized each year, but the data is normally released in the fall of the year following the last year in the series (thus 2009 averages were released in fall 2010). In 2010, five-year averages were released for the 2005–09 period, the first available for small geographic areas since the ACS was established in 2005. However, the 2005 survey did not cover the group quarters population, so the 2006–10

Figure 4.7   ACS subjects, PUMS

Public Use Microdata Sample (PUMS) Files: 2006-2008 ACS 3-Year Subjects in the PUMS

Subjects in the American Community Survey PUMS

Items in the housing record include		Items in the person record include	
• Agricultural sales • Bedrooms • Commercial use • Condominium fee • Cost of utilities and fuels • Family income • Family, subfamily, and household relationships • Fire, hazard, and flood insurance • Food Stamps • Fuels used • Grandparent/grandchild • Household income • Household type • Housing costs • Kitchen facilities • Linguistic isolation • Lot size • Meals included in rent • Mobile home costs • Mortgage • Plumbing facilities • Presence and age of own children	• Presence of subfamilies in household • Property taxes • Property value • Rent • Residence state • Rooms • Telephone in unit • Tenure • Units in structure • Unmarried partner • Vacancy status • Vehicles available • Work • Year householder moved into unit • Year structure built	• Ability to speak English • Age • Ancestry • Citizenship and place of birth • Class of worker • Commuting to work • Education • Fertility • Grandparent/ grandchild • Hispanic origin • Hours worked • Income by type • Industry • Language spoken at home • Last week work status • Marital status • Migration • Military	• Mobility status • Occupation • Place of work • Poverty • Race • Relationship • Sex • Weeks worked • Work • Year of entry

Source: U.S. Census Bureau 2009b, http://www.census.gov/acs/www/Products/PUMS/PUMS3.htm

averages (scheduled release in fall 2011) are the first complete small-area ACS data. Cross-tabulations are released at the census geography levels outlined in chapter 1.

Public use microdata sample

Census and ACS data are also released as microdata files, enabling researchers to investigate relationships among characteristics without the constraints imposed by the published cross-tabulations (U.S. Census Bureau 2009b). Microdata are individual records for housing units and people, rather than summaries of cross-tabulated totals. Figure 4.7 shows the subjects for which public use microdata is released.

For instance, if we were interested in the school enrollment, school drop-out rates, and employment rates in families who migrated to the area from another state or country, available cross-tabulations are of little use. However, PUMS provides the sort of cross-sectional detail that could be used to estimate the proportion of children of recent immigrants who have not completed high school and are not enrolled in school. We could apply those proportions to neighborhood-level data on immigrant families to estimate the number of children in the neighborhood who meet these criteria. The estimates would be approximate, but a reasonable basis on which to plan for supplementary education or employment and training programs.

Microdata has limitations. To protect confidentiality, only samples of the data are released at quite broad spatial scales. ACS PUMS provides a 1 percent sample for single-year averages (e.g., 2007), a 3 percent sample for three-year averages (e.g., 2005–07), and a 5 percent sample for five-year averages (e.g., 2005–09). The PUMS data is released for PUMAs, which generally have a population of at least 100,000 (Gaines 2009). Figure 4.8 shows how PUMAs differ in size in states with different population densities. In Montana, PUMAs include several counties; meanwhile, New Jersey has several PUMAs in each county.

For the 2000 and earlier censuses, PUMS data is available as a 5 percent sample for PUMAs and as a more detailed 1 percent sample for super–public use microdata areas (Super-PUMAs), which are much larger in size (about 400,000 population). Super-PUMAs are composed of contiguous PUMAs and do not cross state lines.

Several other methods of disclosure limitation are used to protect confidentiality, including data swapping, top-coding of variables, age perturbation, and collapsing of categories (U.S. Census Bureau 2003a). Data swapping, for instance, involves replacing some data for a sampled household with data from another household, matched on key variables. Top-coding involves truncating variables like income. Data in the PUMS dataset is also synthesized, using models to replace attributes for respondents for whom confidentiality may be threatened (e.g., a family of eight that emigrated from Africa to a central Salt Lake City PUMA in 2007).

The 1 percent samples of housing units were drawn from ACS records stratified by several variables, including PUMA, interview type, tenure, housing unit type, and householder demographics, among others. Records were sampled based on a systematic random sample. For 2000 and earlier censuses the two samples (1 percent and 5 percent) were drawn independently. For the ACS PUMS, annual 1 percent samples are added to produce the 3 percent and 5 percent samples.

Records are weighted to allow users to estimate the frequency of a particular characteristic or set of characteristics for the population. The PUMS sample is drawn from the ACS sample, so it will have an additional level of sample error. Except for the variables controlled by ratio-estimates (occupancy status of housing units and male and female persons in households), PUMS estimates will not necessarily be the same as ACS estimates. Weighting methods are described in more detail in the technical documentation for each PUMS release. For instance, methods for the 2008 ACS PUMS release are available on the U.S. Census Web site (U.S. Census Bureau 2010b).

Other major census demographic and social datasets

Although the ACS now provides annual data releases of the demographic and social characteristics of places, it is not the source of annual estimated population for states, counties, cities, and towns.

Population estimates program

The Census Bureau's Population Estimates program is responsible for these estimates, which provide a benchmark to which ACS estimates are controlled (in other words, the number of total people reported in the ACS is based on the population

Figure 4.8 Super-PUMAs, Montana and New Jersey

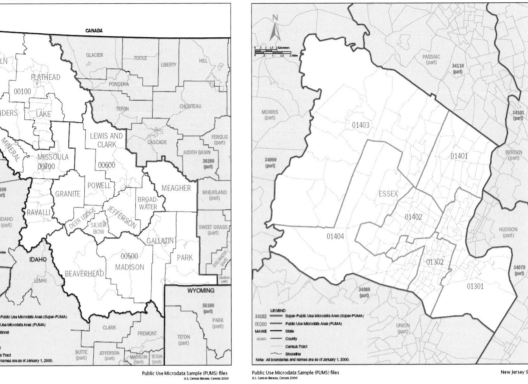

Source: U.S. Census Bureau. 2003d, http://www.census.gov/geo/www/maps/puma5pct.htm

estimates program, not the ACS survey responses). However, the ACS does contribute to the program through the improved insight it offers into international migration patterns and fertility (U.S. Census Bureau 2010c).

Population is estimated at the state and county levels using components of population change methods (essentially, projecting population forward from the previous year based on assumptions and data about fertility, mortality, and migration). Separate projections are constructed for the population under and over sixty-five years of age. Population estimates are also constructed for major race and ethnic groups. County- and state-level population estimates are controlled by the overall national population estimate. At the local government level, subcounty estimates are based on housing unit estimates and group quarters population counts controlled to the county total (in other words, estimates of total numbers for subareas are adjusted to add up to the estimated county population). Subcounty housing units are estimated based on new construction, demolition, conversion, and mobile home placement, combined with assumptions about occupancy rates and household size. Detailed descriptions of the population estimates program methodology are available on the U.S. Census Web site (U.S. Census 2010c).

Population estimates are adjusted to incorporate special censuses, which are sometimes conducted for local areas in between decennial census years, and the results of successful challenges to census counts.

Hurricanes Katrina and Rita in 2005 posed a major challenge for the population estimates program in the 117 affected counties, because the scale of destruction and displacement undermined the base on which estimation models rely—the previous period's population. In addition, administrative sources such as tax filings were no longer very helpful, because most residents of the stricken counties took advantage of IRS automatic filing extensions. Census Bureau strategies to deal with these challenges have evolved over time (U.S. Census Bureau 2010d).

National, state, and county populations are estimated using a components-of-population-change method to estimate how population has changed, drawing on a variety of administrative data sources, such as IRS records of tax return addresses and registers of births and deaths from members of the Federal State Cooperative Program for Population Estimates, or FSCPE. Estimating international migration flows has always been challenging given the United States' permeable borders and that emigration is not recorded.

The ACS data improves these estimates in several ways. It provides information on residence one year ago for foreign-born respondents, who are assumed to be immigrants if they were living in a different country then. The expected foreign-born population for the year is estimated based on that of the previous year; the residual (the difference between the expected number of foreign-born residents and the number estimated in the ACS) becomes the estimate of foreign-born emigration. In combination, the ACS and the Puerto Rico Community Survey (PRCS) are used to estimate flows between the United States and Puerto Rico.

Population estimates for smaller counties and places may be decidedly approximate. Census Bureau evaluations of intercensal estimates against population counts in the next census identify far more errors for smaller counties. Error is also more likely in places undergoing rapid change.

Current Population Survey

The Census Bureau conducts the monthly Current Population Survey (CPS) for the Bureau of Labor Statistics. The Annual Social and Economic Supplement (ASEC) of the CPS (conducted annually in March) provides additional detail on social characteristics such as household structure. Until the ACS was introduced, the CPS was the major source of updated intercensal estimates on social and demographic trends. However, with a sample size (for the March supplement) of just under 100,000, the CPS ASEC cannot be used at a finer spatial scale than the state level. For most social and demographic analyses, the ACS will be preferable to the CPS. The CPS is used primarily as a source of official data on employment patterns; it is discussed in more detail in chapter 6.

Conclusions

Is it possible to develop meaningful measures of complex and fluid social phenomena? A closer look at many familiar demographic variables suggests they are ambiguous and mutable rather than precise and universal. Can we argue that the biracial affiliations reported during the era of President Barack Obama will mean the same thing in the 2010 census as they did in the 2000 census, when many African American commentators were deeply suspicious of new racial definitions that were seen by some as an attempt to dilute starker racial categories, and divide racial minorities by separately identifying people who considered themselves biracial?

A healthy skepticism for the timelessness and universality implied in many analyses of demographic data need not lead to the conclusion that all numbers are equal. Concepts of ethnicity, sexuality, and disability will continue to be contested political and academic territory (Nagel 1994; Brown and Knopp 2006), but if we abandon measuring them we would also abandon the possibility of discussing meaningful solutions to the inequalities with which they are associated. The demographic concepts included in the census reflect an evolving public agenda of concern.

Chapter 5

Analyzing housing data

Census data provides a valuable resource for many parts of the housing industry and local government. In the late 1980s Congress proposed cutting costs by dropping most housing items from the census. City and state governments protested, and industry organizations such as the National Association of Realtors offered to volunteer their members to collect this information if the Census Bureau could not afford to do the work (Lavin 1996). Each decade, the battle continues over information versus costs versus paperwork reduction versus privacy. The housing questions on the ACS are justified by various pieces of legislation that require the data for allocating funds or setting priorities. For instance, cities prepare consolidated plans to qualify for HOME Investment Partnership or Community Development Block Grant (CDBG) funds from the federal government. Consolidated plans rely on census information on housing affordability and adequacy, and estimates of need are based on special tabulations of census data. Allocations of Low-Income Housing Tax Credits (LIHTC) are higher in census tracts identified as Difficult Development Areas or Qualified Census Tracts, which are determined based on income and housing cost information from the census and other sources. Bank regulators use census data on home-ownership rates, demographic and economic characteristics, and housing type to evaluate financial institutions' performance under the Community Reinvestment Act.

Developers use census and ACS data to analyze local housing markets, projecting demographic and economic trends to assess the type, quantity, and characteristics of new housing that would meet future demand. Community planners, nonprofit housing organizations, and human service providers (such as homeless shelters) analyze housing needs and gaps in supply to provide the justification for grant applications and to decide on future priorities. Real estate agents target their marketing based on the characteristics of neighborhood residents and housing stock. Housing markets are intensely local; spatially detailed information is needed to distinguish trends in adjacent neighborhoods with very different housing stocks and economic trends.

Census data is integral to many sorts of housing policy, investment, and funding decisions. The 2010 census reports information on tenure and housing occupancy; the ACS provides annually updated estimates of more detailed data such as the characteristics and costs of the housing stock.

This chapter begins by describing the major housing measurement concepts used in the 2010 and earlier censuses, and in the ACS. The housing data discussed here is available in the same formats as the demographic and social data described in chapter 4. Published tabulations for the ACS

cover many more combinations of variables than in previous decennial censuses, although the level of detail may differ by county size. PUMS data can be used to investigate record-level relationships among housing variables for PUMAs (see chapter 4 for a detailed discussion of microdata). We discuss several other important spatially detailed housing datasets gathered by the U.S. Census Bureau, the U.S. Department of Housing and Urban Development (HUD), and the Federal Reserve Board.

Understanding housing data

A substantial amount of housing data once collected in the long form of the decennial census has now been shifted to the ACS. Only data on housing unit counts, tenure, and occupancy status are reported in the 2010 census. An advantage of the ACS is that data on detailed housing characteristics and costs will now be gathered continuously, providing an updated estimate of how local housing markets are changing. Annual estimates of housing characteristics required for several state and federal programs—such as Fair Market Rents (FMRs), the basis for rental assistance—have been enriched by the availability of ACS data. A disadvantage of the ACS's smaller sample is that precision is reduced, and housing data at the census-tract level now reflects five-year averages rather than a point-in-time profile. In this section, we explain the basic measurement concepts used to describe local housing markets and conditions. More detailed definitions are available in the cited publications.

Two types of variables are discussed here: the basic housing measures collected in the 2010 census (and in the short form of previous decennial censuses), and the sample measures reported in the ACS.

Basic housing measures

The census gathers information on three housing characteristics: number of units, occupancy, and tenure. The ACS also collects information on these three characteristics, but the variables are not directly comparable because the ACS is based on a different universe of respondents.

Number of units

What is a housing unit? The question is not trivial. The concept of a housing unit is different from the more inclusive concept of living quarters. Living quarters include all kinds of group living arrangements—from sheltered care facilities and college dormitories to prisons—and all kinds of structures—from those intended for human habitation to a variety of nonresidential structures or places such as abandoned warehouses, tents, vans, and the streets. A housing unit, in contrast to a place where people live, is a residential structure such as an apartment, single-family home, or mobile home where a household lives separately from other households that may occupy the structure and has direct access from the outside or through a common hall that is not part of anyone else's living space (U.S. Census Bureau 2008). For vacant units, it may be difficult for the enumerator to decide whether these criteria apply. If so, the judgment is based on the previous occupants (U.S. Census Bureau 2004). Residential structures include boats, recreational vehicles, tents, or vans, if they are occupied by someone as their usual place of residence. If they are occupied only temporarily or are vacant, they are not housing units.

Occupied and vacant units

Vacancy rates are useful indicators of housing supply, but they are also used as a measure of neighborhood blight. Mortgage foreclosures and economic crisis have likely increased vacancy rates significantly in the worst-hit communities, but tracking changes over time is complicated because vacant units are defined differently in different datasets. Consistent historical comparisons require analysts to understand these differences. Chapter 4 explained how the ACS concept of place of residence differs from that used in the 2010 (and earlier) censuses. For the ACS, a housing unit is a place of residence (and thus an occupied unit) if its occupants intend to stay there for at least two months. If they are staying for a shorter period, it would be counted as vacant (U.S. Census Bureau 2006c). For the 2010 census, a housing unit is occupied if it is the usual place of residence of the occupants, the place they spend the majority of the year (U.S. Census Bureau 2008). Thus a home could be classified as occupied in the 2010 ACS but vacant in the 2010 census. Comparisons between 2000 and 2010 should be based on census rather than ACS data. Because only five-year average ACS data is available at the census tract level, detailed spatial comparisons of vacancy rates before and after the mortgage foreclosure crisis—that is, from about 2006 to 2010—are not possible for all except a handful of counties for which ACS test data was collected in the first half of the decade.

In both the ACS and 2010 census, vacant units are those not occupied by anyone at the time of the survey unless their residents are temporarily away, perhaps on vacation or business (U.S. Census Bureau 2006, 2008). Homes sold or rented but not yet occupied are vacant. So are homes under construction if they have all exterior windows and doors installed, and usable floors. If even one window or door is missing, they are not yet housing units, and thus would not be vacant. Condemned homes and those that have deteriorated to the extent that they are open to the elements are not counted as housing units and thus are not counted as vacant. But boarded-up homes are still counted as units, and thus would count (U.S. Census Bureau 2009a).

The ACS's administrative procedures make it less likely that vacant units will be identified, compared with the decennial censuses. Sampled units for which a paper return is not received are selected for follow up by telephone in the second month of the survey cycle, then by an in-person visit in the third month if there is still no response. Vacant units would only be identified during the third month. By that time, they might be occupied and thus would not be counted as vacant. In comparison, in-person follow up after the decennial censuses is continuous, beginning

the month after the survey date, so vacant units would be identified sooner, and thus the overall count of vacant units is likely higher in the decennial censuses than in the ACS (U.S. Census Bureau 2004; ORC Macro 2002). An alternative source of updated local estimates of vacant units (the Metropolitan Area Quarterly Vacancy Report, based on U.S. Postal Service data) is discussed in the next section.

Tenure

Home ownership rates are often used to measure prosperity and neighborhood stability, but ownership has many variants. Owners include

- occupants of mobile homes paying installment loans to dealers for a unit on rented land;

Figure 5.1 Homeownership rate changes, Florida, 2005–07

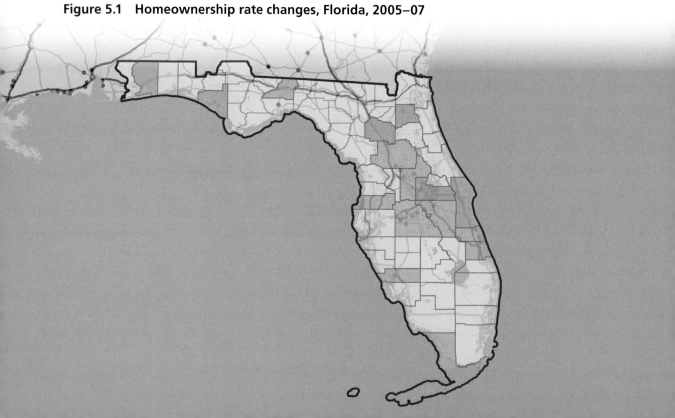

- tenants with a contract to purchase the home they're leasing, often at an exorbitant interest rate with few legal protections; and
- owners with negative equity in declining markets.

As the recent subprime lending crisis has demonstrated, home ownership is not necessarily stable. Figure 5.1 shows the rapid changes in home ownership rates between 2005 (the peak of what we now see as the housing bubble) and 2007 for counties in Florida. Home ownership rates declined in several counties and increased in others over this period. However, it is important to consider the effect of the imprecision in the ACS data on which these estimates are based. The counties outlined in heavier lines indicate those where changes are statistically significant (see chapter 2 for a discussion).

All occupied units are defined as either owned or rented. If the owner or co-owner lives in the house, it is owner-occupied, even if that person has only a contract to purchase, an installment loan, or a purchase agreement rather than a mortgage (U.S. Census Bureau 2008). Owners with home equity loans are counted as owning a home with a mortgage, even though they may have paid their original mortgage off (U.S. Census Bureau 2009a). Owner-occupied homes may be on leased or rented land such as a mobile home lot, or a community land trust home on land held by a separate agency. All other occupied housing units are counted as rented, even if the occupant pays no cash rent, such as in military housing or caretaker apartments.

Sample housing measures

In addition to these basic measures, the ACS gathers information on the physical characteristics of the housing stock (its configuration, condition, and attributes) and its economic characteristics (the value of homes and the costs of owning and renting).

Units in structure

The configuration of the local housing stock is one of the most important defining characteristics of housing markets. Many government housing assistance programs are targeted to only some types of units: for example, CDBG funds cannot be used to renovate mobile homes. Mortgage financing options differ between multifamily and single-family homes. Projections of energy use are based on the particular mix of homes within a community. Analyses of supply and demand are only useful indicators of market conditions if they are differentiated by type of housing unit.

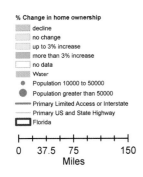

% Change in home ownership
- decline
- no change
- up to 3% increase
- more than 3% increase
- no data
- Water
- ● Population 10000 to 50000
- ● Population greater than 50000
- —— Primary Limited Access or Interstate
- —— Primary US and State Highway
- ☐ Florida

0   37.5   75   150
Miles

Source: Calculated from 2005 and 2007 ACS

In this typology, structures are buildings separated from neighboring buildings by space or by walls that extend from ground to roof (U.S. Census Bureau 2009a). Stores, office spaces, and other nonresidential uses are not counted as housing units, but structures that contain a variety of uses (such as retail and residential) are not identified separately in the census tables. The major housing types follow:

- Single-family units, which may be detached units surrounded by land, or attached units separated from others by a ground-to-roof wall. Two- to four-unit structures (including four-unit apartment buildings) are technically groups of single-family homes. Mobile homes with a permanent room addition, or with a permanent foundation, are single-family detached units, not mobile homes.

- Multifamily units, which are not separated from one another by space or by ground-to-roof walls, such as apartments and stacked duplexes. Multifamily structures have five or more units.

- Mobile homes, which do not have permanent attached structures or permanent foundations. Mobile homes used only for business or as extra sleeping space are not counted as separate housing units. In contrast to conventional homes, completed mobile homes for sale on a dealer's lot are not yet counted as housing units. HUD defines mobile homes as a type of manufactured housing that includes a range of prefabricated, modular, and factory-built homes that would be classified as single detached units once installed on a permanent foundation (HUD 2009). The practical distinction rests on whether the unit could be moved, even if this would require the addition of wheels. In most states, tax assessors treat mobile homes as personal property, and identical units on permanent foundations are classified (and taxed) as real estate. Cross-tabulations of unit type by tenure refer to the structure only—owner-occupied mobile homes include those on a rented lot in a park and those placed on the owner's land.

- Other types of structures including boats, recreational vehicles, vans, and the like that are occupied as housing units. Only structures occupied as permanent living quarters are counted as units in this definition; vacancy rates for this category of units are thus always zero.

Structure type is sometimes confused with ownership type. Row houses, town homes, or single-family attached homes may be owned as condominiums. Condos are not a type of structure but a form of ownership under which residents own their individual units, but all common spaces are owned by a condominium association, a particular form of homeowner's association (U.S. Census Bureau 2009a). In the case of an apartment building in condominium ownership, residents own a box of air, with all land, common spaces, and the exterior of the structure owned by the condominium association. Apartments or even single-family homes may be owned as cooperatives. Residents own a share in a corporation, which gives them the right to occupy a particular unit owned by the corporation. Row houses or attached units separated by ground-to-roof walls could be owned through fee-simple ownership as zero-lot line units. In this case, the householder owns the land on which the unit is placed, and there is no common property unless it is owned by a separate homeowners association. It is also possible to own the home but lease the land on which it sits.

Such distinctions are important. Traditionally, mortgage lenders have offered different loan products for different types of structures. Structures with four or fewer units are treated as single-family units eligible for lower-priced mortgages if they are owner-occupied. Structures with five or more units are classified as multifamily, and loans are usually made on different (less lenient) terms than single-family loans, even for owner-occupants (Schnare 2001). Loans for rental housing are made on commercial rates. Mobile homes classified as real estate are in principle eligible for more attractively priced single family loans. Those classified as personal property—that is, those not on a permanent foundation—are usually financed through dealer installment loans, or high-priced personal loans. The type of financing available to mobile home owners may have an important effect on long-term value appreciation or depreciation (Genz 2001).

Farms, businesses, and homes

Two questions are used to distinguish primarily residential units from farms. Acreage is reported in three categories: less than an acre (in which case the household is not questioned about agricultural sales in the previous year), more than one but less than ten acres, and ten acres or more. Occupants of homes on more than an acre are asked for the value of agricultural sales in the previous twelve months (U.S. Census Bureau 2009a). Respondents are also asked whether a business is on the premises. Businesses must be easily recognizable from the street. A private consultancy operated out of a home office with no distinguishing sign would not classify the property as a business premises. A dentist's office with a small sign would, however (U.S. Census Bureau 2009a). Acreage, farm sales, and the presence of a business are also used to

adjust the estimates of home value (discussed in the following section), eliminating the distorting effect that very large acreages or commercial properties could have on housing value.

Year structure built

Age is sometimes used as a proxy for housing condition, but this measure is often inaccurate. Neighborhoods with many old but well-preserved historic homes offer far better housing quality and value appreciation than suburbs made up of deteriorating 1960s- and 1970s-era homes. Homes built in the 1960s may be more likely to have lead paint than older homes, for instance (Jacobs et al 2002). The year the structure was built is not necessarily the year it was converted to a housing unit. For mobile homes, houseboats, recreational vehicles, and so on, year built is the manufacturer's model year (U.S. Census Bureau 2009a). Because this variable relies on the memory (or guess) of the occupant, it may be an unreliable measure. The 2000 census eliminated the optional response "don't know," but it is unclear whether this improved the accuracy of responses for older homes (U.S. Census Bureau 2004). Imputation rates for the year the structure was built are far higher than they are for other variables such as tenure or housing type, which are much easier questions to answer.

As chapter 3 explained, people do not always answer every question on the census (or ACS survey), so the Census Bureau fills in, or imputes, missing answers based on the other characteristics of the respondent. Table 5.1 compares 2000 Census of Population and Housing imputation rates for tenure, housing type, and year of construction, for counties in Massachusetts. So, in Barnstable County, Massachusetts, for instance, 11.37 percent of surveys in the 2000 census lacked

Table 5.1 Imputation rates for tenure, units, year, Massachusetts, 2000

County	Tenure	Units in Structure	Year Built
Barnstable	4.06	2.18	11.37
Berkshire	4.48	2.65	8.41
Bristol	4.38	3.85	14.73
Dukes	2.35	0.65	9.21
Essex	5.41	5.11	13.63
Franklin	3.01	2.27	9.57
Hampden	5.03	5.26	16.29
Hampshire	4.08	4.25	11.11
Middlesex	3.90	4.04	12.17
Nantucket	3.22	0.93	34.83
Norfolk	3.87	3.65	9.89
Plymouth	4.85	4.41	11.36
Suffolk	4.99	5.96	22.74
Worcester	3.26	3.76	12.06
Note: All figures in percentages.			

Source: Calculated from 2000 Census of Population and Housing

information about the age of the dwelling; this information was estimated (or imputed) based on the age of nearby dwellings of a similar type.

In some counties, more than one of five answers about the age of the structure are imputed, and imputation rates are likely to vary even more widely among census tracts. The table illustrates the importance of checking imputation rates to assess the reliability of the data. Consequently, comparisons about the age structure of the local housing stock over time are more difficult than comparisons of other housing variables.

Number of rooms and bedrooms, and occupants per room

This group of variables is essential to market analyses and assessments of the adequacy of the housing supply. They form the basis for estimates of overcrowding, one of the few housing quality indicators in the ACS.

Rooms are enclosed areas suitable for year-round use. This category includes kitchens (but not Pullman or strip kitchens), finished recreation rooms or enclosed porches. Unfinished attics and basements, bathrooms, halls, foyers, or utility rooms are not considered habitable rooms. Rooms are enclosed by a floor-to-ceiling partition (not just shelves or cabinets) but need not have a door (U.S. Census Bureau 2009a).

Bedrooms would be rooms listed as such when advertising a home for sale or rent, even if the room is used for some other purpose now, such as a study. An efficiency apartment has no bedroom. Before 1990, bedrooms had to be used for sleeping; a room used as a study, for instance, was not a bedroom (U.S. Census Bureau 2009a). This small change in definition matters if you are using census data to identify trends in home size over time.

Dividing the number of people in the household by the number of rooms in the dwelling provides a measure of overcrowding. HUD defines units with more than one person per room as overcrowded; those with more than 1.5 people per room are severely overcrowded. Like the definition of affordability (discussed later in this chapter), this is in part a cultural standard based on assumptions about housing adequacy (Blake, Kellerson, and Simic 2007).

Overcrowding is an important measure of housing quality. While it is a minor problem in most places, it has grown in significance in very high-priced markets, and in places with high concentrations of very poor households. The financial crisis of the past few years has likely also resulted in higher rates of overcrowding, as households who have lost their homes to foreclosure (or lost jobs) move in with family or friends. However, because overcrowded households are usually only a small proportion of all households, the ACS may not be precise enough to chart changes in overcrowding over time at a detailed spatial scale (MacDonald 2006). Figure 5.2a shows the proportion of renter households who were overcrowded in San Diego in 2000. In many inner city and inner suburban tracts, more than 35 percent of renter households had more than one person per room. Smaller but still substantial proportions of renter households were severely overcrowded, as figure 5.2b shows. Comparisons with the situation in 2010, which would highlight the effects of the most recent economic crisis, will be difficult because the ACS reports only five-year averages at the census tract level. If the crisis is sustained for a full five-year cycle, these effects could be identified, but if acute levels of overcrowding are dissipated as housing prices fall and the economy stabilizes, peak effects will be smoothed out in the averages reported for census tracts. One-year averages for cities would be a better choice to compare the impacts of economic crisis on rates of overcrowding overall.

Plumbing and kitchen facilities

These are the only measures of housing condition included in the decennial census. As measures of housing quality, the presence of complete kitchens and bathrooms is a very limited indicator. The American Housing Survey (AHS) provides much more detailed information on housing condition, including assessments of the condition of the roof and siding, the presence of leaks, and so

on. However, the AHS is available at only a broad geographic scale. Variables with very small numbers of reported units will be more difficult to track in the ACS, because the margins of error around these estimates are likely to be very wide. Thus, though some federal programs, such as CDBG funding, use these two measures to distribute funds, the lesser precision of the ACS measures may reduce their usefulness (ORC Macro 2002).

Complete plumbing facilities include hot and cold piped water, a flush toilet, and a bathtub or shower, located inside the unit but not necessarily in the same room (U.S. Census Bureau 2009a). In most states, only small proportions of homes lacked complete plumbing, which may be associated with groundwater contamination. However, states with more remote communities and infrastructure challenges, Alaska in particular, have much higher proportions of homes without complete plumbing. Figures 5.3a and 5.3b compare the incidence of homes without complete plumbing in Alaska with the incidence in a more typical state, such as Missouri.

Complete kitchen facilities include a sink with piped water, a range (or cooktop and oven), and a refrigerator. Homes with a microwave or portable cooking equipment but no range, or an icebox but no refrigerator, have incomplete kitchens. This variable is cross-tabulated with data on whether meals are included in rent, so units that do not require complete kitchens, such as in independent living facilities, can be identified (U.S. Census Bureau 2009a).

Telephone available

Estimating homes without telephones may be useful for identifying particularly vulnerable households and for determining whether a telephone survey would reach an adequate sample of

Figure 5.2a Overcrowded renter households, San Diego, California, 2000

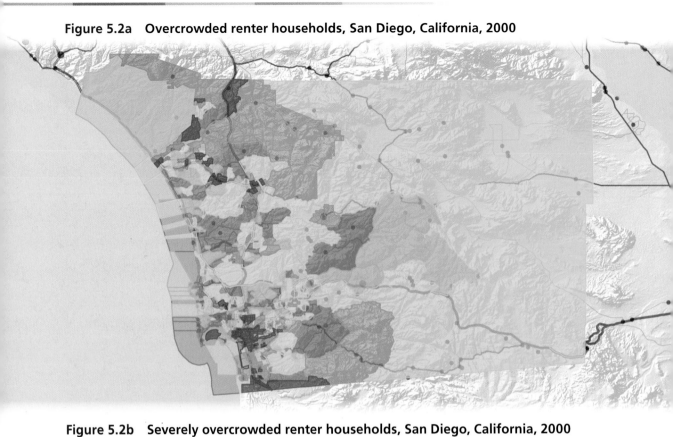

Figure 5.2b Severely overcrowded renter households, San Diego, California, 2000

**% Over-crowded
renter households**

☐ 5% or less

☐ more than 5% to 10%

☐ more than 10% to 20%

☐ more than 20% to 35%

☐ more than 35%

☐ Water

• Population less than 10000

● Population 10000 to 50000

● Population greater than 50000

— Primary Limited Access or Interstate

— Primary US and State Highway

— Secondary State and County

0   5   10   20
         Miles

Source: 2000 Census of Population and Housing SF3

**% Severely over-crowded
households
(More than 2 people per room)**

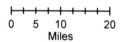

☐ 5% or less

☐ more than 5% to 10%

☐ more than 10% to 20%

☐ more than 20% to 35%

☐ more than 35%

☐ Water

— Primary Limited Access or Interstate

— Primary US and State Highway

— Secondary State and County

• Population less than 10000

● Population 10000 to 50000

● Population greater than 50000

0   5   10   20
         Miles

Source: 2000 Census of Population and Housing SF3

different types of households. Emergency services also take this information into account. As of 2003, the ACS definition changed so that households with only cell phones are recorded as having a telephone available, even though they do not have land lines (U.S. Census Bureau 2008).

Year householder moved into unit

Migration patterns and neighborhood stability can be estimated from this indicator of mobility. It always refers to the most recent move to the current home (not, for instance, to another apartment at the same address). Renters and owners usually have different rates of mobility. Rapid turnover may indicate a neighborhood in economic decline, a new suburb, a neighborhood dominated by mobile young adult renters, or one that is gentrifying (Lee, Oreposa, and Kanan 1994). The demographics of the population, trends in housing prices, physical and economic factors, and the balance between rental and owner-occupied households need to be considered (alongside rates of new construction) to explain the causes of higher or lower mobility rates. For instance, a neighborhood may grow rapidly because it offers comparatively low-cost housing, or vacant developable land, or amenities appealing to young singles, or because it is close to a job growth area. Projecting future growth should be based on a clear understanding of the reasons for past growth. Is it reasonable to expect that housing will still be a bargain as the neighborhood becomes established? Are there remaining developable lots? Do demographic projections suggest there will be a large enough cohort of young singles to replace current residents when they move out to more family-oriented neighborhoods? Will the industries responsible for the job growth continue to prosper or expand in this location?

Figure 5.3a   Homes without complete plumbing, Alaska, 2000

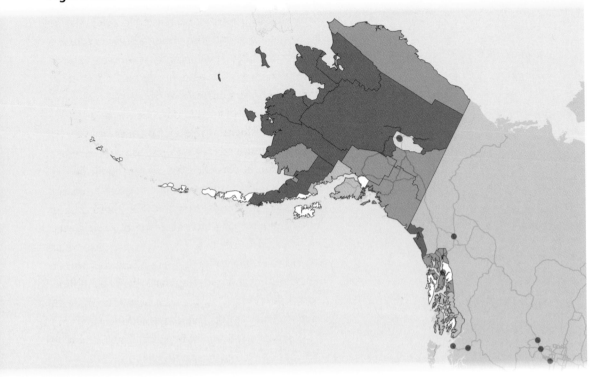

Figure 5.3b   Homes without complete plumbing, Missouri, 2000

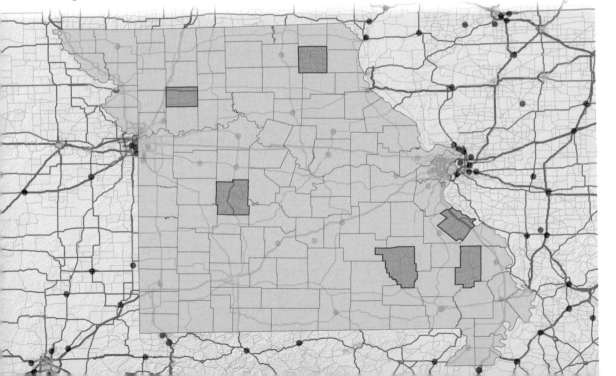

House heating fuel

In high-cost heating environments, reliance on electricity or wood may also indicate a housing-quality problem. Fuel source also helps identify environmentally vulnerable places (U.S. Census Bureau 2009a). Data about fuel can be correlated with other more detailed data on costs and usage from the Residential Energy Consumption Survey (which is designed based in part on this variable). Each home is classified by the one type of fuel used most often to heat the home. Solar energy was included as a possible response beginning in 1990. In locations that require heating, units that report no fuel used may provide another indicator of poor housing quality, but advances in green building technology complicate this assumption. Although the ACS collects information about energy costs, this is not shown in the summary tables. It is reflected only in the calculation of monthly housing costs or gross rent.

Contract rent, gross rent, and rent asked

These are slightly different measures of rental housing costs, another essential component of market analyses and assessments of housing affordability and need. Rental units are all those not occupied by an owner, not only those for which rent is paid. Homes occupied as a condition of employment, such as a minister's house or caretaker's apartment, or those owned by a friend or family member who allows the occupant to live there rent-free, are rentals with no cash rent (U.S. Census Bureau 2008).

The difference between contract rent (the monthly rent contracted for, regardless of the kinds of services included, such as utilities or meals) and gross rent is important. Gross rent is derived from several questions: it includes the contract rent and the average estimated monthly cost of utilities (electricity, gas, water, and sewer),

% Homes without complete plumbing

☐ 5% or less
☐ more than 5% to 10%
☐ more than 10% to 20%
☐ more than 20% to 35%
■ more than 35%
● Population 10000 to 50000
— Primary US and State Highways

0   125   250   500
            Miles

Source: 2000 Census of Population and Housing SF3

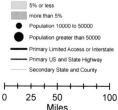

% Homes without complete plumbing

☐ 5% or less
☐ more than 5%
● Population 10000 to 50000
⬤ Population greater than 50000
— Primary Limited Access or Interstate
— Primary US and State Highway
— Secondary State and County

0   25   50   100
          Miles

Source: 2000 Census of Population and Housing SF3

fuels, and condominium fees, if these are paid by the renter (U.S. Census Bureau 2009a). Of the two, gross rent provides a better measure for comparison. Contract rent distributions may be skewed by including units with and without paid utilities.

Contract rent is the total paid from all sources. A tenant with a government housing subsidy, or with a roommate who pays half the rent, would therefore report the total paid, not just the individual share. For units that include business premises, contract rent is the amount paid for the residential portion of the unit only.

Aggregate gross rent is tabulated separately for units with and without meals included. Where there are many congregate housing units (not group living quarters, which are not counted as housing units), it would be helpful to separate the number of units with meals included. Average rents could be calculated for units without meals included to adjust the overall gross rent distribution. Gross rent is also reported for units of different sizes. A strong correlation often exists between gross rent and the incidence of overcrowding. Figure 5.4 shows median gross rents in 2000 by census tract in San Diego.

Rent asked can be a useful indicator of the supply of units. For instance, vacancy rates may be around normal (in stable housing markets, about 5 percent would be the expected vacancy rate), but units with affordable rents may be in tight supply.

Figure 5.4 Median gross rent, San Diego, California, 2000

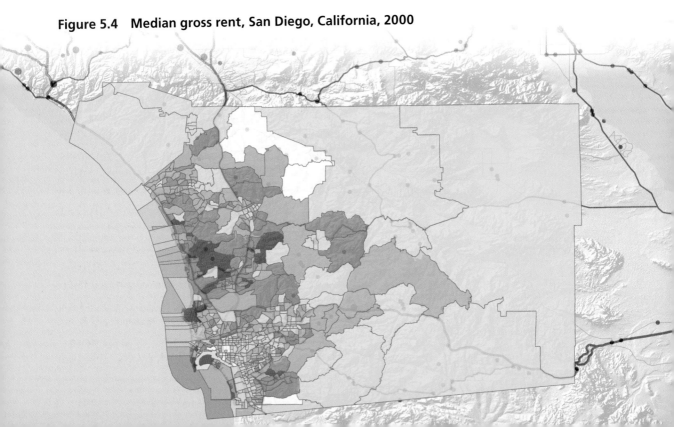

However, this variable often has quite high imputation rates (see discussion that follows), which may limit its precision.

Gross rent as a percentage of income

The gross rent as a percentage of income ratio measures the affordability of the housing stock. Federal, state, and local housing programs assume that households paying more than 30 percent of their gross income in rent are cost-burdened. Those paying more than 50 percent for rent are defined as severely cost-burdened. Housing assistance is usually targeted to very low-income, cost-burdened households (HUD 2010). Cross-tabulations by race and ethnicity, income, householder age, and type of unit make it easy to identify the households most likely to have affordability problems. Figure 5.5 shows the proportion of cost-burdened renter households in counties in Massachusetts on average during the 2005–07 period. Since 2000, the percentage of cost-burdened renter households increased significantly in most counties.

Units with no cash rent and households that reported no income or a net loss in 1999 are not included in this ratio. The ratio is based on gross rent as a percentage of gross income, not tenant payments. Households with housing assistance may therefore be shown as cost-burdened, even though they may pay no more than 30 percent of their income in rent (U.S. Census Bureau 2009a). Accurately reflecting affordability problems in a local housing market requires additional data on the numbers of households receiving assistance. Local public housing authorities would be the best source of this information.

Value

The distribution of home values is important for market analyses, but census and ACS data have some limitations. Estimates of home value are gathered for all owner-occupied homes and vacant homes for sale (U.S. Census Bureau 2009a). Estimates of the value of vacant units may be more reliable than estimates for occupied units, because value is based on a sales or asking price (although it does not differentiate between new and existing homes for sale). For occupied units, it is based on the owner's estimate of the home's value. It is easy to see how value could be under- or overestimated unless the owner has a relatively current appraisal. Owners who bought their homes decades ago and have little knowledge of the local real estate market might do either. Property tax-based estimates of market prices from local assessors and

**Median gross rent
by tract**

- $500 or less
- $501 to $750
- $751 to $1000
- $1001 to $1500
- $1501 to $2001
- Water
- • Population less than 10000
- ● Population 10000 to 50000
- ⬤ Population greater than 50000
- ▬ Primary Limited Access or Interstate
- — Primary US and State Highway
- — Secondary State and County

0   5   10   20
         Miles

Source: 2000 Census of Population and Housing

sales records from the local board of Realtors may be helpful checks.

Value includes the value of the land and the home. If the home is owned but not the land, respondents are asked to estimate the combined value of home and land. This may be difficult to do for parcels of land that are rarely sold separately, such as a rented lot in a mobile home park.

A variable may have very different values depending on the universe for which it is tabulated. Specified owner-occupied (or vacant for-sale) units include only single-family homes (not mobile homes) on fewer than ten acres, without a business or medical office on the premises. Thus, specified units would include single-family condominium units but not those in multiunit structures. Approximately 80 percent of all owner-occupied

homes are included in this definition (Bonnette 2003). Value is tabulated separately for mobile homes (which also include estimates of the value of the land, even if the home is on a rented lot), and for all owner-occupied units (including those excluded from the above description). "All owner-occupied units" includes homes in multiunit structures and single-family homes on more than ten acres, as well as mobile homes (U.S. Census Bureau 2009a).

Mortgage status and selected monthly owner costs

Mortgage status distinguishes between homes owned free and clear and those with a loan secured by the property. Loans include deeds of trust, land contracts, home equity loans, and conventional

Figure 5.5   Cost-burdened renters, Massachusetts, 2005–07

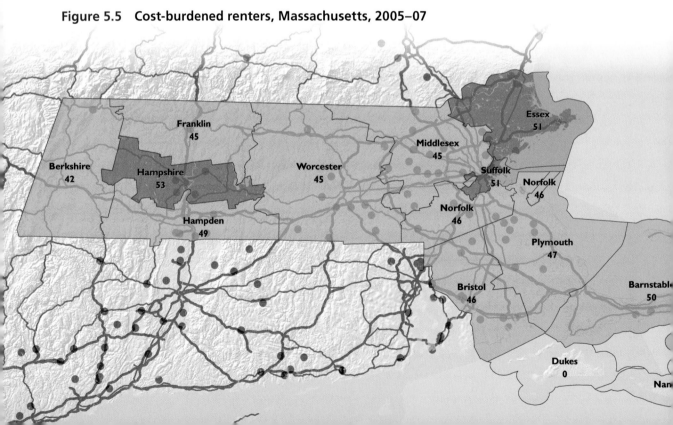

mortgage loans. Data is collected separately on each loan, and monthly owner costs are tabulated separately for owners with and without a mortgage.

Like gross rent, monthly owner cost is estimated from several questions. It is the sum of payments for

- all loans secured by the property,
- real estate taxes,
- property insurance, and
- utilities and fuels.

It may also include

- monthly condominium fees,
- installment loan payments (not secured by the property), and
- lot rent and other charges associated with mobile homes.

% Cost burdened renters

- no data
- 25% or less
- 25% to 40%
- 40% to 50%
- 50% or greater
- Water
- ● Population 10000 to 50000
- ● Population greater than 50000
- Primary Limited Access or Interstate
- Primary US and State Highway

0   12.5   25   50
Miles

Source: 2005-2007 ACS (3 year averages)

Monthly costs are tabulated separately for all owner-occupied units, selected owner-occupied units, and owner-occupied mobile homes (U.S. Census Bureau 2009a). Mortgage status and owner costs were collected from all sampled units beginning in 2000, not just single-family owner-occupied units, mobile homes, and condominium units.

Monthly owner costs as a percentage of income

The ratio of monthly owner costs to income measures the affordability of home ownership, but should be used with more caution than the rental affordability ratio. Rents tend to increase regularly to reflect market prices, but home ownership costs do not. Protection from inflation in housing costs is one of the benefits of ownership, although owners are of course not protected from the effect of sharp declines in home value. Thus the ratio of housing costs to income reflects a wide range of situations, from long-established owners who spend a minor share of their income on housing, to new homeowners struggling to afford "as much house as they can buy" (Megbolugbe and Linneman 1993). Overall, housing costs make up a lower share of owners' incomes than it does for renters; more than two-thirds of owners spent less than 30 percent of their income on housing in 2009, compared with only 40 percent of renters. The median ratio of housing costs to income was 21 percent for owners and 34 percent for renters (U.S. Census Bureau and HUD 2009). The year the household moved in may significantly affect owner costs and affordability. Another complicating factor is that the estimate includes all mortgage payments. Home equity loans and other mortgage-type debt may be used for consumer expenditures, but this skews estimates of ownership costs upwards. Owner costs are estimated separately for households with a mortgage and those

Figure 5.6a Cost-burdened owners with mortgages, Massachusetts, 2005–07

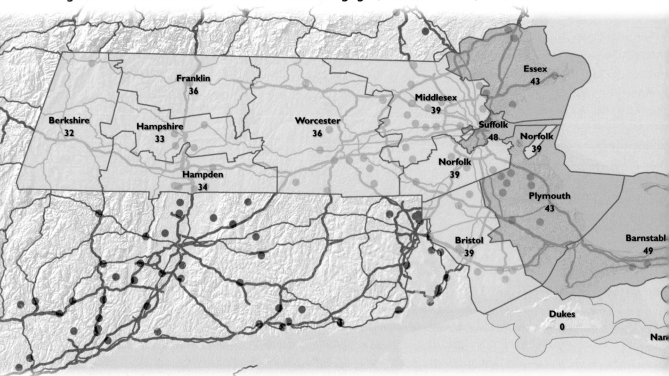

Figure 5.6b Cost-burdened owners without mortgages, Massachusetts, 2005–07

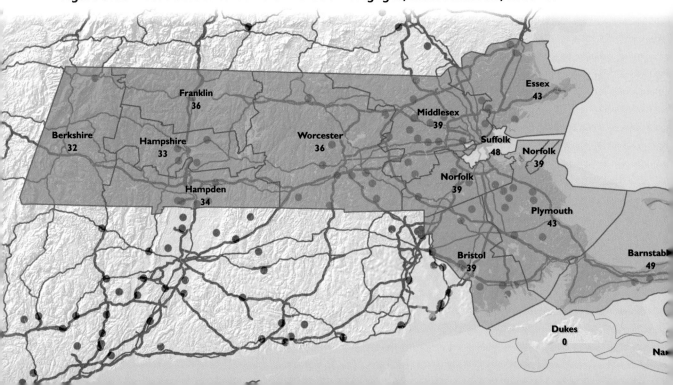

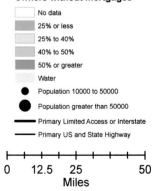

**% cost burdened
owners with mortgages**

- no data
- 25% or less
- 25% to 40%
- 40% to 50%
- 50% or greater
- Water
- Population 10000 to 50000
- Population greater than 50000
- Primary Limited Access or Interstate
- Primary US and State Highway

0   12.5   25   50
Miles

Source: 2005-2007 ACS (3 year averages)

**% cost burdened
owners without mortgages**

- No data
- 25% or less
- 25% to 40%
- 40% to 50%
- 50% or greater
- Water
- Population 10000 to 50000
- Population greater than 50000
- Primary Limited Access or Interstate
- Primary US and State Highway

0   12.5   25   50
Miles

Source: 2005-2007 ACS (3 year averages)

without. Figures 5.6a and 5.6b show the percent of cost-burdened owner households with and without mortgages in Massachusetts over the 2005–07 period. As with renters, most counties saw significant increases in the percent of cost-burdened owner households compared to 2000.

Traditionally, lenders used a ratio of housing costs to gross income to calculate how much debt a household could afford. These ratios are flexible; a typical standard is 28 percent of income for housing, but the increased use of subprime mortgages in the 2000s pushed the bounds of acceptable debt-to-income ratios. Recent regulatory reforms aim to reestablish the link between incomes and debt payments, for instance, in the Mortgage Reform and Anti-Predatory Lending Act of 2010, Title XIV of PL 111-203.

A general note about imputation of housing costs: monthly housing costs and rents are important indicators of problems in local housing markets. They are widely used to evaluate changing market conditions and identify areas for intervention, for instance, by providing more rental assistance or subsidizing affordable housing development. We have discussed the limitations on precision imposed by the smaller sample size of the ACS compared with previous decennial censuses; for variables with fewer observations, margins of error may be much wider than those for larger categories. This is often an issue for renters, who account for a smaller share of residents in most communities than homeowners.

However, an additional methodological consideration is the wide variance in imputation rates among different housing variables. (We have already discussed imputation rates for housing age in this chapter, and imputation rates in general in chapter 3.) When respondents are unavailable or unable to answer a question, an answer

Table 5.2   Imputation rates for housing cost variables, Massachusetts, 2009

County	Rent Asked	Gross Rent	Value	Price Asked	Mortgage Status	Housing Costs (Mortgage)	Housing Costs (No Mortgage)
Barnstable	61.40	13.94	4.89	5.48	0.58	35.51	31.71
Berkshire	24.67	22.52	7.44	7.10	1.16	31.24	25.68
Bristol	32.53	17.78	10.54	48.63	1.52	34.88	29.38
Essex	46.84	17.84	9.36	67.74	1.40	36.28	29.21
Franklin	0.00	9.48	6.46	0.00	0.78	37.10	23.85
Hampden	15.80	17.07	8.65	22.51	1.03	34.17	24.06
Hampshire	46.27	15.21	7.47	23.20	1.64	34.66	26.03
Middlesex	41.00	18.51	7.77	23.15	1.19	34.06	29.79
Norfolk	33.63	19.23	8.94	15.25	1.52	36.83	29.44
Plymouth	46.80	21.64	8.67	20.86	1.74	38.55	31.14
Suffolk	30.03	20.44	14.12	11.57	1.79	35.81	23.60
Worcester	39.49	16.76	7.41	18.15	1.03	32.39	27.84
Note: All numbers in percentages.							

Source: Calculated from 2009 American Community Survey 1-year file

is imputed based on the characteristics of similar dwelling units. Table 5.2 summarizes imputation rates for several components of housing cost data from the 2009 ACS for counties in Massachusetts. Most housing cost variables include substantial proportions of imputed responses in most counties, though some (such as mortgage status) have very low imputation rates. Consequently, although housing cost indicators may be an acceptable general guide, data from the census or ACS is no substitute for careful analysis of actual sales, rents, and housing costs.

Other sources of housing data

Housing market trends drive segments of the construction, real estate, and finance industries, and are an important part of local government revenue sources, through their effect on property taxes. Housing subsidies and incentives are key parts of state and local economic development strategies. Governments and industry argue that because many of their housing-related decisions rely on locally specific and current information on trends, the cost of gathering more spatially detailed data in addition to that collected in the ACS is justified (U.S. Congress 2003). Two main sources of data are discussed in this section:

- data collected through the Construction Division of the Census Bureau (housing starts and building permits)
- data collected or estimated by the Department of Housing and Urban Development and other federal agencies

Other important datasets report information at much broader spatial scales. The American Housing Survey (AHS), conducted by the Census Bureau for HUD, is based on a sample of about 55,000 units nationally. It is also conducted in forty-seven metropolitan areas every six years (the sample in each metropolitan area is about 4,100 units). The AHS provides detailed information on the housing stock, which can provide a valuable context for geographic analyses. It is not discussed in detail here because its geographic applicability is limited. The Housing Vacancy and Homeownership Survey (HVS), conducted alongside the Current Population Survey, is based on a sample of about 80,000 households. Information from the HVS is reported for 75 metropolitan areas. Like the AHS, it provides a valuable picture of broad trends but limited geographic applicability.

Building permits

The Construction Division of the Census Bureau collects and reports monthly information on building permits for places issuing permits (about 20,000 cities and counties). Data reported includes the following:

- number of permits issued for residential structures of different types (single unit, two to four units, and five or more units)
- number of units within each type of structure
- value per unit (not necessarily the same as cost per unit or ultimate sales price)

Building permits are useful in analyzing trends in residential construction and to update estimates of the housing stock. Unfortunately, information on demolition is no longer collected and must be obtained from local sources to construct accurate estimates of the current housing stock between decennial censuses. Permits are reported at the place but not the census-tract level. Permits

issued in the unincorporated portions of counties are reported separately in a single category for each county. Not all local governments issue permits, and even where required they may be unevenly enforced. Monthly building permit reports are obtained from only a sample of smaller jurisdictions, whereas all 20,000 permit-issuing jurisdictions are surveyed for annual permit activity, so annual data is more reliable for smaller places than monthly data (U.S. Census Bureau 1990).

The Survey of Construction (SOC) is based on a sample of building permits and construction in nonpermit issuing areas. Builders are interviewed to gather information on the start and completion dates of construction, the date of sale, and other characteristics such as home size. The sample is not large enough to report data at the place level, but a new SOC microdata file is available that identifies units by the nine census divisions and whether they are inside or outside a metropolitan area. Annual files are available starting in 1999. The forty characteristics reported include substantial details about construction materials, cost and price, and amenities (U.S. Census Bureau 2010h).

Housing starts

Building permits are different from housing starts and completions, and have a few inconsistencies with census concepts. Some of the structures that local governments classify as multiunit would be classified as single-family attached units in the ACS (such as townhouses). Not all building permits result in housing starts, especially during economic downturns. Developments may be redesigned to produce more or fewer units than specified in the permit. Overall, the Census Bureau estimates that there were 2.5 percent fewer starts than permits for all units, 2.5 percent more single-family starts than permits, and 22.5 percent fewer multifamily starts than permits, on average during the period from 1999 to 2004 (U.S. Census Bureau MMCS 2006a).

Not all housing starts were completed: of all units, there were 4 percent fewer completions than starts, 3.5 percent fewer for single family units and 7.5 percent fewer for multifamily units (U.S. Census Bureau MMCS 2006a.). Thus, using place-level building permit data to estimate additions to the local single-family housing stock, we could adjust the annual single-family building permits reported for the place upward by 2.5 percent to estimate starts, then reduce the estimate of starts by 3.5 percent to approximate the number of single-family units completed. But these relationships are volatile. Figure 5.7 shows trends in building permits, housing starts, and completions for single detached structures for the month of May from 2004 to 2009. The relationships among the three measures vary over time, because completions lag starts, which lag permit applications. The massive recent declines illustrate the difficulty of projecting trends when economic circumstances change dramatically.

Building permit and construction data are used along with mobile home shipments and estimates of housing losses to develop the Census Bureau's annual estimates of housing units for states and counties. These estimates are the basis for the subcounty population estimates described in chapter 4.

Fair market rents

HUD develops annual estimates of FMRs for counties and metropolitan areas to set maximum rents covered by housing assistance vouchers and other subsidy programs. FMRs are estimates of gross rent (shelter plus all utilities) for a moderately priced two-bedroom unit of standard quality

Figure 5.7 Building permits, starts, and completions, 2004–09

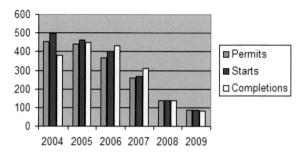

Source: U.S. Census Bureau MMCS 2006b., http://www.census.gov/const/www/newresconstindex.html

(which are then adjusted for units of different sizes). HUD's methodology for calculating FMRs relies quite heavily on the ACS, updating the previous year's estimates based on the ratio between current and previous year ACS estimated rents. HUD uses the ACS differently for categories of areas based on whether the ACS sample includes at least 200 cases of two-bedroom standard quality rents or not. The precise FMR methodology used is explained for each county (U.S. Department of Housing and Urban Development n.d.a).

Subsidized housing

HUD offers a variety of other census-tract level information, which has been extensively updated and supplemented in recent months. Data on assisted and subsidized housing is available for 2008, and data on Low Income Housing Tax Credit projects has been updated for 2010. Related sources include the official list of Qualified Census

Tracts (QCTs) and Difficult Development Areas (DDAs), a statutory designation based on several census variables. QCTs are high poverty areas, and DDAs are high housing cost/low income areas. Information on the physical quality of properties owned, insured or subsidized by HUD is now available, with location data (HUD n.d.b).

Vacancy data

An interesting new data source is based on U.S. Postal Service delivery data. Vacant addresses (identified for mail delivery purposes by USPS carriers) are aggregated quarterly at the census-tract level to estimate total vacancy rates in the Metropolitan Area Quarterly Vacancy Report compiled by HUD. Residential vacancy rates are distinguished from business vacancy rates, and the average number of days vacant is calculated for each tract. A high proportion of rural homes do not receive mail. These, along with homes under construction or in the process of demolition, are identified by the USPS as "no-stat" addresses rather than vacant addresses (HUD n.d.c).

The data for vacancy rates measures something different than the data measured by the ACS or the decennial censuses; it includes only addresses vacant for at least 90 days, and it does not distinguish between seasonal or permanent homes or between homes for rent and for sale. A large number of rural addresses are excluded. Figure 5.8 shows estimated residential vacancy rates by census tract for the first quarter of 2009, for the Gary, Indiana, metropolitan area.

Because the data is quarterly and published quite rapidly, it provides a more timely estimate of vacancy rates, and thus of the economic stability of neighborhoods. The data may also be a better indicator than the ACS, given the problems with the ACS vacancy variable. The availability of

business address vacancies provides a spatial dimension to economic development data that we have lacked until now.

Home mortgage data

The Home Mortgage Disclosure Act (HMDA) requires most mortgage lenders to report information on each loan application they receive. HMDA's main purpose is to show the volume of mortgage credit flowing into particular neighborhoods, but it can also be used as good indicators of where different types of people are buying or refinancing homes and the size and type of loans they are obtaining. The HMDA covers banks, savings and loans, credit unions, and mortgage brokers with assets more than $30 million if they have headquarters in a metropolitan area. The data is incomplete in nonmetropolitan areas, but in recent years as the mortgage lending industry has consolidated, HMDA's coverage in nonmetro areas has improved. HMDA data provides information at the census-tract level. It includes demographic information on the race and gender of borrowers and co-borrowers, household income, and the loan amount. Since 2004, HMDA has reported details of some high-cost loans, which provided a basis for estimating the locations of subprime mortgages (Federal Financial Institutions Examination Council 2010a).

Researchers used this data to investigate whether particular neighborhoods were being targeted by predatory lenders and to forecast the locations where subprime mortgage foreclosures were likely to be concentrated (Li and Ernst 2006; Immergluck 2009; Schuetz, Been, and Ellen 2008). But the research had little impact because the data they used (available only since 2004) relied on indirect proxies for subprime mortgages and lacked a crucial variable—applicant credit scores. It was easy for lenders to dismiss allegations that some borrowers were receiving loans on worse terms than they deserved because there was no information on borrower credit scores. The GAO's recent assessment of regulatory failures in Fair Lending enforcement concluded that regulators did not have adequate information to enforce the law (GAO 2009). As this book goes to press, Congress is debating legislation that will expand the data required under HMDA. Expansions are likely to be vigorously resisted by mortgage lenders, who argue that new data reporting requirements are costly.

It is possible that HMDA will be significantly expanded: the last dramatic expansion occurred in 1989 after the savings and loan crisis.

The mortgage lending data story illustrates the intensely political nature of public information. A similar source of home financing information is the public use database on the government-sponsored enterprises (GSEs). Fannie Mae and Freddie Mac are secondary mortgage markets, now government-owned, but still known collectively as the GSEs. They purchase loans from mortgage lenders with funds raised through securities and

Figure 5.8   Residential vacancy rates, Gary, Indiana, first quarter 2009

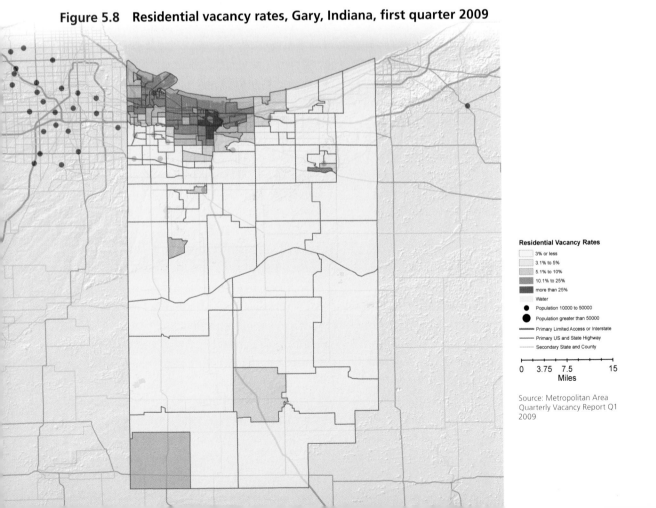

bond issues, and this dataset reports the location and several other characteristics of the loans they purchase. The GSE data is provided in different formats, for single-family (one to four units) and multifamily (five or more units) loans. For each type of mortgage, one file has a census-tract identifier along with demographic information about the borrower (age, race, gender, income, and whether the borrower was a first-time buyer). As with HMDA, the loan amount is shown, but not the original sales price of the home (Federal Housing Finance Agency 2010b). Although the GSEs also report the loan-to-value ratio and other characteristics of loans purchased, this information is not linked to the geographic identifiers. Because GSE data covers only some home financing activity, it is less useful as a general indicator of neighborhood trends but may be of interest for specific questions about patterns of investment.

Conclusions

The census and ACS provide spatially detailed data on housing markets that enables market analyses, needs assessments, and many other sorts of research on urban development patterns. State and local governments, the housing related industries, nonprofit organizations, and academics are some of the major users of this data, in addition to the federal government programs under which it is authorized. Although the data is probably as good quality as possible within the constraints of funding, it suffers from important limitations that analysts should be aware of. The traditional limitations on census data take new forms in the ACS. In addition, the data that gets collected and the ways it is reported also reflects broader political forces; banks resisted reporting sufficiently detailed information on loan terms that would have enabled regulators to see broader patterns of subprime lending emerging, for instance. Similarly, some of the limitations imposed by the introduction of the ACS have a political basis: they reflect Congress's assessment of the worth of funding better quality national data.

Chapter 6

Analyzing economic data

Economic indicators are at the heart of many of our policy decisions. The dramatic effects of quarterly unemployment estimates on politicians' approval ratings, or the use of poverty rates to identify target neighborhoods for a plethora of antipoverty programs, result in part from economic data. Income, employment, and poverty rates define much of our understanding of particular places and our judgment of whether current policy directions are working. But most nonspecialists are unsure where the data for various indicators comes from, how it is constructed, and how and when to use the various sources for key indicators.

Understanding economic data

Unlike social and demographic data, economic data is collected in a wide variety of formats and time periods. Economic data is needed at both the household and the establishment (or firm) level, because we care about the economic circumstances of people, places, and industrial sectors. The ACS is one but not the only source of economic information about people, households, and the communities in which they live (the 2010 census did not collect any economic data).

The Economic Census collects information about businesses based on firm location. It is conducted every five years, in years ending in two or seven. A series of monthly surveys conducted by the Census Bureau and the Bureau of Labor Statistics provide other sources of official data on economic trends. Some of these data sources are based on where people live, and some on where they work. This chapter begins with a discussion of economic data collected at the household level then discusses data collected at the establishment level.

Economic data collected at the household level

Economic data about households is collected in the ACS and other Census Bureau surveys but not in the decennial census. Because the ACS is based on continuous measurement, economic variables such as income, poverty, and employment will be defined somewhat differently that they were in 2000. These differences are important considerations when doing analyses over time.

Income

Income is a key indicator of social prosperity and one of the most widely required pieces of information for policy and resource distribution. Income is requested from all household members age fifteen or older. In decennial censuses before 2010, respondents were asked for their income during the previous calendar year (1999 in the case of the 2000 census). Because the ACS is a continuously administered survey, the question is structured differently, asking people to report their income for the previous twelve months. Thus, the one-year ACS estimate of household income in 2010 represents an average of incomes reported during a period from December 2008 to November 2010. Consequently, the income estimates are adjusted for inflation (using the consumer price index) to refer to the survey period (2010). A similar strategy is used for three-year and five-year ACS releases; incomes would be expressed in 2007 dollars for the 2005–07 estimates and in 2009 dollars for the 2005–09 estimates (U.S. Census Bureau 2006).

Income is defined differently in the decennial censuses and the ACS compared with other sources, such as the Current Population Survey Annual Social and Economic Supplement (Webster 2007). Total census income includes the following: gross earnings (wages or salary, or self-employment income); interest and dividends; rents and royalties; trusts and estates, Social Security or retirement, survivor or disability pensions; Supplemental Security Income (SSI); and public assistance or welfare payments (other sources not excluded). Total census income excludes: capital gains; money from the sale of property (unless it was the sale of a person's business); in-kind income from food stamps, housing assistance, medical care, and so on; loans; tax refunds; support from family members living in the household; gifts and inheritances; and other lump sum amounts. Unearned income, such as interest, dividends, net rental income, and public assistance, is more likely to be underreported. The Census Bureau uses procedures to correct for these deficiencies based on responses to questions about employment and other characteristics (U.S.

Census Bureau 2010e). Income-related questions have varied only slightly in their wording since 1970. Since 1996 the ACS has asked respondents whether they received food stamp benefits but did not ask them for the equivalent cash value of the food stamps.

It can be confusing when the income estimates in the ACS differ from the official income estimates that HUD and other agencies use to define program eligibility. Although the ACS provides annual estimates of income, the CPS ASEC is the official source of national, regional, and state estimates of income and poverty. The ASEC surveys a smaller population than the ACS (about 100,000 addresses versus 3 million), but it investigates income in greater detail. Respondents are asked about more than fifty sources of income and noncash benefits (U.S. Census Bureau 2010e). The Survey of Income and Program Participation (SIPP) is a longitudinal survey based on about 61,000 addresses, which gathers even more detailed income data, asking respondents about eighty-one sources (Westat 2001). Income estimates from these two sources are not comparable with ACS estimates.

Census-reported income is also distinct from other administrative data sources:

- IRS-reported income for tax purposes includes several sources (capital gains, for instance) that the census excludes, and people with very low incomes are exempted from filing tax returns, but not from completing the census or ACS.
- Social Security Administration earnings data is based on employers' reports and tax returns of self-employed people. It excludes some classes of workers, and thus is not comparable with ACS income data.
- The Bureau of Economic Analysis of the Department of Commerce publishes income data based on business and government

sources, and as with tax data the concept is defined differently than it is in the ACS.

The Small Area Income and Poverty Estimates (SAIPE) program uses statistical methods to adjust ACS income data using other surveys and administrative sources to guide the allocation of funds to school districts. Estimates are available at the state, county, and school district levels.

The Department of Housing and Urban Development also estimates median family incomes for states and counties, as a guide for several housing assistance programs. These estimates are updated annually based on ACS income data; the methodology used varies depending on the size of the locality, and HUD income estimates may not be identical to ACS estimates. Thus, the appropriate income data source will vary depending on the research purpose; if your project involves estimating the proportion of renters eligible for Section 8 housing assistance, for instance, it would be best to use HUD's income limits rather than the ACS limits. Even though the HUD limits are based on the ACS data, they use other sources as well and are likely to be slightly different.

Poverty status

Poverty status is calculated from questions about income. Poverty measures are important tools for determining eligibility or priority needs for a wide variety of federal programs, from Head Start to the Low-Income Home Energy Assistance Program. The poverty threshold (*poverty level* is a widely used but less precise term) is defined nationwide by the federal government. Poverty thresholds vary by household size, composition, and age of members; there are forty-eight possibilities. Table 6.1 shows the various thresholds. These are updated annually using the CPI, but do not vary by location. This may make it difficult to compare estimates of poverty across places (Slack 2010).

Table 6.1　Poverty thresholds, 2007

Size and Type of Family	Weighted Average Income Threshold	Number of Related Children under 18						
		0	1	2	3	4	5	6
Single:	10,590							
Under 65	10,787	10,787						
65 or older	9,944							
Two:	13,540							
Householder under 65	13,954	13,884	14,291					
Householder 65 or older	12,550	12,533	14,237					
3	16,530	16,218	16,689	16,705				
4	21,203	21,386	21,736	21,027	21,100			
5	25,080	25,791	26,166	25,364	24,744	24,366		
6	28,323	29,664	29,782	29,168	28,579	27,705	27,187	
7	32,233	34,132	34,345	33,610	33,098	32,144	31,031	29,810
8	35,816	38,174	38,511	37,818	37,210	36,348	35,255	34,116
9 or more	42,739	45,921	46,143	45,529	45,014	44,168	43,004	41,952
Note: All figures in dollars.								

Source: Census Bureau, http://www.census.gov/hhes/www/poverty/data/threshld/thresh07.html

Originally, poverty thresholds were calculated based on an estimated minimum food budget (Fisher 1997). The official measurement of poverty included several obvious flaws. Apart from the lack of regional variation, the measure excludes the effects of taxes (income tax and the Earned Income Tax Credit) and transfer payments such as food stamps and housing assistance. Many have pointed out that the original derivation of the poverty threshold from a minimum quality food budget in the 1960s does not consider that food now accounts for only about 13 percent of family budgets compared to about 30 percent in the 1960s (Cauthen and Fass 2007). Housing, transportation, health care, and child care now account for a much larger share of household costs, and the poverty threshold has not been revised to reflect this.

Because the threshold is not adjusted for regional, state, or local variations in the cost of living, many federal programs base program eligibility on the area median income instead. The Department of Health and Human Services uses a different version of the measure, using poverty guidelines to simplify poverty thresholds, with different guidelines for Alaska and Hawaii, two high-cost states.

More information on poverty guidelines is available at the HHS Web site.

For families, total family income is used to decide whether individual members are in poverty or not. For those living in nonfamily households, the decision is based on the individual's, not the household's, income. However, poverty status cannot be determined for everyone. People in some group quarters (such as prisons or nursing homes, college dormitories or military barracks), or those who do not have conventional housing, are not included in the ACS estimates of poverty status. However, estimates do cover people living in noninstitutional group quarters (such as boarding houses, migrant worker dormitories, and homeless shelters). Income information is not collected for children younger than fifteen. Although children living in households with related family members would be included in poverty estimates, if they are not living with a relative (for instance, if they live with foster parents) their poverty status would not be determined. Thus, aggregate estimates of people in poverty exclude some individuals we might think of as very poor (such as an indigent person in a nursing home, or people living in their cars) and include some individuals who we would not think of as poor (for instance, a nonearner in a wealthy unmarried partner household). Poverty is an approximate category, and changes in poverty rates may not always mirror the reality of peoples' circumstances. For instance, although more families have moved in with relatives as a result of the recent mortgage foreclosure crisis and unemployment, we may not see a corresponding rise in local poverty rates because family members would be classified according to the poverty status of their relatives, not their own economic circumstances.

Published tables address the dissension over poverty definitions to some extent by breaking out those within 125 percent of the poverty threshold and reporting income deficits (the amount by which incomes of those in poverty fell below the appropriate threshold for that person or family). Income deficits measure the degree of impoverishment of those in poverty. The SAIPE (discussed earlier) is the official source of poverty estimates for states, counties, and school districts. Figure 6.1 shows the SAIPE estimates of school-age children in poverty for unified school districts in Arizona in 2007.

Health insurance

Information is now collected (in the ACS since 2008) on the type of health insurance coverage for each person in the household. This is an important supplement to information on income because it is a key indicator of material disadvantage and played an important role in the debate surrounding recent health-care reform legislation. Data on health insurance coverage by demographic and income characteristics was a key element of the Congressional Budget Office's estimates of the long-term costs and budgetary impacts of the legislation (the Patient Protection and Affordable Care Act, Public Law 111-148, and the Healthcare and Education Reconciliation Act of 2010, Public Law 111-152) (Congressional Budget Office 2009). Debate was heated over the distribution of costs, the constitutional implications, and the impacts on insurance companies; the Kaiser Foundation produced a useful comparison of the various versions of reform legislation proposed (Kaiser Family Foundation 2010). Health insurance coverage is also collected in the CPS ASEC (discussed earlier) and the SIPP, both of which have limited geographic coverage but, like income, are based on more detailed questions about coverage types. As with income data sources, health insurance estimates may differ depending on the source of the data. The ACS provides reasonably current estimates at a fairly detailed geography, but may not be as accurate as ASEC or SIPP estimates, that are only available at state or regional levels. For a table comparing the three sources, see the Census Web site (U.S. Census Bureau 2010f).

Model-based estimates of health insurance coverage for counties are developed in the Small Area Health Insurance Estimates program (SAHIE, similar to the SAIPE), using data from the CPS ASEC, other administrative sources (such as Medicaid participation and federal tax returns)

and County Business Patterns data (described in the next section). Figure 6.2 presents estimates of health insurance coverage for near-poverty residents in counties in Missouri for 2006, based on the SAHIE.

Employment and labor force status

Employment estimates are one of the most significant indicators of political success or failure, and thus employment rates are one of the most scrutinized

Figure 6.1   Poverty rates among school-age children, unified school districts, Arizona, 2007

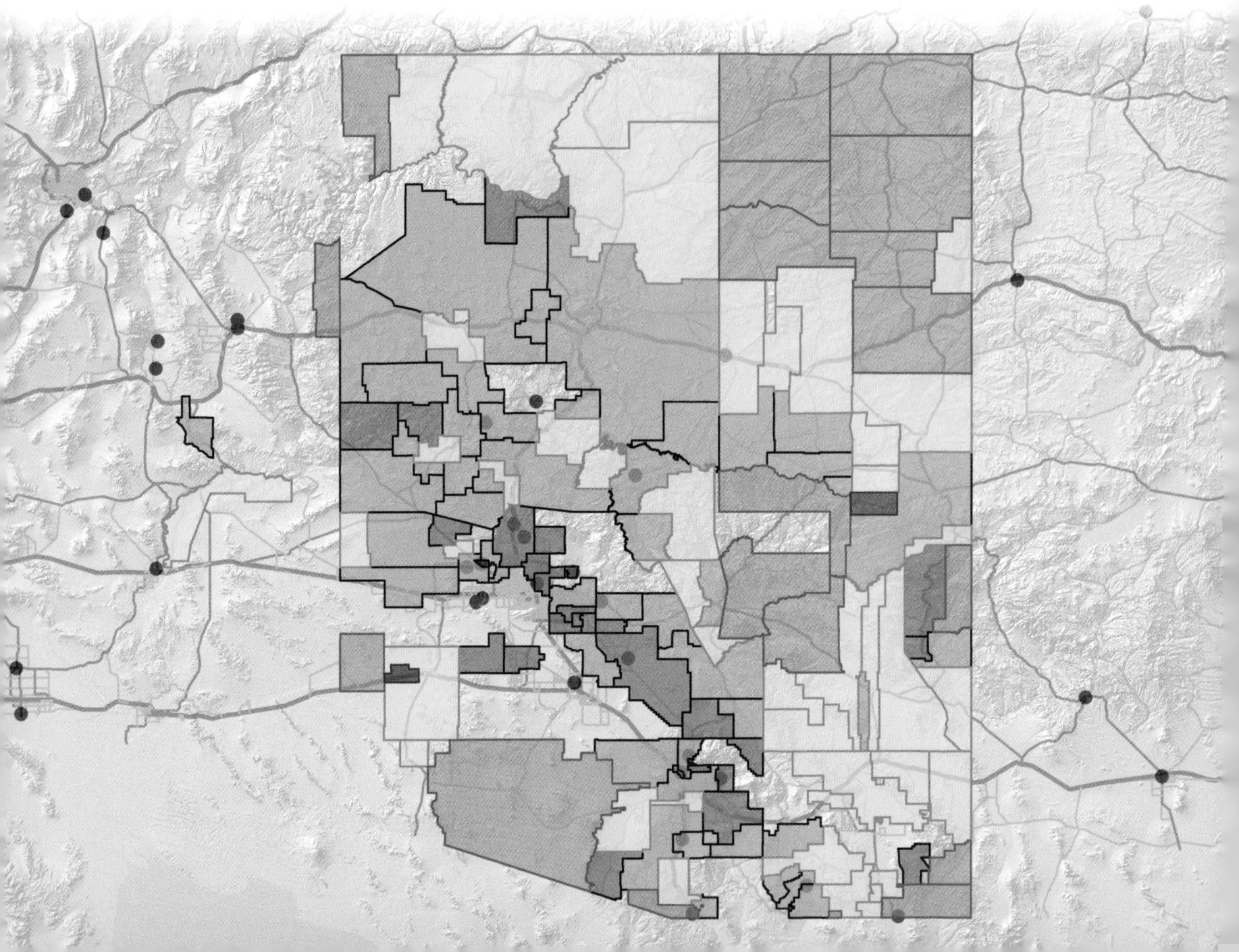

(and contested) of official statistics. But, as with income and poverty, sources of employment data are numerous and give us slightly different information in different formats. Differing estimates can confuse public debates about the evidence in support of or against a particular policy direction. The following discussion aims to guide readers through these differences, making it easier to decide which data source would be appropriate for a particular issue.

The ACS, and before it the decennial census, is only one source of employment estimates; the Current Population Survey provides the official estimates of national and state employment rates. Employment questions are asked of people sixteen years or older. Unlike the income questions, employment questions ask people about their experience during a *reference week*, the calendar week before the week of the survey. Thus alignment between the ACS employment question concept and that in previous decennial censuses is much closer than for income, meaning that it is simpler to compare employment trends over time from the 2000 census with current ACS releases. Employed people include those who

- worked at any time for pay during the reference week,
- did more than fifteen hours unpaid work for a family business or farm, or
- were temporarily absent from work (for vacation or illness, for example) but not laid off.

Unemployed people include

- temporarily laid-off workers who expect to return to their jobs within six months (or at a specific date) and who were available for work during the reference week, and
- those who did not have a job but were actively looking for work during the reference week or the previous three weeks and were available for work (U.S. Census Bureau 2009a).

The labor force includes the employed and the unemployed; unemployment rates are calculated based on people in the labor force, rather than other measures such as all adults of working age. The civilian labor force excludes people on active duty in the U.S. armed forces; this information is particularly useful in places with a military base, because it allows researchers to track employment trends without the skewing effects of trends

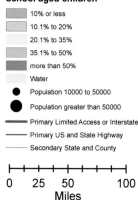

% Poverty rates among school aged children

- 10% or less
- 10.1% to 20%
- 20.1% to 35%
- 35.1% to 50%
- more than 50%
- Water
- Population 10000 to 50000
- Population greater than 50000
- Primary Limited Access or Interstate
- Primary US and State Highway
- Secondary State and County

0   25   50   100
Miles

Source: 2007 ACS

in military deployment. The labor force does not include people who were

- involved in unpaid work around the home, such as childcare or home repairs, or unpaid volunteer work, unless they were actively seeking work and available for employment;
- full-time students without a job and not seeking a job;
- seasonal workers interviewed in the off-season who were not looking for work;
- in institutions, even though they may have worked during the reference week, perhaps in a sheltered employment program; and
- doing fewer than fifteen hours of incidental unpaid work for a family business or farm (U.S. Census Bureau 2009e).

Thus, high rates of unemployment would not be adequately explained by high numbers of full-time parents, or full-time students, because these groups may not be actively seeking work, and thus would not be counted in the labor force.

Although ACS employment data is useful for profiles of community employment trends and for investigating relationships with other demographic and social variables (such as with "educational attainment"), it is not the official source of employment estimates. The monthly CPS is the source of official estimates of national and state employment and unemployment rates. The survey (based on an overlapping sample of about 73,000 households monthly) asks far more detailed questions about employment and labor force status. Its

Figure 6.2 Near-poverty, uninsured population, Missouri, 2006

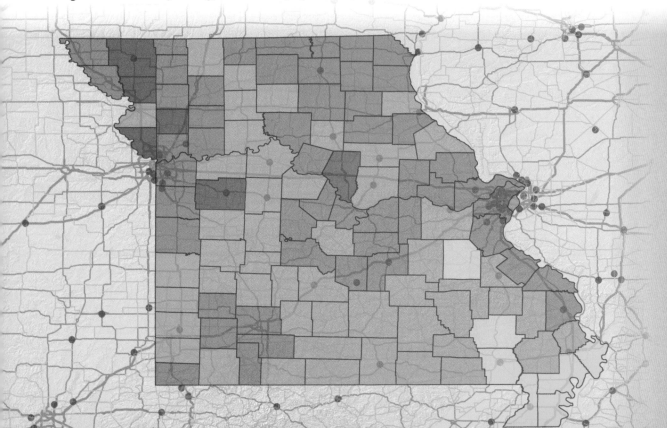

estimates of unemployment tend to be somewhat lower than the ACS. Annual average CPS estimates of employment are released for the fifty largest metropolitan areas and seventeen cities, but the sample size is not large enough to provide the geographic detail offered by the ACS and the survey does not cover the same elements included in the ACS (U.S. Department of Labor 2009a). Employment data is also collected in SIPP (introduced earlier), a longitudinal survey aimed at understanding households' economic dynamics over time. SIPP defines participation in the labor force differently (over a four-month period rather than a single week) and uses different questions than the CPS and the ACS. Because of its small sample, SIPP is not geographically detailed. However, it offers more in-depth data on several economic characteristics. SIPP would be an appropriate source to investigate correlations among the income of other family members, labor force participation, and earnings, for instance, but it would not do this at a detailed spatial scale.

The Local Area Unemployment Statistics (LAUS) program provides model-based estimates of unemployment for counties and cities with populations of 25,000 or larger and all cities and towns in New England (because cities and towns throughout New England are independent of counties). It is based on data from the CPS and the ACS, using CPS definitions of place of residence and employment. Like the CPS, it provides monthly estimates, but at a much finer spatial scale. It thus incorporates the advantage of ACS labor force and employment estimates that are tied to many other socioeconomic and demographic characteristics not included in the monthly CPS (U.S. Department of Labor 2009b). The LAUS, like the SAHIE and the SAIPE, is another example of *synthetic* data—small-area estimates that protect confidentiality and overcome limitations such as small sample sizes through statistical construction of data based on several different sources. Synthetic data can provide geographically detailed estimates of key indicators such as unemployment using a consistent methodology; it is one of the strategies developing to address the lower precision of the ACS while making use of its timeliness. We discuss synthetic data in more detail below.

The complex array of labor force and employment statistics can be confusing. Considerable dissension can arise over "real" unemployment rates during periods of crisis; alternative definitions (for instance, those used in Japan and western Europe) that include discouraged workers and others would substantially increase U.S. unemployment estimates (Engel 2010). Choosing

% Near-poverty uninsured

    20% or less
    20.1% to 35%
    35.1% to 50%
    more than 50%
    Water
●   Population 10000 to 50000
⬤   Population greater than 50000
——— Primary Limited Access or Interstate
——— Primary US and State Highway
——— Secondary State and County

0   20   40   80
        Miles

Source: 2006 Small Area Health Insurance Estimates

Figure 6.3   Measures of employment, Rhode Island, 2007

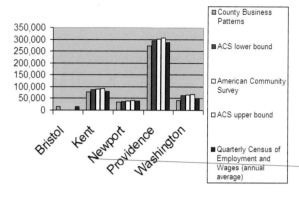

Source: Authors' compilation based on County Business Patterns data 2007; American Community Survey 2007; Quarterly Census of Employment and Wages 2007.
Note: ACS data for Bristol County is not available for 2007 because county population is less than 65,000.

the right data series for the question at hand is important. If your goal is to examine how welfare reform legislation affected labor force participation and employment rates over the last decade, SIPP would be a more appropriate source than the ACS. If you are interested in variations in employment rates among high immigrant neighborhoods in your city, the ACS would be a more appropriate choice. Just as important, though, is avoiding comparisons across sources. Although it may be defensible to compare unemployment rates from the 2000 census with those from the 2005 or 2010 ACS, it would not be appropriate to compare the 2000 census with official unemployment rates for any year. Figure 6.3 shows the disparities across three different estimates of employment for counties in Rhode Island in 2007. And although it is sometimes tempting to use whatever data is available for a particular period, switching from County Business Patterns data for 2002–04 to ACS data for 2005–07, for example, would likely create

an artificial increase in unemployment rates that neither data source would support.

Work status and experience

The potential labor force in most places is larger than the actual labor force at any one time. People may prefer to work only seasonally (for instance, in retail over the holiday season or during summer holidays). The ACS gathers information on work status to estimate the size of this potential labor force and to estimate how many people are full-time versus part-time workers (U.S. Census Bureau 2009a). Full-time workers are likely to travel further to work than part-time workers, for instance, and to earn more. They are also more likely to be concentrated in particular industries and occupations (Turner and Niemeier 1997). A shift from full-time to part-time work may indicate hidden underemployment (Engel 2010).

In contrast to employment questions, work status questions ask about work history during the previous twelve months: whether people worked, for how many weeks, and the usual or average hours of work per week. People sixteen or older who worked at least one week during that time are classified as "worked in the past twelve months." However, they may not be counted as part of the current labor force, because they may be neither employed nor looking for work. Work is defined in the questions about employment and does not include unpaid work in the home. Full-time, year-round workers are those usually working thirty-five hours a week or more, at least fifty weeks out of the year (U.S. Census Bureau 2009a).

Place of work

Understanding job locations (relative to home locations) is essential for modeling commuting patterns. Knowing the number of people working in a particular location also provides a basis for estimating the daytime population of that area, which is useful for emergency planning (for instance, to plan evacuation routes in the event of a disaster).

The ACS asks people who worked at some time during the reference week for the exact address (or nearest street or intersection), whether the place was inside city limits, and the county, state (or country), and ZIP code of their job location. If people worked in more than one place during the week, they are asked to report the location at which they worked for the majority of the week. For people with more than one job, it would be the location of the job where they worked the most hours. People who worked in several locations regularly (for instance, plumbers) are asked for the place where they began their workday. People with jobs but not at work in the reference week are not included, so "place of work" does not necessarily reflect total local employment (U.S. Census Bureau 2009a).

Place of work is summarized by whether people worked within or outside the county, place, state, or metropolitan area where they lived. Within metropolitan areas, places inside or outside the central city are distinguished. For residents of twelve selected states, place of work is also shown by the Minor Civil Division (MCD, usually cities, towns, and townships) of their homes. Place of work defines the commuting shed around employment centers and is one of the components used to revise definitions of metropolitan and micropolitan areas.

Place of work is also the basis for other questions about the journey to work, which are explained in chapter 7. For employment and commuting analyses, we often need to know not where people live but where they work. The Census Bureau also reorganizes place of work information in this way and summarizes it to the place of work.

This is published in a separate dataset, the Census Transportation Planning Package, showing the spatial distribution of jobs. The CTPP is discussed in detail in the next chapter.

Industry and occupation

The industries where people work and the occupations they hold are important indicators of economic structure. Industrial restructuring can transform cities. The shift from manufacturing to services caused economic disaster in Rust Belt cities in the 1980s. The rise of information industries in the 1990s and 2000s, and of information-analyzing occupations, was argued by some to represent the rise of a new "creative class" (Florida 2002). That argument became the basis for numerous city regeneration strategies and marketing campaigns. Industry and occupation data were some of the key indicators Richard Florida used to develop his classification scheme. Changes to industrial and occupational structure also provide a basis for forecasts about future economic trends.

The ACS collects industry and occupation data at the household level and the Economic Census collects it at the establishment (the branch of a company or corporation) level. *Industry* describes the type of activity at a workplace, and *occupation* describes the type of work that a person does there. For instance, a single factory may forge metals. All employees, no matter what they actually do, will be classified as working in the metal forging industry. Some may tend metal furnaces; others may be secretaries, janitors, media spokespersons, accountants, or supervisors. Each person is also classified by occupation. Industry, occupation, and class of worker are reported for the job held during the reference week (or for an unemployed person, the most recent job). Like place of work, the descriptions of industry and occupation are also limited

Figure 6.4a   Workers in professional, scientific, technical services industries, Boulder, Colorado, 2000

Figure 6.4b   Workers in professional occupations, Boulder, Colorado, 2000

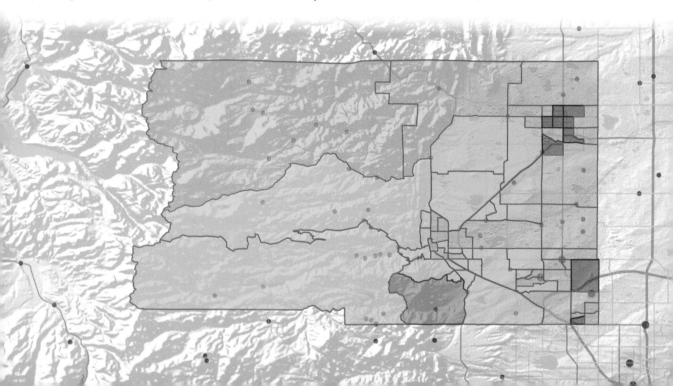

% Employed professional, scientific, & technical

less than 10%

10.1% to 20%

more than 20%

Water

Pimary Limited Access or Interstate

Primay US and State Highway

Secondary State and County

● Population Less than 10000

● Population 10000 to 50000

● Population greater than 50000

0   3   6   12
Miles

Source: 2000 Census of Population and Housing SF3

% employed in professional occupations

less than 20%

20.1% to 35%

35.1% to 50%

more than 50%

Water

● Population less than 10000

● Population 10000 to 50000

● Population greater than 50000

Primary Limited Access or Interstate

Primary US and State Highway

Secondary State and County

0   3   6   12
Miles

Source: 2000 Census of Population and Housing SF3

because they refer to the primary job, not all jobs held. Figures 6.4a and 6.4b contrast the proportion of workers in professional services industries in Boulder, Colorado, and the proportion in professional occupations in the county. Many more people are in professional occupations, but those jobs are in a range of industries, such as construction, education, or health care.

Analyses of industrial and occupational restructuring are usually based on time-series analyses, which require several data points. Although the census and ACS offer an ideal basis for such analyses, a change in the classification for industry and occupation in 1997 make comparisons more complicated, because we need to ensure we are comparing like with like (table 6.2 illustrates the complexities of comparisons in one industry).That year, the twenty-category North American Industrial Classification System (NAICS), which standardizes classifications within the North American Free Trade Area (NAFTA), replaced the fourteen-category Standard Industrial Classification code (SIC). Both systems are hierarchical, meaning that sectors of the economy are broken down into increasingly narrow subsectors. Table 6.2 presents an example of how one industrial sector was redefined. The Standard Occupational Classification system (SOC) was restructured in similar ways.

The reclassification reflected a significant social shift. SIC divisions were based on an economy structured around producing and transporting goods such as washing machines, frozen peas, and shoes. But many of the most profitable (if volatile) firms of the past decade have dealt in more ephemeral goods. The production and distribution of information—through software development, the creation of hedge and derivative financial products, or nightly talk shows—add far more value to the economy than the production of the television sets or computers that deliver the information.

Table 6.2 Recreation-, arts-, entertainment-sector classification schemes

SIC Classification	NAICS Classification
791–Dance studios, schools, and halls	711–Performing Arts, spectator sports, and other industries
	111–Performing arts companies (theater, dance, music, and others)
792–Theatrical producers, bands, orchestras, and entertainers	
7922–Theatrical producers	7113–Promoters of performing arts, sports, and similar events
	7114–Agents and managers for artists, athletes, entertainers, and others
7929–Bands, orchestras, and entertainers	7115–Independent artists, writers, and performers
793–Bowling centers	
794–Commercial sports	7112–Spectator sports (sports teams, racetracks, and others)
7941–Professional sports clubs and promoters	
7948–Racing, including track operation	
799–Miscellaneous amusement and recreation services	713–Amusement, gambling, and recreation industries
7991–Physical fitness facilities	
7992–Public golf courses	
7993–Coin-operated amusement devices	
	7132–Gambling industries
7996–Amusement parks	7131–Amusement parks and arcades
7997–Membership sports and recreation clubs	
7999–Amusement services not elsewhere classified	7139–Other

Source: U.S. Department of Labor 2009c

The industries of the so-called new economy are part of what the NAICS seeks to capture. But economic change is continuous; the classification system, like geographic classifications, must evolve constantly. This offers benefits (new sorts of enterprises are reflected in local economic profiles) and challenges for the analyst, who must deal with constant transition.

Concordance tables for historical comparisons are available at the U.S. Census Web site (U.S. Census Bureau 2009c). The 2000 census and the ACS use a modified set of industrial and occupational classifications, with fewer detailed categories (which are more relevant at the establishment level than at the household level). Crosswalks (tables that allow translation between the various coding schemes) can be also found at the Census Bureau site (2010g). The crosswalks can be downloaded, saved, and converted into databases allowing fairly straightforward conversions among the various industrial coding systems and somewhat more difficult conversions among the occupational systems. Spreadsheet versions of some of the crosswalks are also available.

Class of worker

A community's economic profile is also defined by its mix of workers in the public and private sectors. For instance, in some small midwestern towns, government employees make up a majority of the workforce, and the private sector has received little investment for some time. In other communities, a higher-than-average proportion of self-employed workers and small businesses may reflect a strong entrepreneurial culture. This information can provide a useful guide for targeting economic development efforts to resolve low rates of private investment and support local entrepreneurs.

Based on their primary jobs, workers are classified into the following categories:

- private wage and salary workers, which includes people working in the for-profit and nonprofit sectors, and owners of incorporated companies who are paid a wage by the company;
- government workers, including those working for federal, state, or local agencies, such as school teachers and members of the armed forces
- self-employed people in an unincorporated business, such as private dentists or farmers; and
- unpaid family workers, who worked for fifteen hours or more in a relative's business or farm (U.S. Census Bureau 2009a).

Economic data collected at the establishment level

Examining establishments, or firms, provides a different set of insights into local economies. Several data sources gather economic data from firms rather than individuals.

The Economic Census

The Economic Census is conducted every five years (in years ending in two or seven). Instead of surveying households, it surveys business establishments: that is, a single plant (or part of a plant devoted to one type of output that keeps a separate set of books), in contrast to an enterprise (an entire company), which could consist of many establishments in many different industrial sectors. Economic Census data enables researchers to analyze trends in business conditions (such as the impact of increased energy, finance, or labor costs on profitability), structure (such as patterns of firm consolidation and ownership changes), and business models (such as diversification in particular industries). These are important for forecasting economic growth, tax revenues, and sometimes population. They are also used to determine the need for particular types of assistance (such as tax cuts for industries that are struggling, for instance).

The 2007 Economic Census was really a hybrid of a census and a survey, gathering data for every large and medium-sized firm and every multi-establishment firm in the nation. Some firms were sampled, and very small firms were counted using administrative records (such as from the IRS), so the Economic Census provides information on all firms even though it does not survey every firm.

Like the decennial census, answering the Economic Census is mandatory, and similar confidentiality protections govern the publication of the data. Consequently, detailed data is rarely available for small areas. Data is reported at different geographic scales for different industry sectors, as table 6.3 outlines. Within consolidated cities and counties, data is reported separately for incorporated places with more than 2,500 residents and for the balance of the consolidated city (or county) for all smaller places. Although data is geocoded to the census tract and block level, data is not tabulated at this level, because it would be very likely to violate confidentiality. For the 2007 census, data is also released for CDPs (census designated places) with at least 5,000 residents or 5,000 workers.

Sectors are defined based on the NAICS classification described earlier. Reflecting the continuing restructuring of economic activity, the 2007 Economic Census introduced two new industries, research and development in biotechnology and executive search services, and consolidated several industries in the information sector.

All establishments provide some information: the physical location of activity; number of employees; payroll; and the value of sales, receipts, or the equivalent. However, a variety of questionnaires are designed for different industries: 530 versions of the form gather data specific to particular industries or subsectors. The data collected focuses on several broad categories of issues:

- cost of labor (including fringe benefits, subcontractors, hours worked)
- cost of supplies (materials, purchased services)
- operating expenses (rent, fuel, and so on)
- depreciable assets, capital expenditures, and debt payments
- inventories and value of assets
- sources of revenue

- employment by occupation
- legal form of organization, ownership, and control

In 2007, new data was gathered on business owners, including whether they were born in the United States (which helps forecast the impact that future immigration may have on business starts) and when and how they acquired the business. Totals will once again be reported for minority business owners, and tables will show business owners who are veterans. Counts of businesses owned by minority groups provide a base for estimates of how well banks may be meeting their Community Reinvestment Act, Public Law 95-128, obligations by providing finance for businesses throughout their market area, regardless of the business owner's race. The Small Business Administration evaluates the effectiveness of programs targeting small business startup assistance to veterans, as required in the Veteran's Entrepreneurship and Small Business Development Act of 1999, Public Law 106-50 (Small Business Administration 2004). International business links (sales and outsourcing), languages in which business is conducted, use of the Internet, and employee fringe benefits offered are new business characteristics added for 2007. They help identify the sorts of skills and infrastructure needed by business and new costs that businesses bear.

The Economic Census is published in three main data series: industry, subject, and geography (or area). The first provides detailed information on the various NAICS sectors with limited geographical breakdowns. The second provides data on more specialized topics, such as merchandise line sales for the retail sector. The third provides geographic data down to the place (population greater than 2,500) and ZIP code levels. The 2007 and 2002

Table 6.3   Geographic coverage for establishment-based economic data

2007 Economic Census Sectors	States	Metropolitan	Areas	Counties	Places	ZIP Code
Mining	•					
Utilities	•	•				
Construction	•					
Manufacturing	•	•	•	•	•	
Wholesale trade	•	•	•	•	•	
Retail trade	•	•	•	•	•	•
Transportation and warehousing	•	•				
Information	•	•	•	•	•	
Finance and Insurance	•	•				
Real estate rental and leasing	•	•	•	•	•	
Professional, scientific, and technical services	•	•	•	•	•	•
Management of companies and enterprises	•					
Administration, support, waste management and remediation services	•	•	•	•	•	•
Educational services	•	•	•	•	•	•
Health care and social assistance	•	•	•	•	•	•
Arts, entertainment, and recreation	•	•	•	•	•	•
Accommodation and food services	•	•	•	•	•	•
Other services (except public administration)	•	•	•	•	•	•
Other economic programs						
Annual survey of manufactures	•					
Commodity flow survey	•	•				
County business patterns	•	•	•	•		
Nonemployer statistics	•	•	•	•		
Survey of business owners	•	•	•	•	•	
ZIP code business patterns	•					•

Source: U.S. Census Bureau, 2007b

economic censuses are available on American FactFinder; previous economic censuses are available on CDs and in print versions.

Although Economic Census data is used most often at the state and state region scale to identify issues with competitiveness, market share, and so on, it is also useful for questions relying on a finer spatial scale. For instance, community residents are increasingly concerned about the types of businesses in their community. In some communities, grocery, hardware, pharmacies and other retailers are in short supply, forcing residents to travel longer distance or pay higher prices for poorer quality goods (Proscio 2006). Some retail businesses are seen as essential for community development efforts, and city governments have offered subsidies to attract them. Other retailers, such as liquor stores and pawn shops, are sometimes seen as a neighborhood detriment, generating noise and sometimes criminal behavior, creating a phenomenon known as *liquorlining* (Pacific Institute 2009). New license applications or rezoning efforts often focus on residents' concerns to attract "good" retailers and exclude "bad" ones. Figure 6.5 uses data on retail establishments from the 2002 Economic Census to chart the ratio of grocery stores to liquor stores in counties in Maryland. In some counties, especially Baltimore, there are nearly as many liquor stores as there are grocery stores, and in others three times as many grocery stores as liquor stores. Maps like this can provide a basis for considering either incentives for new grocery stores or zoning restrictions to limit liquor stores.

Figure 6.5   Grocery stores and liquor stores, Maryland, 2002

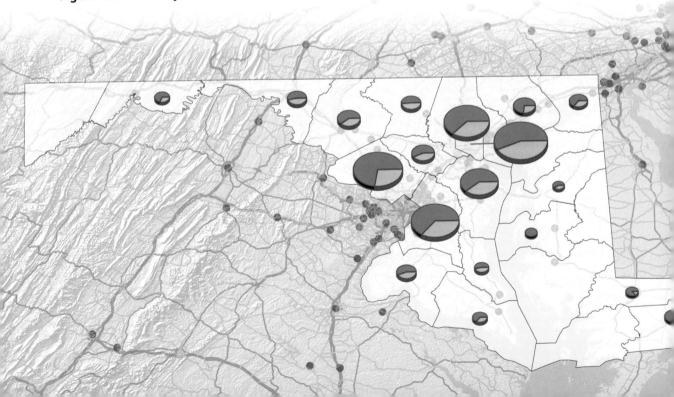

County business patterns

This is an annual series on employment based on full- and part-time workers who are on the payroll on March 12, payroll and number of establishments by industry for states, counties, metropolitan areas, ZIP codes, and the United States. It is widely used for economic analysis down to the county level. It is useful because it ties together data on establishments along with data on workers and provides a more frequent and spatially detailed set of some of the information contained in the Economic Census. It excludes self employed persons, employees of private households, railroad employees, agricultural production workers, and most government employees. Thus, it does not provide employment estimates similar to those in the ACS or BLS datasets.

County Business Patterns data is extracted from the Census Bureau's Business Register, a file of all known companies. The Annual Company Organization Survey and Economic Census provide individual establishment data for multilocation firms. Data for single location firms is obtained from various programs including the Economic Census, the Annual Survey of Manufactures (ASM), and the Current Business Surveys, together with records of the Internal Revenue Service, the Social Security Administration (SSA), and the Bureau of Labor Statistics (BLS) (U.S. Census Bureau 2010i). The data provides a reasonably current way to estimate trends in the local economy. Figure 6.6 shows estimates of changes in the number of firms that were single-family residential construction general contractors in Florida, from 2005 to 2007. The map provides a snapshot of one of the economic impacts of the recent mortgage foreclosure crisis.

Current Employment Statistics

The Current Employment Statistics (CES) series from the Bureau of Labor Statistics is the basis for a monthly news release, the "Employment Situation," showing trends in earnings and wage-related inflation, demand for labor, and the overall health of the economy. The CES counts people employed at each establishment, based on a monthly survey of nearly 400,000 establishments. CES has some limitations. A person with two jobs could be counted twice. Some types of workers, including private household workers and the self-employed, are excluded. People under sixteen may be included in CES employment estimates, but excluded from the CPS and ACS. The CES also reports hours worked and earnings; data is reported for more than 300 metropolitan areas (U.S. Department of Labor 2010). As explained

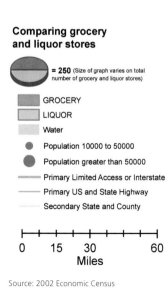

Comparing grocery and liquor stores

= **250** (Size of graph varies on total number of grocery and liquor stores)

■ GROCERY
□ LIQUOR
Water

● Population 10000 to 50000
● Population greater than 50000
— Primary Limited Access or Interstate
— Primary US and State Highway
— Secondary State and County

0   15   30   60
Miles

Source: 2002 Economic Census

earlier, CES data is based on different definitions and sources than ACS data; it is more useful as a current metropolitan-wide indicator of economic health but less useful as basis for understanding such questions, for instance, as the causal relationship between education and earnings.

Unemployment insurance data

Unemployment insurance data (ES202) provides an alternative geographically detailed estimate of employment. Based on administrative data collected directly from establishments paying unemployment insurance for their workers rather than a survey, it is used as a benchmark for the CES. Consequently, some researchers believe that it is a better source for local employment estimates. Because it is tied to establishments, it provides a

way to investigate links between broader economic changes, such as increases in the minimum wage, and employment outcomes (Card and Krueger 2000). It excludes several categories of people, including those who have exhausted their benefits but are still looking for work, new workers not yet eligible for benefits, and people who lose jobs not covered by unemployment insurance, such as domestic servants, farm laborers, or the self-employed. But the estimates also may include people who worked only a few hours during the week, if they are eligible for benefits. The census would count these people as unemployed.

Local Employment Dynamics series

An alternative to small-scale and fragmented datasets is another example of synthetic data:

Figure 6.6 Construction firms, Florida, 2005–07

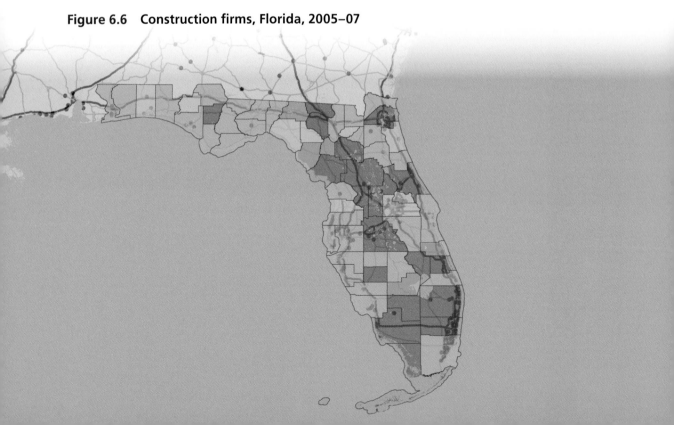

a model-based estimate of local employment at the county and subcounty level developed by the Census Bureau and forty-six participating states and published quarterly. The Local Employment Dynamics series integrates existing data from censuses, surveys, and administrative sources and uses sophisticated confidentiality protection methods (such as data perturbation) to produce useful synthetic data on employment trends. The Quarterly Workforce Indicators product shows trends in employment, job growth and decline, and earnings. It is broken down by age, gender, and industry at detailed geographic levels. OnTheMap, an interactive mapping program based on the Local Employment Dynamics series, shows employment and home locations for workers (we discuss this in more detail in chapter 7). Synthetic data has

tremendous potential to provide near real-time information broken down by meaningful geographies and demographic categories, while protecting confidentiality. Figure 6.7a shows a sample analysis of employment concentrations in Portland, Oregon, using OnTheMap. Figure 6.7b is a sample analysis of the Portland labor shed (showing where workers live).

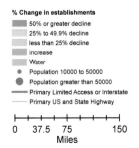

% Change in establishments
- 50% or greater decline
- 25% to 49.9% decline
- less than 25% decline
- increase
- Water
- ● Population 10000 to 50000
- ● Population greater than 50000
- ▬▬ Primary Limited Access or Interstate
- ── Primary US and State Highway

0   37.5   75   150
            Miles

Source: Calculated from 2005 and 2007 County Business Patterns

Figure 6.7a Employment concentrations, Portland, Oregon

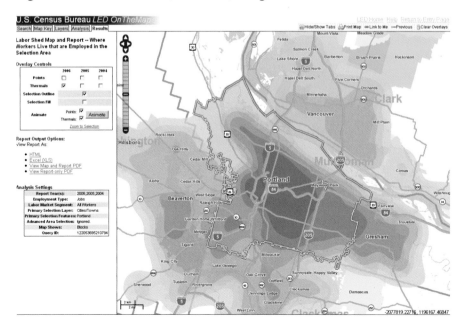

Source: Sample Work Area Profile Analysis, OnTheMap version 3, Local Employment Dynamics Program, http://lehd.did.census.gov/led/datatools/doc/OnTheMapSampleAPAnalysis.pdf

Figure 6.7b Labor sheds, Portland, Oregon

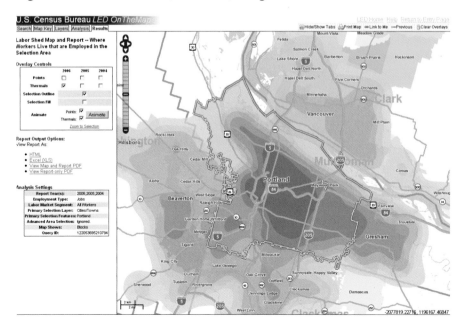

Source: Sample Labor Shed Analysis, OnTheMap version 3, Local Employment Dynamics Program, http://lehd.did.census.gov/led/datatools/doc/OnTheMapSampleShedAnalysis.pdf

Conclusions

Many of our decisions about the public good revolve around economic issues: how a policy change will affect people at different income levels, whether a new program will stimulate or retard economic growth, or how political consolidation may alter local economic competitiveness. Those are fundamentally political choices, but they can be better informed by careful analysis that outlines their economic implications. Debates may be enriched if we have a clearer idea of the likely outcomes of particular actions. Given the centrality of economic indicators to our definition of the public good, a plethora of relatively current economic data sources are available to inform these debates. They have pitfalls for those who treat them interchangeably, but they are valuable resources to improve the quality of public debate over sometimes contentious choices.

Chapter 7

Analyzing
transportation data

Understanding people's travel patterns can help us evaluate infrastructure investment needs, identify mismatches between homes and jobs, and predict patterns of suburban growth. Increasingly, commuting data is used to evaluate and forecast the environmental impacts of policy changes and transportation investments. The ACS, like earlier decennial censuses, gathers only a few pieces of information about travel and transportation resources. Yet by combining this information with demographic and economic data, transportation planners can analyze the spatial implications of several important questions about how travel behavior differs among various groups.

The ACS reports travel information cross-tabulated with far more variables than the 2000 and previous censuses did. Another major change is that most commuting data is now reported at the workplace and at the place of residence. So, for example, we can now see how modal split and trip length differ for central business district workers compared to suburban workers (rather than only people living in suburban or central areas), which can help when we plan new public transit investments and evaluate the impacts of prior investments. The ACS data is reported in a variety of formats; two formats that are particularly relevant to travel analysis are the CTPP and the PUMS.

CTPP reports information gathered through the ACS for travel analysis zones, based on place of residence and place of work. Because the CTPP represents travel flows and static trip origin and destination data, it is well suited to several transportation planning tasks, including updating travel demand forecasting models for a particular city and investigating commuting patterns along a particular corridor. The inclusion of demographic characteristics improves the quality of forecasts. For instance, recent immigrants may have different travel patterns compared with the population as a whole, and the community's future travel patterns may follow different trajectories depending on projected immigration rates.

PUMS is a file, rather than tabulation, based on a sample of ACS responses. It provides individual and household-level data that can be analyzed much more flexibly than the standard cross-tabulations allow. For instance, PUMS enables us to estimate the likelihood that someone with a particular income, gender, occupation, and industry would travel to work alone in a car rather than take a bus or train. However, to protect confidentiality, PUMS data is released only for PUMAs, typically consisting of at least 100,000 people, so it cannot be used for the sorts of spatial analyses for which CTPP is well suited.

Understanding census travel data

Decennial censuses have asked about peoples' journeys to work since 1960. The ACS has gathered this information for all U.S. locations since 2005; however, no transportation questions were asked in the 2010 census (the questions are asked in the ACS surveys). The ACS's smaller sample and thus less-precise spatial estimates raise a few challenges for transportation analysis, especially for smaller categories of responses such as public transit usage (MacDonald 2006; Murakama 2007; Cambridge Systematics et al. 2007). The first two chapters of this book dealt with the basic principles of sampling approaches and the issues of accuracy, standard errors, and confidence intervals we will refer to here.

ACS transportation data has other important limitations. Because only work trips are covered, a significant amount of travel (including travel by children, the elderly, and others neither in the labor force nor unemployed) is not reflected in this data. Other types of transportation issues (transportation infrastructure, freight movement, long-distance travel, and so on) are not reflected in decennial census data either, although aspects of these are covered in the Economic Census and other sources.

Transportation data collected at the household and individual level

Information about journey to work characteristics is collected for each employed person sixteen or older, and information about vehicles available is collected for households.

Place of work

Data for place of work is used to estimate commuting destinations and to link trip origins and destinations so that we can create a network of typical trips. Because the ACS collects only information on the time people spend commuting (not the trip distance), data for place of work is the only way we can estimate the actual distance people travel. This data is also the basis for understanding cross-county flows, which in turn is the basis for the commute-sheds that define metropolitan areas. Understanding where people work (in a suburban office park or a central business district) allows us to ask interesting questions such as how the urban form of a city affects travel choices, congestion, and emissions (Boarnet and Crane 2001). The question is asked of people age sixteen years and older who worked during the week before completing the questionnaire. They are asked for the primary place of employment for the job they worked that week, and information is collected on the exact street address, place (if the job was located in an incorporated place), county, and metropolitan area (if applicable) (U.S. Census Bureau 2009a). This information allows us to understand commuting flows. For instance, figure 7.1 displays the proportion of central-city residents of Hennepin County, Minnesota, who were reverse commuters (that is, commuted to jobs in the suburbs of the metro area) in 2000. Increased reverse commuting may help alleviate peak traffic congestion, but it may be more difficult for workers to use public transit for trips to suburban work locations.

The data for place of work does not cover a specific week. It also excludes the work trips of employed people who were away from work during the previous week and work trips to a second job. Thus, place-of-work data is not an accurate estimate of the total number of jobs in a particular place. If someone, for example, a construction worker, travels to different job sites, the worker is asked to report the place where the majority of work time was spent. This may produce a temporary spike in the number of work trips to a particular place. Data for place of work can be a rough basis for estimating the daytime population of employment centers, in combination with data for time leaving home, which can be useful for emergency management.

Usual means of transportation

For people who were sixteen or older and worked outside their homes in the previous week, information is collected about the primary travel mode (means of transportation) used for the home to work trip. This is the basis for estimates of modal split (the proportion of people commuting by public transit, traveling alone by car, carpooling, and so on). Historical data on modal split enables transportation planners to forecast the traffic likely to be generated by future development and thus estimate whether additional resources are needed to deal with the impacts (such as an additional highway lane, a new bus route, or a bicycle lane). Tying information on modal split to demographic and employment information allows us to analyze how labor markets might be defined by public transit availability and to forecast demand for different sorts of travel (Sanchez 1999; Giuliano and Narayan 2003).

However, the variable does not provide a complete picture of modal split. Only one travel mode is reported. If respondents used more than one kind of transportation, such as driving to a park and ride and then riding a train to complete the journey, they were required to report only the one used for the longest distance (U.S. Census Bureau 2009a). This limits the information because it does not capture any multimodal trips. People driving to a train station and completing their trip by train could report either but not both modes, limiting the data's effectiveness for estimating demand for park and ride facilities, for instance. The ACS now reports travel mode (and other travel) data at the worker's residence and the place of work. Figure 7.2a shows the percentage of county residents who took public transport to work over the 2005–07 period in New Jersey. Figure 7.2b shows the percentage of people who commuted by public transport to jobs in New Jersey counties during that period. Because there is likely to be substantial cross-county commuting, the workers whose trips are shown in figure 7.2a are likely to be quite different than those shown in figure 7.2b.

The ACS is based on a smaller sample than previous decennial censuses, so in some places it has become more difficult to identify changes in some commuting modes. Estimating trends in travel mode is a useful way to measure the impact of transit investments or other programs such as carpooling schemes (Transportation for America 2010). Increases in transit usage may demonstrate the impacts of system changes, and declines may identify problems (such as the effect of increasing congestion on bus trip times). New Jersey has a high proportion of public transit users, and several counties demonstrate statistically significant changes in public transit work trips from 2000 to 2005–07 (shown in figure 7.3a). In contrast, Missouri has far smaller shares of public transit work trips, and statistically significant changes can be demonstrated in only a handful of counties, as figure 7.3b shows.

Figure 7.1   Reverse commuters, Hennepin Co., Minnesota, 2000

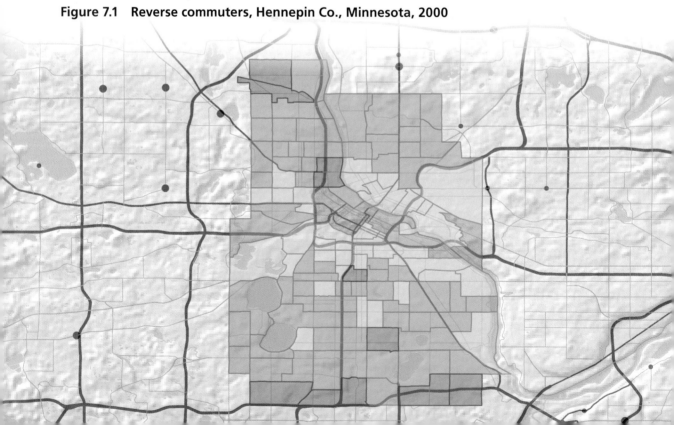

Number of persons in vehicle

Vehicle occupancy rates provide important data for measuring progress toward attaining Clean Air Act travel reduction goals; increasing the number of people riding in each vehicle is a goal of travel demand management (TDM) programs. People driving alone in cars increases traffic, congestion, and emissions on the road network. Carpooling increases vehicle occupancy rates and is one way to reduce the load on the road network. Ride-matching schemes are often combined with incentives such as reserved lanes or free parking for high-occupancy vehicles (Concas and Winters 2007). Vehicle occupancy rates are reported for those who traveled to work by car, truck, or van. This data, along with the estimates of total workers, allows us to calculate the number of vehicles being used for the home to work trip.

% Reverse commuters

20% or less

25.1% - 35%

35.1% - 50%

50.1% or greater

Water

• Population less than 10000

● Population 10000 to 50000

● Population greater than 50000

—— Pimary Limited Access or Interstate

— Primay US and State Highway

— Secondary State and County

0 1 2 4

Miles

Source: 2000 Census of population and Housing SF3

Time of departure for work

The time a person leaves home to travel to work is reported separately. This data lets researchers calculate peak work-travel hours, which is helpful for forecasting peak travel demand and thus congestion. Typical work hours vary by industries (for example, hospital workers versus office workers) so peak hours may vary depending on the industry mix. One TDM strategy encourages employers to introduce staggered work hours, which can help alleviate peak hour congestion (Downs 2004). The data collected may not be precise because it relies on the memory of the person responding (who is not necessarily the worker). Some evidence suggests that responses are rounded to the nearest quarter hour (U.S. Census Bureau 2009a). This is only an issue when using microdata, as the ACS reports even peak-hour times in half-hour categories. A different limitation is that respondents are asked to report only one typical time at which they begin their trips to their primary jobs. The data will be imprecise for people who work flexible or variable hours or more than one job.

Although the decennial census covers only work trips, according to the 2001 National Household Travel Survey, work and work-related trips in fact make up only a minority of daily trips, 17.7 percent, versus nearly 45 percent of trips for personal and family business. At 27.1 percent of daily trips, even social and recreational trips outrank work trips (U.S. Department of Transportation 2003). Consequently, the most trips are not made during the morning peak hour (between seven and eight in the morning, when about 6.2 percent of all trips are made). The busiest hour is from three to four in the afternoon, when about 8.3 percent of all trips are made. A higher proportion of daily trips are made each hour between eleven in the morning and seven in the evening than are made from seven to eight in the morning (U.S. Department

Figure 7.2a   Work trips by public transport (residence), New Jersey, 2005–07

% Work trips by public transit

- 5% or less
- 5.1% to 10%
- 10.1% to 15%
- 15.1% to 20%
- more than 20%
- Water
- ● Population 10000 to 50000
- ● Population greater than 50000
- —— Primary Limited Access or Interstate
- —— Primary US and State Highway
- —— Secondary State and County

0   15   30   60
Miles

Source: 2005–2007 ACS
(3 year averages)

Figure 7.2b   Work trips by public transport (workplace), New Jersey, 2005–07

% Work trips by public transit
(Workplace)

- 5% or less
- 5.1% to 10%
- 10.1% to 15%
- 15.1% to 20%
- more than 20%
- Water
- ● Population 10000 to 50000
- ● Population greater than 50000
- —— Primary Limited Access or Interstate
- —— Primary US and State Highway
- —— Secondary State and County

0   15   30   60
Miles

Source: 2005–2007 ACS
(3 year averages)

of Transportation 2003, table A-12). Trends in nonwork travel are important in forecasting peak congestion periods, and nonwork trips are more likely to be made by modes such as walking or bicycling compared to work trips (Kwan 1999).

Usual travel time to work

The other data item needed to model and forecast peak travel is the length of the work trip, which is reported in minutes rather than by distance, and thus takes congestion and other factors into account. In larger cities with more trips, congestion periods usually last longer. Again, this data relies on the memory of the person responding (not necessarily the worker), and some evidence indicates that responses are rounded to the nearest five-minute interval (U.S. Census Bureau 2009a). This may affect the precision of a travel forecasting model calibrated with microdata and may affect the aggregate time traveled reported in the ACS. However, this is likely random error. Reported travel time can be interpreted as peoples' perception of the length of their trips. Figures 7.4a and 7.4b summarize changes in the proportion of commuters making short (less than fifteen minutes) and long (more than forty-five minutes) work trips from 2000 to 2007 for counties in the Portland metropolitan area.

Travel time will vary based on trip mode: bus trips take longer than train trips to cover the same distance, for example. Part-time workers are less likely to spend as much time commuting as full-time workers, so job structure influences these outcomes (Schwanen and Dijst 2002). Women continue to have shorter work trips than men because of several factors: they are less likely to work full-time and are likely to earn less and have greater household responsibilities (Crane 2007). A growing proportion of commuters with time-consuming commutes may reflect increasing suburban sprawl, worsening traffic congestion, a shift to slower modes (such as buses), an expanding labor shed, or even (as with all survey data) errors in reporting and processing the data.

Vehicles available

Vehicle availability may reflect household wealth, household composition (for instance, households with subfamilies are likely to have more cars), land-use patterns (low-density suburbs with few local services may make residents more car-dependent), or the availability of public transit. Households with more vehicles available may have better access to employment opportunities, and thus their members may have higher labor force participation rates (Raphael and Rice 2002). Researchers have argued that labor force participation rates can be depressed in neighborhoods where there is a spatial mismatch between home and work locations, especially for poorer households with fewer cars available (Ihlanfeldt and Sjoquist 1998). The variables discussed have all referred to the work trips of individuals; data for "vehicles available" is collected for households. The number of vehicles available for all uses by household members is reported, not the number of vehicles owned. Employer-owned cars kept at home would be counted if they could also be used for nonwork trips, but vehicles that may be used only for business purposes would not be counted. Cars, vans, and trucks of one-ton capacity or less are included, but motorcycles, larger trucks, and dismantled or immobile vehicles are not (U.S. Census Bureau 2009a). Numbers of vehicles per household may be used to estimate trip generation rates: households with four cars generate more trips (for instance, by teenagers) than those with only one car. This allows transportation planners to forecast travel patterns based on the demographic and economic characteristics associated with car ownership.

Figure 7.3a **Change in work trips by public transport, New Jersey, 2000 to 2005-07**

% Change in work trips by public transit

- decline
- up to 10% increase
- 10.1% to 25% increase
- 25.1% to 50% increase
- more than 50% increase
- Water
- Population 10000 to 50000
- Population greater than 50000
- Primary Limited Access or Interstate
- Primary US and State Highway
- Secondary State and County

Note: Counties with statistically significant changes highlighted in white

0   15   30   60
Miles

Source: Calculated from 2000 Census of Population and Housing and 2005–2007 ACS (3 year averages)

Figure 7.3b **Change in work trips by public transport, Missouri, 2000 to 2005–07**

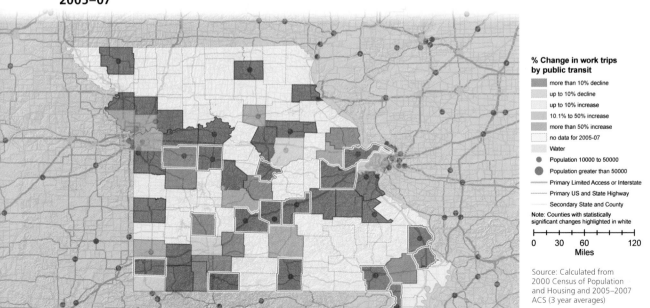

% Change in work trips by public transit

- more than 10% decline
- up to 10% decline
- up to 10% increase
- 10.1% to 50% increase
- more than 50% increase
- no data for 2005-07
- Water
- Population 10000 to 50000
- Population greater than 50000
- Primary Limited Access or Interstate
- Primary US and State Highway
- Secondary State and County

Note: Counties with statistically significant changes highlighted in white

0   30   60   120
Miles

Source: Calculated from 2000 Census of Population and Housing and 2005–2007 ACS (3 year averages)

Major formats in which journey-to-work data is reported

Data gathered in the ACS is reported in a variety of specialized formats suitable for various sorts of spatial analyses. ACS tabulations summarize commuting patterns by place of residence and place of work. Three other specialized data formats are available: CTPP, county-to-county flows, and PUMS data. In addition, a new source of model-based estimates provides a more precise picture of the geographic patterns of flows.

Census Transportation Planning Package

The CTPP is a special tabulation by the Census Bureau designed for transportation analysis. The 2000 CTPP was based on the Census 2000 long form. Some CTPP profiles have been released based on one-year and three-year ACS averages (the most recent is for the 2005–07 ACS cycle). A spatially detailed CTPP comparable with the 2000 CTPP will be released annually based on the five-year ACS averages. Although administrative data can be used to estimate travel flows (such as actual traffic counts), survey-based data offers the advantage of linking travel to demographic, social, and economic characteristics. It provides a basis for forecasts; if a community faces reductions in retail employment in some locations and increases in others, those land-use changes can be expected to alter travel patterns. CTPP data on the work trips of retail industry employees broken down by income categories, occupational groups, and gender, can help estimate how travel patterns will change as retail uses change, for example. Figure 7.5 shows the change in the proportion of retail industry workers commuting to work by car in Rhode Island counties according to the 2005–07 ACS-based profile.

CTPP files are organized in three parts:

- place of residence: the data is summarized by the area (county, place, and so on) where the worker lives.
- place of work: the data is summarized by the area (county, place, and so on) where the worker works.
- journey-to-work (JTW): these are matrix tables measuring flows between homes and work places summarized to some area level (county, place, and so on).

The three file formats can be used for different sorts of analyses, depending on the topic of interest. Researchers concerned with analyzing whether the spatial mismatch between home and work is more severe in minority neighborhoods compared with low-income neighborhoods might use the "place of residence" file (Sanchez 1999). Those concerned with how urban form affects travel patterns might use both "place of residence" and "place of work" files (Giuliano and Narayan 2003). Journey-to-work matrices would be useful for estimating the change in interdependence between inner city and suburban locations (Hewings, Okuyama, and Sonis 2001).

The CTPP uses a special geographic unit, the traffic analysis zone, for tabulating the results. A TAZ is a spatial aggregation of census blocks. State departments of transportation (DOTs) and metropolitan planning organizations (MPOs) define the number and geographic boundaries of local TAZs using the same boundary features used to define census blocks. The size of a TAZ is in part a function of population. A TAZ can be as small as a single city block in areas with high population density or many times larger than a city block in areas with low population density (U.S. Department of Transportation 2002). TAZs are most useful for travel analyses if they are contiguous, compact, include homogenous land use and demographics,

Figure 7.4a   Change in work trips (less than 15 minutes), Portland, Oregon, 2000 to 2005–07

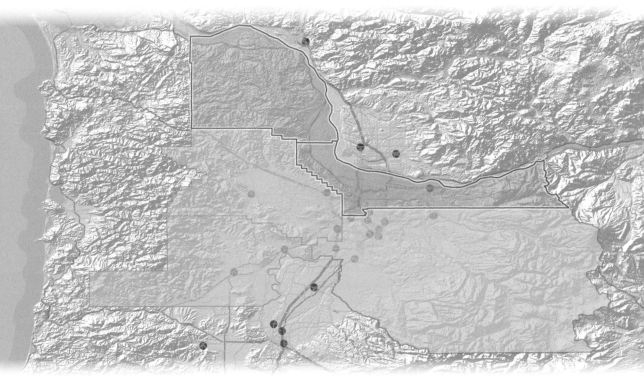

Figure 7.4b   Change in work trips (more than 45 minutes), Portland, Oregon, 2000 to 2005–07

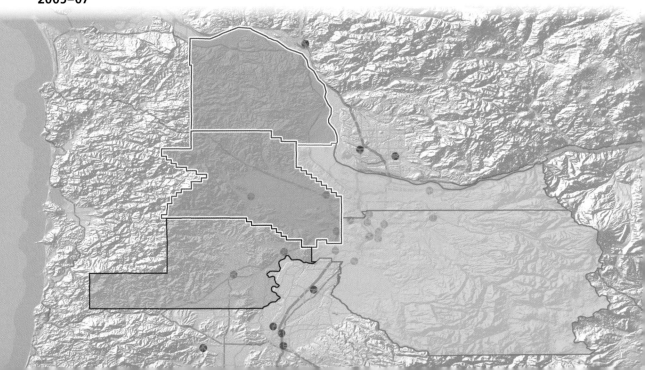

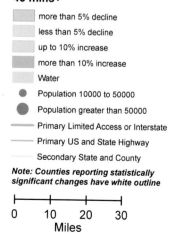

% Change in Commuters

- more than 5% decline
- less than 5% decline
- increase
- Water
- Population 10000 to 50000
- Population greater than 50000
- Primary Limited Access or Interstate
- Primary US and State Highway
- Secondary State and County

Note: Counties reporting statistically significant changes have white outline

```
0    10    20    30
         Miles
```

Source: Calculated from 2000 Census of Population and Housing and 2005–2007 ACS (3 year averages)

% Change in Commuters 45 mins+

- more than 5% decline
- less than 5% decline
- up to 10% increase
- more than 10% increase
- Water
- Population 10000 to 50000
- Population greater than 50000
- Primary Limited Access or Interstate
- Primary US and State Highway
- Secondary State and County

Note: Counties reporting statistically significant changes have white outline

```
0    10    20    30
         Miles
```

Source: Calculated from 2000 Census of Population and Housing and 2005–2007 ACS (3 year averages)

and do not include natural and constructed land features that physically restrict access.

Using existing census blocks to define TAZs may not meet all the cited criteria. Blocks are not defined based on homogeneous land uses and demographics, and their boundaries are not necessarily defined by natural or constructed features that limit accessibility, such as bridges. TAZs can vary widely in size, and changes in metropolitan definitions can mean recent additions to a metro area will have far less detailed TAZs for historical data. Figure 7.6 shows the number of women workers who earned less than $25,000 for TAZs in the Austin, Texas, metropolitan area in 2000, using the 2004 definition of the metro area. In two of Austin's suburban counties, there was only one 2000 TAZ, whereas the other three counties have considerable spatial detail. In the three counties with detail, more specific analyses about whether women workers face a spatial mismatch would be possible compared with the two counties with no detail.

It is unclear as of this writing whether the ACS-based CTPP will provide enough spatial detail to enable transportation planners to meet their statutory planning responsibilities, which require data at the census-tract and block-group levels (Cambridge Systematics et al. 2007; TCBPEP 2007; MacDonald 2006). Concerns about confidentiality will limit available cross-tabulations with means of transport to work to five variables: travel time, household income, vehicle availability, the person's age, and times leaving home and arriving at work. The seasonal variation the ACS introduces in standard transportation variables is another source of difference (Parkany 2004).

Transportation planners argue that they need a range of demographic and economic detail to understand travel patterns and forecast how they will change. For instance, commuting patterns are likely to change as women's labor force participation continues to grow and the number of workers with disabilities increases. The American Association of State and Highway Transportation Officers (AASHTO) requested eighteen cross-tabulations. A recent AASHTO-sponsored project examined how synthetic data methods could be used to substitute for the detailed cross tabulations that the Census Bureau did not agree to provide (Cambridge Systematics, Fienberg, and Love 2009). The Local Employment-Household Dynamics Program (discussed in a later section) is an example of how this might work.

County-to-county worker flows

The County-to-County Worker Flow census file summarizes the number of workers by place of residence and place of work. Home and work locations are identified by county and minor civil division. For each state, two files are available. One shows where people work by their county of residence, and the other shows where people live by the county they work in. Files are also available for worker flows by minor civil division for the twelve states that have MCDs. Worker flow data identifies statewide commuting patterns that are helpful in determining infrastructure expansion needs. They are also used to identify patterns of suburbanization and labor sheds, and form the basis for the Office of Management and Budget's definition of metropolitan areas. Figure 7.7 summarizes workplace destinations for residents of two Maryland counties, Alleghany and Montgomery. Montgomery County residents are far more likely

Figure 7.5 Change in retail industry workers driving alone to work, Rhode Island, 2000 to 2005–07

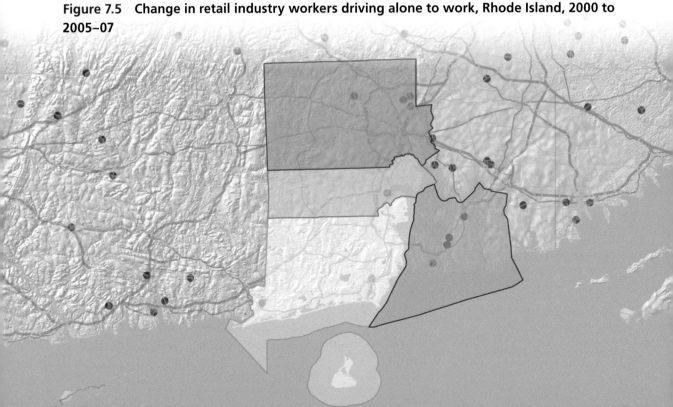

to work outside their county of residence. Similar analyses of county-to-county worker flows are useful for studies of the potential market for new housing in the counties where a majority of workers commute in from surrounding areas; people who work but do not live in a particular place may find housing in that location attractive (Schmitz and Brett 2001).

Public use microdata sample

The PUMS are samples of the ACS responses—in other words, a sample of a sample. They consist of individual records for people and households, rather than summaries of distributions by place, as we explained in chapter 4. Unlike the summary tables, PUMS allows users to create their own descriptive summaries and to test for relationships

between variables (U.S. Census Bureau 2009b). Microdata is an improvement over the fixed summary tables for analyses involving statistical or econometric models. For example, the relationships between people's choice of travel mode and personal characteristics, such as income and access to vehicles, can be used to calibrate a discrete choice model.

PUMS data are released for PUMAs, which consist of approximately 100,000 people. Geographic aggregation is an important technique used to protect confidentiality, but other techniques such as top-coding or data swapping, are also used to ensure that ACS responses cannot be tied to individuals.

The PUMS records contain the complete responses from the ACS. As with other census products, household and population characteristics are released in two separate data files. The population and household files are linked through a common data field (the serial number), that links individuals to their households. Because PUMS is a weighted sample of responses from the ACS, which is itself a sample, the issue of sampling error is even more important, especially if the data is used for statistical or econometric models.

Other transportation data

The census-based data we have discussed so far covers only one major transportation issue, the journey to work. However, another important policy concern is the issue of nonwork travel and travel by people who are unemployed or not in the labor force (especially trips by people who are disabled, elderly, or very low-income). Nonwork trips account for a majority of traffic. The journey-to-work data collected in the ACS does not reflect this, nor does it reflect long-distance travel.

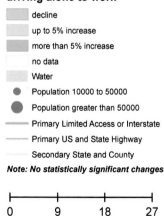

% Change in retail workers driving alone to work

[ ] decline
[ ] up to 5% increase
[ ] more than 5% increase
[ ] no data
[ ] Water
● Population 10000 to 50000
● Population greater than 50000
----- Primary Limited Access or Interstate
— Primary US and State Highway
— Secondary State and County
Note: No statistically significant changes

0   9   18   27
Miles

Source: Calculated from 2000 Census Transportation Planning Package (place of residence) and 2005–2007 Census Transportation Planning Package (place of residence)

The transportation infrastructure, including congestion, safety, environmental impacts, and freight movement, are important topics covered by other data sources. The following section briefly reviews data sources that supplement the information collected in the decennial census.

National Household Travel Survey

The National Household Travel Survey (NHTS), conducted for the first time in 2001 and more recently in 2009, collects information on daily and long distance travel for the nation. It combines the coverage of two previous surveys: the National Personal Transportation Survey and the American Travel Survey. Like PUMS, the data is made up of individual records for each member of the households surveyed.

NHTS collects information on all trips, not just work trips. Trips for personal, family, social, and recreational purposes make up a majority of daily trips, which was estimated at 72 percent in 2001 (U.S. Department of Transportation 2003). The survey also reports information on demographic characteristics, trip characteristics (mode, length, time and day of week, and vehicle occupancy), and vehicle characteristics (model year, annual miles driven, and so on). Many aspects of travel

Figure 7.6   Low-income female workers, Austin, Texas, 2000

behavior can be cross-tabulated with household and individual characteristics. Data on long-distance trips is broken down by purpose and by mode and distance. NHTS data enables researchers to answer a wider range of questions such as whether men and women have different trip-chaining patterns, and differences in travel patterns by children or the elderly (McDonald 2008).

The NHTS covers a limited sample of households (25,000 nationwide), and thus is not useful at a more detailed spatial scale than the nine census divisions. However, localities may cover the costs of sampling their jurisdictions at a higher rate. Additional surveys were conducted for

about twenty states or metropolitan planning organizations in 2009. In these places, the NHTS can be used for a wider range of local analyses, such as developing more detailed travel demand models (Kane 2004.).

Longitudinal employer-household dynamics program

The Longitudinal Employer-Household Dynamics program (LEHD) provides spatially detailed estimates of home and work locations (and potentially also journey-to-work flows) based on several sources of federal and state administrative data and

Figure 7.7   Work destinations, Allegheny and Montgomery Cos., Maryland

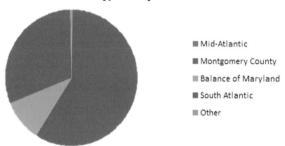

Work destinations, Montgomery County, Maryland

- Mid-Atlantic
- Montgomery County
- Balance of Maryland
- South Atlantic
- Other

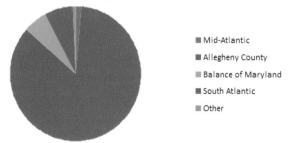

Work destinations, Allegheny County, Maryland

- Mid-Atlantic
- Allegheny County
- Balance of Maryland
- South Atlantic
- Other

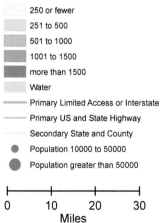

Low income female workers

- 250 or fewer
- 251 to 500
- 501 to 1000
- 1001 to 1500
- more than 1500
- Water
- Primary Limited Access or Interstate
- Primary US and State Highway
- Secondary State and County
- ● Population 10000 to 50000
- ● Population greater than 50000

0   10   20   30
Miles

Source: 2000 Census Transportation Planning Package (place of residence)

Source: County-to-County Work Flows, 2000, http://www.census.gov/population/www/cen2000/commuting/index.html

Census Bureau surveys. Several data manipulation techniques are used to protect confidentiality, providing essentially synthetic data. Given the challenges transportation planners now face developing spatially precise travel models, because of the reduced spatial precision of ACS-based datasets, synthetic data produced through programs like the LEHD may offer an alternative source of timely but spatially detailed data. Synthetic data can enable researchers to investigate topics such as how differences in access to job locations may affect earnings over time by gender and race, without risking the loss of privacy that real data disaggregated by so many characteristics might (Andersson, Holzer, and Lane 2002). Assessments are under way about methodological issues and the potential of LEHD to provide a basis for a local program equivalent to the Local Employment Dynamics program discussed in chapter 6 (Murakama 2007; Cambridge Systematics, Feinberg, and Love 2009).

Other household-based sources

Data on commuting costs is collected in some of the economic databases described in chapter 6. The Survey of Income and Program Participation, for instance, includes valuable national level information on transportation issues faced by people receiving public assistance and those making the transition from welfare to work.

Special purpose surveys are also conducted periodically. In 2002, the Bureau of Transportation Statistics surveyed a sample of about 5,000 people with and without disabilities to identify differences in their transportation needs in the 2002 National Transportation Availability and Use Survey. Researchers used this information to identify the specific transportation problems faced by people with disabilities and recommend solutions (Rosenbloom 2007). In 2005, the Federal Highway

Administration (FHA) surveyed 2,600 people in the Traveler Opinion and Perception Survey, aimed at identifying overall levels of satisfaction and areas for improvement; similar surveys had been conducted in 1995 and 2000. Some states added to this survey; for instance, Idaho gathered information about its residents' perceptions of road safety and their opinions about alternatives to manage growth (Northwest Research Group 2005). None of these surveys can provide spatially specific data, but the topics they cover are important for many local transportation planning issues, such as whether public transit or subsidized taxi services would be better to increase the employment opportunities of people with disabilities, and can be a helpful supplement for local analyses.

Transportation impact and infrastructure data

The Aerometric Information Retrieval System data from the National Air Quality Database, sponsored by the Environmental Protection Agency (EPA), is a valuable source of data about ambient concentrations of air pollutants at monitoring sites in cities and towns throughout the United States, collected annually since 1996. Air quality data is reported to the EPA as the basis for its evaluation of the compliance of states and metro areas with the Clean Air Act. Localities that consistently violate air pollution standards risk losing federal highway funds. The data has been used to evaluate the impact of changing travel patterns on pollution, develop models of the causes and impacts of climate change, and evaluate the exposure of pedestrians to pollution (Murazaki and Hess 2006; de Nazelle and Rodriguez 2009).

The Highway Performance Monitoring System provides a wealth of information on arterial and collector roads, and more limited data on all public roads, summarized by urbanized, small urban, and rural areas. The FHA collects the information in partnership with state and local governments and metropolitan planning organizations. Data on highway condition, performance, future investment needs, and air quality are available annually, enabling states to develop highway adequacy ratings to plan priorities for upgrades and repairs. The Highway Congestion (Urban Mobility) study provides information on trends in mobility and congestion for sixty-eight urban areas. Driver-hours of delay, traffic-rate index, and congestion cost per year are some of the analytic indicators provided. These enable evaluations of the effects that transport investments and TDM programs have on relieving congestion. Transit advocates have used the data to estimate the economic costs of congestion; one study concluded that the average peak period commuter wastes the equivalent of eight working days in congestion delays annually (APTA 2005). The Fatality Analysis Reporting System provides information on crashes involving fatalities, including vehicle and personal characteristics, which is used for developing targeted road safety campaigns.

Freight movement data

The Commodity Flow Survey (CFS), sponsored by the Bureau of Transportation Statistics (BTS) and the Census Bureau, estimates the flow of goods and materials by mode of transportation. In addition to providing a basis for projections of freight traffic, it also offers a way to understand regional trade flows and industrial links (Batten and Boyce 1987). The CFS surveys mining, manufacturing, wholesale trade, selected retail industries and selected auxiliary establishments, such as warehouses, for the value, weight, mode of transportation, and the origins and destinations of the commodities

shipped. The survey has been conducted since 1963 more or less every five years, with major revisions in 1993 and 1997. The data is released at several geographic levels, including states, and can be broken down into selected metropolitan areas and the rest of the state. The Economic Census provides data on transportation companies and commodity movement. Data includes operating revenue, percentage of motor carrier freight revenue by commodity type, weight of shipments handled, country of origin and destination of the shipment, and inventory of the vehicle fleet.

The BTS publication, *National Transportation Statistics* (U.S. Department of Transportation 2002), lists additional specialized data sources. States and MPOs also collect and disseminate transportation data though the type, quantity and quality vary widely. Larger urban areas have local MPOs that are more actively involved in the collection and analysis of transportation data.

Conclusions

Census and ACS-based data is far less costly than survey data and offers spatial comparability, consistency over time, and quality control. However, administrative and survey data are essential for some questions, particularly when specific programs or policies are being evaluated. For instance, national-level data about travel barriers for people with disabilities would need to be supplemented with specific local surveys to evaluate the effectiveness of a particular solution. Census and ACS data play a valuable contextualizing role, where the lack of either spatial precision or currency is less important.

But precise and current data is needed for some analyses. As transportation planners respond to the challenges of the new data environment, two complementary paths deserve serious consideration. First, synthetic data may be a reasonable solution to the dilemma of protecting confidentiality while using precise and current information (Abowd and Lane 2004; Cambridge Systematics, Fienberg, and Love 2009). In the past, CTPP data was fairly precise at the TAZ level but almost never current (2000 CTPP data became publicly available in mid-2004). Transportation analysts adjusted the data, projecting flows forward to reflect current circumstances and forecasting trends into the future. Most analysts did this carefully and responsibly, but forecasting is a difficult art, and as many commentators have noted, forecasts are only as good as the assumptions on which they based (Isserman 1993). Would it be any less problematic to use widely scrutinized and rigorously debated statistical methods to develop timely and precise synthetic data from the variety of available survey and administrative data?

Second, the potential to digitize, standardize, and share administrative data (from the rich array of transportation-related sources) as a substitute for survey-based data is tremendous. Growing ITS (intelligent transportation system) capabilities offer an alternative to the relatively vague and often subjective data gathered in surveys, because they offer real-time counts of traffic flows and can provide a comprehensive picture of the origin, destination, and time of each trip. They lack links to demographic and socioeconomic information gathered in surveys, but other administrative data sources have the potential to bridge this gap. Confidentiality concerns are an obvious barrier, but confidentiality could be protected by linking administrative data before analysts get access to it, and summarizing it at similar spatial units to survey data. Could administrative sources offer a supplement or substitute for census and ACS data? This is a political rather than merely a technical question, but one of particular interest as transportation analysts adapt to the ACS era.

Chapter 8

Making sense of the data

Effective, targeted responses to disasters depend on careful assessment of evidence. Spatially detailed information from the 2000 census improved relief efforts in New York City's Chinatown after the 9/11 attacks. Chinese American residents of Chinatown were particularly vulnerable to the economic freeze after the attacks, with restrictions on public access and basic services affecting some businesses for up to three months afterward (U.S. Census Bureau 2003c). Chinatown's predominately low-income immigrant residents relied on the jobs provided by local businesses, but only 40 percent of them lived within the relief zone defined in the days following the disaster. Mapping the community that relied on the businesses that had been shut down by the disruption (see figure 8.1) enabled the redefinition of the area in which cash relief was provided until economic activity resumed (U.S. Census Bureau 2003c).

Figure 8.1 Chinese American population, New York City's Chinatown

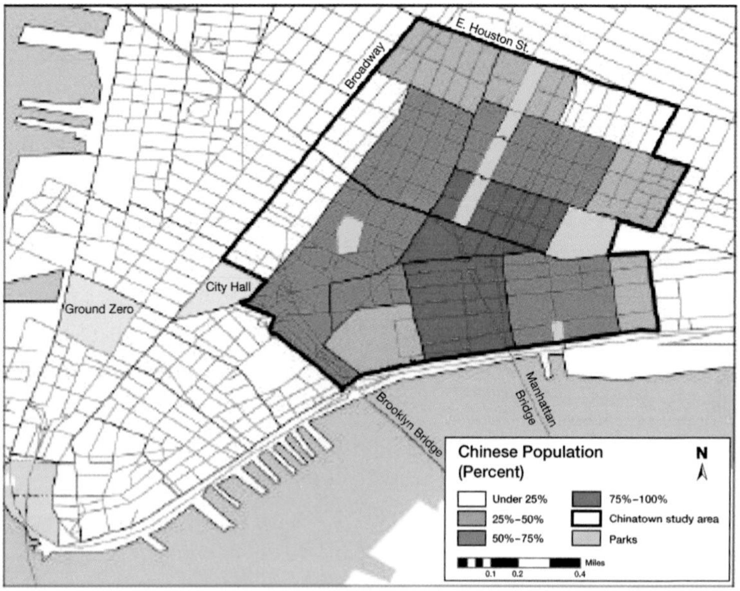

Source: U.S. Census Bureau 2003c, 3

Few urban policy questions are as dramatic as those New York City faced in the last months of 2001. But careful assessment of evidence still matters; making assumptions about the dimensions and extent of the problems we set out to resolve often leads to inappropriate or ineffectual responses. As this book has explained, census and ACS data can provide much of the evidence needed to frame choices for action. But, as we noted in chapter 3, data only becomes useful as evidence once we grasp how it is constructed, what it can and cannot tell us, and how to communicate it meaningfully.

The preceding four chapters focused on these issues in relation to each of four substantive topics. In this chapter, we demonstrate how the questions outlined in chapter 3 can be applied to make sense of geographic data for spatial analyses. We develop four hypothetical policy research designs to illustrate how to construct studies within the possibilities and limitations of available census and ACS data. Although hypothetical, these case studies are based on actual research projects. In each case, census and ACS data play a valuable role, but supplementary data is needed. The final section of the chapter briefly discusses the potential for incorporating administrative data into analyses. The chapter's conclusion reflects on the lessons these cases suggest for evidence-based policymaking and discusses their implications for the spatial analysis of urban policy decisions in the ACS era.

Case 1. Demographic and social policy: Planning for child-care facilities in a small but growing community

In this scenario, a coalition of subsidized child-care providers is concerned with the declining enrollment faced in some day-care facilities, combined with long waiting lists at others. Informal feedback from low-income parents has highlighted a mismatch between working hours and hours of child-care availability. The coalition is based in a fringe county of a small but rapidly growing metropolitan area. The county housing stock is lower priced, so it has a fairly large concentration of younger lower-wage working families.

Recent efforts to increase child-care funding to deal with the unmet need have failed, because elected officials anxious to limit expenditure pointed to the excess capacity at several facilities. Grant applications to state-level sources are likely to face stiff competition from other localities that have absolute shortfalls in child-care spaces. Another concern is that emerging needs, such as for dual-language facilities, more comprehensive family support services, and services to children of families who are homeless or near-homeless, are not being met within the existing decentralized network of small-scale child-care providers. Opportunities to train more child-care providers and help them establish home-based businesses are being lost because the county cannot demonstrate enough overall need in comparison with other counties competing for the same funding.

Within the coalition, members debate two options: first, closing existing undercapacity services and consolidating child care in a central location where a variety of services (including training for new providers) could be concentrated; or, second, redesigning the decentralized network of small-scale providers to better match areas of residential growth.

Study questions

We begin by breaking down the complex multifaceted challenges in this scenario into a series of discrete questions to guide the study design:

- What is the current total demand for child care? What share of it is being met by existing services? Would different services (e.g., options for longer days and evening care) tap demand that isn't being met currently?
- How will demand for different sorts of services change over the short to medium term? What is the projected increase in the lower-income family population the coalition targets? How will that increase be distributed among segments of need (e.g., single parents with long working hours, non-English-speaking families, or families vulnerable to homelessness)?
- How is current demand distributed spatially? Will this distribution change as a result of future residential growth?
- Where are the mismatches between current facilities, and current and future demand?
- What are the pros and cons of concentrating services in a single location? What are the pros and cons of continuing with a decentralized service network?

Study design

In this section, we discuss the availability and limitations of data that could help answer the child-care planning questions just posed. We then outline the sorts of analytic approaches that might be appropriate and discuss their limitations.

Defining and understanding current demand

Administrative data could address part of this by showing trends in current enrollment and waiting lists for child-care spaces. It could tell us how many children are in different types of child care. But this question also asks about the potential current demand. To estimate this, we need to answer questions such as the following:

- How many children under age six live in the county? How many are part of low-income families?
- How many low-income families have two parents, one parent, or no parent present?
- What role do grandparents play in caring for children?
- How many women and men with children under age six work full or part time outside the home?
- How many parents of children under age six are not in the labor force?
- How have parents' work patterns changed? How many are in full- or part-time employment? How are they distributed by industry and occupation? What are the typical pay and working hours for the most common industries and occupations (e.g., retail versus manufacturing industries, health-care versus clerical and administrative occupations)?
- Where do most low-income family members work (in or outside their home county)? How do they travel to work?
- Why don't some eligible families use the subsidized child-care services available? Are there services or delivery options that would meet their needs better?

Some of these are social and demographic questions, and some are related to employment, income, and transportation. Several questions cannot be answered through census or ACS data.

County Business Patterns is a better source of data on prevailing wages and hours by industry. Information on typical work hours could be gathered from business listings, large employers, advertisements for vacant positions, and employment agencies. Understanding family preferences and reasons for not using services would require a household survey or focus groups. Child-care providers may also provide some insight into unmet needs based on inquiries they receive. However, relying entirely on this last source for evidence of need may attract criticism that providers have an incentive to exaggerate the need for their services.

In most places, it may be difficult to develop a defensible estimate of the current number of families with special-service needs. Some needs (for instance, from non-English-speaking families) can be estimated from census or ACS data (although the differential undercount may compromise the quality of these estimates). Others, such as the homeless or near homeless or single parents who work long hours, are much more difficult to estimate. The 1990 and 2000 censuses failed to develop an adequate estimate of the homeless population; even the count of people living in homeless shelters was probably unreliable (GAO 2003). Whether the 2010 census and the ACS improve substantially on this record is still questionable. The homeless population is particularly difficult to count because it is fluid (people move into and out of homelessness over time), mobile, and underserved. The near-homeless population (those at risk of becoming homeless) is even more difficult to determine. People might be at risk for many reasons, ranging from being behind on rent, to being in a bad relationship, to having a job in a vulnerable economic sector. Income, ethnicity, employment, and marital status are inadequate predictors of these sorts of events. Housing affordability measures and displacement are more closely related to the incidence of some but not all near-homeless people. States attempt to count homeless people and families periodically (usually by counties), and local homeless coalitions might have estimates based on an annual one-night count required to apply for funds from the Department of Housing and Urban Development.

An alternative approach might survey a sample of eligible parents to see how many believe they need some of the special services under consideration. Given the gaps in some of the available social and demographic data, a well-designed survey may be a preferable way to estimate specific needs.

Projecting demand

Census data by age and sex, combined with fertility and mortality statistics, provides most of what we would need to project the numbers of the under-six population into the future. Cohort component methods of population projection also require us to estimate migration rates. This could be done using administrative data (such as tax returns, utility connections and disconnections, or change of address forms from the U.S. Postal Service (USPS)). ACS data on "residence one year ago" provides another way to estimate migration into a local area. The traditional approach is to project population from a previous period (for instance, 2000) forward to a period for which we have reliable age and sex data (such as 2010), compare the two population estimates, and treat the difference between our projected estimates and the reported population size as the residual effect attributable to net migration. Many elementary planning methods textbooks explain cohort component population projection methods in detail.

In addition to the total number of children under age six, we are interested in specific subgroups: those who live in income-eligible families, in families where English is not a first language, in those at risk of homelessness, and so on. We are also interested in where future cohorts of eligible families will live in the county. But attempting to project the size of subgroups of children into the future is a bad strategy. Projections become increasingly prone to error at smaller spatial scales, and a laborious projection process will likely result in unusable numbers. There really is no good way to develop meaningful forecasts of small subgroups of need.

The best strategy may be to describe the current distribution of children among categories of need, and assume that their proportionate distribution would remain fairly constant over the next decade. Of course, there may be specific reasons why this isn't the case: a major employer has just folded up, a cohort of international refugees are being resettled locally, or similar. In these cases, the best one could do is argue for a regular reassessment of needs over the near term. Putting precise numbers on future needs is a risky business, and all study conclusions risk being undermined by a single glaringly inaccurate prediction.

Spatial distribution of demand

Administrative records, such as address data for current families, provide a ready source to describe the current distribution of client households. Census data about households that might need subsidized child care but are not currently using it provide some level of spatial detail, but as many of the variables would come from the ACS, spatial precision may be limited. In particular, variables with very small counts (for example, low-income single parents with children under age six) have much wider margins of error. We would also be working with five-year averages of characteristics rather than characteristics at a single point in time.

Distributing projected need among actual locations is also risky but may be based on more solid foundations than projecting the size of subgroups. Examining trends in past annexations, recent new construction, and new subdivision and rezoning approvals can help develop estimates of where new residential, and thus population, growth will be located. It offers a way to allocate the overall estimates constructed at the county level. However, because we are interested in families who are eligible for childcare assistance, areas of new housing growth may or may not be the areas in which these families will live. New homes tend to be more expensive, and lower-income families (and especially some of the subgroups of interest such as recent immigrants or the near-homeless) are more likely to live in the older, more affordable stock in the community. A better strategy in this case might be to examine where the most affordable housing stock is located and where additions are likely to be made (for instance, new family rental housing or mobile home park expansions).

Identifying mismatches

At this point, we should have a fairly clear picture of who the subsidized child-care system currently serves, an approximate estimate of who it could serve if it provided additional services, and the size of future potential demand. We can provide a reasonable estimate of how that demand is distributed now and a rough estimate of how it might be distributed in the future. Although our results are approximate, we can estimate the mismatches (by location and services offered) between this picture of demand and the current services supplied.

Precise numbers, for example, "twelve more places need to be provided for children in long day care" should be regarded with suspicion, but ranges of need (such as "between ten and fifteen new places") are probably defensible. Most important, these estimates could be framed in terms that are easily understood by elected officials and could provide a clear rationale for additional resources (if these are justified).

Evaluating centralization versus decentralization

Based on the ranges of mismatches constructed in the previous stages, we might have a better informed debate about this question. We should also have developed more insight into questions such as whether specialized supportive service needs would justify a centralized child-care facility. We should have a better idea of where current and potential client parents work and thus whether a centralized location might be convenient. However, other elements to consider in such a decision would be the preferences of current and prospective parents and of child-care providers. What do each of these groups see as pros and cons of each choice? Standardized data cannot answer this question, though it can provide a useful context in which the question could be debated.

Focus groups, task forces, and public meetings could discuss the study findings, focusing on the complex questions that belong in the public realm: the weight placed on efficiency versus equity in alternative location choices, and the pros and cons of organizational and institutional change. Too often those debates are sidelined by discussions that research could settle satisfactorily, such as "is there really a demand for specialized services?" or "will demand grow or shrink over the next decade?" Providing sound (if approximate) estimates of the answers to these questions enables stakeholder discussions to focus on the substantive areas where input and debate are most crucial.

The analytic process as described is far from perfect. The social and demographic profile of the target population is more difficult to construct than that of a simpler group, such as all elementary school-age children. Projecting need into the future and estimating spatial distributions based on an approximately defined starting population is likely to magnify inaccuracies. In a small county, the potential for inaccuracies is greater still.

However, this scenario is not an extreme: it is in fact based on a real world example. It reflects the complexity of much local policy-oriented research, and the difficulty that researchers face in developing the sorts of precise numbers that decision makers would like. Too often, the temptation is to provide precise numbers anyway. Precision is usually misleading because it masks the following elements:

- the approximate connection between what the original data measures and the phenomenon of interest
- the approximate nature of an estimate based on a sample
- the impossibility of accurately predicting the future
- the difficulty of predicting the spatial distribution of future populations

Complex social decisions are unlikely to be based on the results of such an analysis, even if the precision were justified. The politics of the situation—which in this example may range from which child-care providers are better connected to the media, to the electoral promises of the county supervisors, to the state governor's perceptions of where legislator loyalties need to be shored up—are likely to override the recommendations of the analysis.

Does this undermine the entire purpose of the analysis? No. In a democratic society, decision makers are held accountable. Decision makers may ignore the evidence, but without evidence it is much less possible to criticize decisions effectively. However, flawed evidence, in particular, evidence that claims more precision than is justified, is much less useful as a basis for criticism.

Case 2. Housing policy: Planning to absorb foreclosed vacant homes in a stagnant housing market

Many communities have faced substantial housing challenges in recent years. Vacant homes in many cases remained on the market for months or years as housing prices fell, property tax delinquencies rose among households in financial distress, and displaced homeowners searched for rental housing. As a result, local community-based housing development organizations faced new stresses, but the downturn was also an opportunity for organizations to expand their housing portfolios and respond to the growing need for affordable rental housing. The combination of low-priced homes on the market and higher rental demand made it a good time for the nonprofit affordable housing sector to buy homes. Such a strategy promised to benefit the entire community by reducing the overhang of unsold homes, bringing residents back to neighborhoods, and stabilizing declining property tax bases.

However, nonprofit organizations could only do this if they could attract the financing needed. Tapping sources of public subsidy and private capital investment or debt depend on a credible analysis about changes in the housing market and how community-based organizations respond to those changes. Projecting market trends is more complex given high levels of uncertainty. In this scenario, the county government is willing to fund a countywide housing market study to inform and strengthen community-based organizations' efforts to develop viable strategies. How should the county structure this study?

Study questions

A countywide housing market study might address the following questions:

- What has happened to the supply of housing during the past two to three years? We would be interested in understanding how supply has changed for different types of units, in various price categories, and in different neighborhoods. Changes in tenure and vacancy status need to be tracked for different segments of the stock.
- What has happened to the demand for different types of housing during the past two to three years? Demand is driven by demographic factors (changes in household composition or age structure) and economic ones (changes in household income and wealth, and employment location). The depth of demand will differ for different types of housing (condominiums for purchase versus apartments for rent), and will also reflect the availability of financing.
- How are patterns of supply and demand likely to change over the next five years? We cannot assume that trends over the past two to three years are a good predictor of the future. Risk tolerance is low now, so projections may be more acceptable if they estimate a range of likely future outcomes and also the probability of each occurring.

Study design

In this section, we discuss the availability and limitations of data that could help answer the housing market questions just posed. We then outline the sorts of analytic approaches that might be appropriate and discuss their limitations.

Identifying recent trends in supply

The ACS offers a starting point for this assessment. Estimates of vacancy rates and tenure by type and age of structures, and the distribution of prices or rents, are key elements of a housing stock profile. However, the ACS's smaller sample means that its estimates are much less precise, especially for small areas such as census tracts and for small categories such as renter-occupied two-to-four unit structures. In the past, housing market analysts would have used the decennial census estimates as a base and updated these using sources such as building permits, rent surveys, and property valuation estimates. The 2010 census provides a reasonably precise number of housing units and their vacancy and tenure status but does not include the more refined detail on how these vary by factors such as type of structure or price. The ACS does, but its estimates are less precise.

Local administrative and industry data will be an important component of the assessment of changing supply. Local real estate boards are a valuable source of data on homes for sale, length of time on the market by type of home (condominium, single-family, or apartment), and trends in price. Data on the location of foreclosed properties can be gathered from the mortgage recorder's office and the county sheriff; in most places this is a labor-intensive process as individual records must be searched and transcribed. Data on recent mortgage transactions and loan size (from the HMDA data) can provide some information on the homeowner market and the locations of some higher-cost loans. Building permits and mobile home registrations provide information on additions to the stock.

Property valuation processes vary by state; this can be a valuable, spatially detailed source of information on home value trends if assessors track the market fairly accurately. Where property tax systems provide a homesteader credit (a tax rebate for owner-occupiers), counts of properties eligible for homestead credit can provide an updated measure of home ownership. The USPS dataset on vacancies is updated quarterly and may be a more current estimate than sources such as the ACS.

A final aspect to understand is the condition of the housing stock. The AHS is the only survey that collects sufficiently detailed information on housing condition; the housing quality measures in the ACS are too limited to be of much use. Unfortunately, AHS data is not available at a sufficiently detailed spatial scale for a neighborhood-focused study like this, even in the metropolitan areas for which the AHS is available. New HUD data on the condition of units that are federally subsidized or insured provides a partial measure of local housing quality, but because housing condition is regulated for subsidized units, we cannot expect this measure to reflect the condition of other homes in the neighborhood. Given the importance of housing condition as an indicator of the adequacy of the stock and the attractiveness of local housing markets, a sample survey is probably justified. GIS can be used to draw a stratified sample of blocks in each neighborhood. Figure 8.2 shows a census block sample drawn for a windshield survey of housing conditions in Scott County, Iowa. Randomly selected blocks (shown in yellow) were surveyed in detail to develop a statistically valid estimate of housing conditions for the census tract. Windshield surveys that rate homes on visible elements (such as roof, foundation, windows, porches, siding, and exterior buildings and landscaping) can be conducted to develop an estimate of the condition of the stock in each neighborhood or tract. If funds are limited, surveys could focus on neighborhoods of most concern instead of conducting a citywide survey.

Identifying recent trends in demand

Current population estimates are a good starting point for understanding a rapidly changing community because they are based on surveys and administrative sources (such as information on tax returns filed by jurisdiction) unavailable to most researchers. Five-year ACS averages could be used to apportion current population to individual census tracts, but care should be exercised where foreclosure and displacement have affected some neighborhoods disproportionately. Five-year averages cannot capture rapid recent change. This is one reason to start with estimates of changes to the housing stock before addressing changes to households and families.

It is probably even more challenging to estimate demand trends than housing supply trends, because households are mobile and their composition can change rapidly. Adults encountering financial difficulty may move back in with parents; families under stress may be more likely to fragment through divorce or the search for work in distant places. The ACS offers a snapshot of how society has looked in the recent past, but there is an inevitable time lag to the present. Furthermore, demographic characteristics are fluid: households may have grown in size and shrunk in number, but may still represent significant pent-up housing demand from subfamily members who cannot afford their own home.

Income data gathered in the ACS refers to income earned in the previous year, creating an inevitable time lag in estimating effective household spending power. HUD's estimates of median family income use the local consumer price index (CPI) to update the previous year's reported income. Administrative data sources could supplement estimates of current housing demand. School enrollment trends, registration for free or reduced price school lunches, housing assistance waiting lists, and trends in rental applications could all be used to estimate current demographic and economic drivers of demand for low-cost housing.

As with housing stock, some aspects of housing demand are difficult to get at without locally

Figure 8.2   Sample frame for survey of housing conditions, selected census tract in Scott Co., Iowa

Tract 107.00

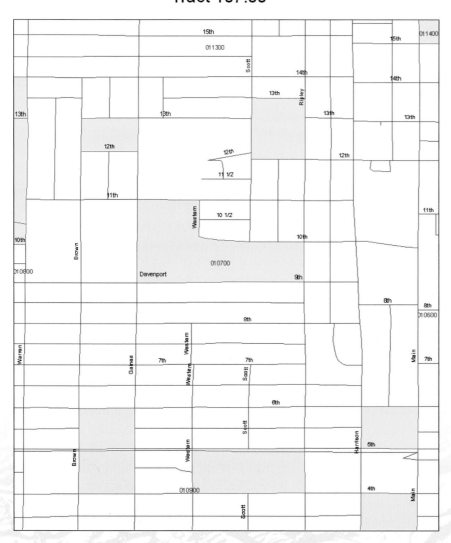

specific information. Perceptions about the quality of amenities like schools can explain how and why demand might differ in neighborhoods with otherwise comparable available housing. Crime rates from local law enforcement agencies can help explain differences in demand, but crime statistics may differ from popular perceptions. Focus groups may be the most effective way to develop a picture of how peoples' perceptions drive demand in particular neighborhoods.

Projecting changes to supply and demand

No method can reasonably forecast an uncertain future. Projections of housing supply and demand typically carry a disclaimer along the lines of "assuming current trends continue." This is not a reasonable assumption during periods of crisis. Developing alternative scenarios and projecting trends under each scenario may be a better strategy. To do this, a clear understanding of the regional economy and its possible future course is essential. During rapid change, economic competitiveness probably will be a more important determinant of population growth or decline and housing market revival or slump than past demographic trends. An interesting resource based on a variety of economic data sources classifies the hundred largest metropolitan areas on several dimensions, developing indicators of economic health. MetroMonitor, an indicator project developed by the Brookings Institution Metropolitan Policy program, is available online at the institute's Web site (Weil and Shearer 2010).

Based on an assessment of regional economic trends, three scenarios might be developed for our hypothetical locality over the short to medium term: a no-growth scenario with continued gradual decline in housing demand, a job-shrinkage scenario with more rapid population losses and rising vacancy rates, and a slow-growth scenario with stable or slightly increasing housing demand but stagnant household earnings. Assessments of the risk of further foreclosures and vacancies, perhaps using indicators similar to those just described, may be adapted to distribute projected economic pain or gain among neighborhoods. This technique does not masquerade as a scientific prediction but instead exposes the speculative nature of any attempts to forecast under conditions of uncertainty. GIS, in this case, becomes a tool to develop a potentially infinite number of what-if scenarios to inform discussion and brainstorming.

Case 3. Economic development policy: Analyzing local economic impacts

Economic development incentives are so widely used to attract firms to particular places that firms often appear to expect them. However, wise decisions about whether to offer incentives should be based on a careful assessment of the likely economic impact of the new facility. Will it add enough new employment to justify spending scarce public resources (or perhaps encumbering future tax revenues) to subsidize the firm's relocation to the community?

In this scenario, a small nonmetropolitan county in the deindustrializing Midwest is being considered as a site for a new component manufacturing plant for school buses that will employ 200 workers. The firm is considering several locations but has approached this local county government because a similar sized manufacturing plant closed in the community about three years earlier. The firm expects that the local labor force would have the skills it needs and that state and local government will offer subsidies to replace jobs that were lost earlier.

The county board of supervisors is expected to make a decision on whether to subsidize infrastructure, plant, or jobs. Before it does so, some supervisors want to see what impact the investment would have on economic growth in the county. One side argues that economic multiplier effects from the new manufacturing jobs will justify large per job subsidies: workers will stimulate the local economy by buying houses, paying taxes, getting their cars fixed and eating in restaurants, thus multiplying the local impact of earned wages. The other side argues that the workers laid off three years ago have left the community, and the jobs will go to outsiders who may not spend their paychecks in or even choose to live in the county. That might justify state subsidies but not local county resources.

Study questions

These questions sort out the various threads in the scenario and form the basis for the study design:

- Where will the firm find the labor force with the required skills and availability? Have the laid-off employees of the departed manufacturing firm found similar jobs locally, have they accepted lower-quality jobs to stay in the community, or have they gone elsewhere for good jobs? If there aren't suitably skilled and available prospective employees in the county, do they exist in the immediate region? If so, are they likely to commute from their current homes or move to the county?
- What are the likely multiplier effects of the 200 new manufacturing jobs? How will these effects be distributed among the economies

of the local county, neighboring counties, and the state? How much of the new taxpaying and spending capacity of the firm and its employees will leave the state altogether?
- What other benefits will be captured locally compared to at the regional or state level? For instance, supporting the continued viability of a local school district by bringing in an influx of new families may be an important social benefit (if not an economic one).
- How do these benefits compare to the projected cost of different types of subsidies? Once potential benefits have been estimated, along with their timing and the probability they will occur, local decision makers should have a sounder basis for evaluating proposed subsidies and deciding on the appropriate timing and form of any supports offered.

Study design

In this section, we discuss the availability and limitations of data that could help answer the local economic impact questions just posed. We then outline the sorts of analytic approaches that might be appropriate and discuss their limitations.

Defining the available labor force and its attributes

ACS data is of limited use to us as a guide to how the labor force has changed since the plant closure three years ago, given this county has a population of less than 65,000. Three-year averages are available from the ACS (the county has a population just over 20,000), but as averages these estimates will include information for surveyed households before, during, and after the plant closure. However, other data sources and a variety of model-based estimates that incorporate ACS data can provide a more current picture of the available labor force.

The datasets discussed in chapter 6 offer some alternatives. County Population Estimates enable us to update ACS estimates of the local population. Local Area Unemployment Statistics provide trends in unemployment rates for the county. Small Area Income and Poverty Estimates provide information on households' economic prosperity. County Business Patterns may be most useful here, as the dataset provides information on employment and payroll by sector, although for a smaller county information may only be available for broad sectors. Covered employment (ES202) data is an alternative, though it may be less preferable because it would exclude categories of workers (such as the self-employed) who may be fairly significant in the county economy. The Economic Census is another potentially useful source of data on establishment-level employment, pay, and benefits, but it may not be available for a recent enough year to be useful, especially given the approximate two-year time lag in releasing results for small areas. The Local Employment Dynamics program may be very useful, if the county is in one of the forty-six participating states, because it combines estimates of workers at their place of residence and at their place of work. A labor shed analysis using this synthetic data would show the locations from which current workers are drawn.

These data sources will be available for surrounding counties and the state as a whole, and thus local trends in employment by sector, wage rates, and so on can be contrasted with those in neighboring communities to identify how the local labor force differs, and the characteristics of the potential labor supply in the immediate region.

Although ACS may be a less satisfactory source for current labor force information, it provides a helpful perspective on education levels, demographic characteristics, trends in mobility, housing availability and cost, and commuting patterns.

Identifying multiplier effects

Ideally, an economic multiplier could be calculated using an input-output or general equilibrium model, but few local economic development specialists have the sort of resources needed to construct a sufficiently complete model of the state and national economy. A solution to this is to purchase information from a specialized economic impact consulting firm. However, economic-base analysis offers a way to calculate an approximate multiplier using easily available information. The multiplier would be based on the ratio of local employment in export sector industries to local employment in other industries.

Export sector industries are those that produce more of a good or service than local demand consumes; non-export sectors produce for local demand. We define export and non-export (or basic and nonbasic) industries using a location quotient, which compares the relative size of a sector locally to its relative size nationally. For example, a cheese production industry that accounts for 6 percent of employment locally compared to a proportion of 1 percent nationally indicates that local firms are producing more cheese than needed for local demand. The local cheese producing industry is thus an export (or basic) sector. In economic theory, basic or export sectors drive local economies: they bring money into the community, which can then be spent on consumption items or services like housing, groceries, car maintenance, and so on.

We would use County Business Patterns to estimate local employment by sector and to calculate a location quotient for each industrial sector. More detailed explanations of the location quotient calculation are available in many economic analysis textbooks (see, for example, Klosterman 1990). Once we have estimated all basic and nonbasic employment in the local economy, we can estimate an economic base multiplier. The multiplier shows how many nonbasic jobs there are compared to basic jobs: in other words, how much local employment is supported by the earnings brought in by jobs in the export sector. In this example, we would use the multiplier to estimate how many other jobs in nonbasic or non-export sectors might be supported by the 200 new jobs in the proposed manufacturing plant. If the multiplier we calculate is 2.5, for example, we would project that the 200 new manufacturing jobs would create 500 other jobs in the nonbasic or non-export sector. These nonbasic jobs might include teachers, health-care workers, car mechanics, bar keepers, and construction workers.

Economic base analysis provides an approximate measure. Different rates of productivity and different levels of per capita income (and thus consumption patterns) in the local area compared with the nation introduce distortion. Richard Klosterman (1990) suggests adjustments to correct for these differences. Productivity differential adjustments, for instance, calculate the ratio of value-added per employee in the sector for the county to value-added per employee for the nation. The most recent economic census reports information on value-added per employee at the county level, though data suppression in small locales means that it may not be provided for the sector of interest, at lower than the state level. Differences in income can be adjusted in a similar way, using SAIPE.

In principle, these adjustments should partly address our questions about how much spending is likely to take place outside, or leak out, of the local economy. A complete input-output model would provide a much better estimate of leakage, because it would incorporate adjustments for local versus state and federal taxes and for underrepresented consumer sectors. For instance, a significant share of car-buying power may leak out of the local economy if most car dealers are located in a nearby metropolitan area. Increasingly, even small-scale goods and services like clothing and haircuts may entail longer shopping trips to regional retail centers.

Several administrative data sources, such as records of sales taxes for retail sectors, are available to help calibrate a more complete model. Lacking such a model in this case, a careful analysis of the geography of current consumption patterns (perhaps using a comparison of sales tax revenues by county) could provide a basis for further refinements to the estimated multiplier.

Identifying noneconomic impacts

Economic development analysts are often under pressure to provide the most favorable picture of local impacts. It is easy to overestimate multipliers, especially in smaller economies with many regional competitors. The pressure to present the rosiest possible picture often results from an expectation that new business investment will provide other unquantified benefits. For instance, local government agencies, school districts, and civic institutions facing declining populations may see their future viability threatened unless population declines can be reversed. Growth at any cost may become the guiding principle for local decisions, and scarce current and future tax revenues may be pledged as incentives for a new investment in the (sometimes misguided) hope that it will bring growth.

A thorough economic analysis should recognize these pressures and address them by providing a separate evaluation of the expected noneconomic benefits of the proposed investment. Is it the community's expectation that the 200 new jobs will bring in 200 new families, with an average of 1.5 children each, providing a massive stimulus to a declining school district? Often, such an expectation is combined with claims that the new jobs will improve earnings and job prospects for under-employed current county residents. Incorporating an analysis of the regional competitiveness of the housing market and likely demographic trends may help clarify whether expectations about noneconomic benefits are justified. The timeliness of the ACS data and its broad scope offer an ideal basis for such analyses.

Comparing estimated benefits to projected costs of subsidies

To the extent that this study provides a sound estimate of different categories of likely benefits, it should help decision makers agree on an appropriate level of incentives. Few of the benefits identified in the preceding steps can be expressed in precise dollar terms, so a traditional cost-benefit analysis is inappropriate. However, quantifying likely benefits (in terms of jobs created, families attracted to the area, and so on) is a useful step because discussion can then focus on how badly the community wants those benefits. When benefits are unclear, it is easy for proponents to claim the investment will single-handedly save the community and for opponents to argue that it will add nothing. Economic impact analysis can offer an alternative to the highly politicized debates that usually result.

These techniques offer rough forecasts rather than firm commitments. The models are approximate, the data is partial at best, and future economic conditions are unknown. Nevertheless, the estimates they offer are better than none. They may also play a useful role in identifying the best timing or format for incentives. If benefits will materialize gradually, providing a large incentive up front in the form of a capital subsidy will place pressure on the county's budget and run the risk that the firm will have too little at stake if times are hard initially. If benefits would be greatly increased if the firm adhered to a policy of local hiring, that could be a requirement of any incentive. Carefully examining likely benefits offers new ways to think about designing incentives to maximize the county's (rather than the firm's) benefit. The wealth of available local economic data is a valuable resource for decision makers at all levels.

Case 4. Transportation policy: Evaluating travel demand management programs in a metropolitan area

Transportation planning is driven in part by federal Clean Air Act goals; in so-called nonattainment areas, transportation planners must find ways to reduce car travel to attain emissions targets (Meyer 1999; Garrett and Wachs 1998). Encouraging drivers to switch to public transit, biking, or walking is an effective way to reduce the carbon footprint of our current commuting patterns. But low-density residential suburbs and scattered office parks make this impossible for many. Land-use patterns lock us into particular travel patterns. However, it may be possible to reduce car travel other ways: for example, encouraging carpooling and increasing the number of people who work at home a few days a week. Carpooling and telecommuting are feasible in lower-density communities with complex, fragmented home and work locations.

In this scenario, a metropolitan planning organization in a rapidly growing Sunbelt location faced a worsening emissions problem in the late 1990s and early 2000s; the number of nonattainment days (when air pollution exceeds Clean Air Act standards) increased each year during that period, endangering federal funding under several programs. In an attempt to reverse this trend, the MPO adopted two initiatives aimed at reducing car travel. First was a carpooling program that consisted of a ride-matching service, a carpool-only lane, and employer education about the benefits of providing carpooling incentives. Second was a telecommute program, aimed at educating employers about the benefits of giving employees the option to work at home several days a week.

Both programs have been in place for five years. During this initial phase, efforts were concentrated on employers in selected suburban employment concentrations and the central business districts of the three largest cities in the metro area. Some industrial sectors were inevitably underrepresented in the program. The original grant that funded the staff position of the program organizer ended. The MPO would like to create a permanent position for the program organizer but to do so must show the programs are effective. This study is intended to evaluate changes in commuting patterns and assess whether there is a causal link with the programs.

Study questions

The questions are relatively straightforward, but answering them will pose several challenges:

- Is there evidence that carpooling rates have increased? Have increases (or declines) been uniform across industries and all parts of the region, or have they been concentrated in just some? Who is most likely to carpool (or, what are the demographic, social, and economic characteristics of people who carpool compared to those who drive alone to work)?

- Has the number of people working at home increased? In what industries and occupations are home-based workers concentrated, and how has this profile changed during the study period? Have those industries grown or shrunk in the recent past? Do some parts of the metropolitan area have a disproportionate share of home-based workers? Who is most likely to work at home?

- Is there evidence that the agency's efforts have contributed to these changes, given the broader changes in the region's employment structure and work-trip patterns? Have the industries and locations that the program targeted demonstrated greater levels of change than those not targeted? Did these changes result from program or other factors?

- Where could further efforts be targeted? Is there any potential to increase carpooling or telecommuting in some industries, some parts of the metro area, or among some demographic groups?

Study design

In this section, we discuss the availability and limitations of data that could help answer the travel demand management questions just posed. We then outline the sorts of analytic approaches that might be appropriate and discuss their limitations.

Determining changes in carpooling rates

Census and ACS data on mode used for travel to work is the obvious source for this data. Employed respondents are asked whether they drove to work alone or with others, and if with others, then how many shared the ride. This gives us the basis to calculate car occupancy rates. However, we may encounter some difficulty using recent ACS data for analyses focused at the traffic analysis zone level (the level of spatial detail that would be needed to assess whether the program had resulted in higher carpooling rates in the targeted employment centers). At best, five-year average data would be available at this scale; to get the before-and-after picture we're seeking, we would have to wait until more than five years had elapsed from program start-up. We could get more recent one-year average data for counties and larger cities in the metro area but not for specific employment concentrations.

The ACS does provide quite detailed cross-tabulations of mode of travel by industry and occupation, by place of residence and place of work. Using industry-specific breakdowns (for the types of industries that predominate in the targeted business districts) may provide a substitute for spatial detail, but the sectoral breakdowns are broad brush (for instance, we would not be able to distinguish the insurance industry from the broader finance, insurance, and real estate sector). We would be able to answer questions about how mode of travel varied by broad demographic and socioeconomic attributes. Similar cross-tabulations would be available only in the 2000 CTPP, not the 2000 census tables.

It would probably be necessary to supplement analyses based on census and ACS trends with data gathered directly from program participants. If employers have incentive programs for employees who carpool, they should have an administrative record that could be used to assess firm-level trends in carpooling rates.

Our best strategy then might be to assess carpooling rates before and after program implementation for broader geographic regions as a baseline analysis and use administrative data from program participants to assess changes attributable to the TDM program.

Determining changes in home-based work

Similar constraints affect our answers to this question. Although recent ACS data on transportation mode is available, it is not at a suitable spatial scale to answer the question as we have phrased it. There is another issue: respondents are asked to report their usual place of work, the location where they work most often. It is fairly clear that people who work at home three or more days a week are home-based workers; but what of the person who works at home only one or two days a week and drives alone to work on the others? They would report their place of work as the firm's location, and drive alone as their usual mode. Most telecommuting occurs only a few days a week, but even avoiding travel one or two days a week can substantially reduce car use if it is widespread.

In this case, program participants would need to provide data to estimate trends in telecommuting. However, employers may not have administrative records of telecommuters: because no actual incentives are used, records may not be kept. Supervisors may need to be surveyed to gather the information on where employees work. Again, the census and ACS data would be useful to chart broader-scale trends in home-based work but would not be sufficient alone to answer the question.

Assessing the effectiveness of the TDM program

Determining trends during the program period is not the same as identifying causal links. We would expect peoples' travel choices to change over time even without any intervention. It is possible carpooling (or telecommuting) has become more (or less) attractive for several reasons unrelated to the TDM program. In both cases, we would need to separate ambient levels of change from the change attributable to the program. (In an ideal world we would have designed a controlled experiment to do this, but few program directors have this luxury). To some extent, the strategies proposed above try to do this. They assess trends in carpooling and home-based work at the county and city level (where current ACS data is available for comparison). More specific information from participating employers could then be compared against these ambient levels of carpooling and home-based work to identify how travel patterns changed for program partners in contrast to the entire community.

However, if the program targeted substantial employment concentrations, its effects may indeed be evident in countywide or citywide trends. If the program targeted specific industries, and carpooling or home-based work potential was different in nontargeted industries, it may be difficult to attribute the difference to the TDM program. Different carpooling or telecommuting rates may reflect fundamental differences among industries. Manufacturing and construction workers obviously have far less potential to work from home than workers in the finance, insurance and real estate, and professional services industries.

It may be necessary to supplement the analysis with survey data, gathering qualitative data from targeted employers and a random stratified sample of employees in targeted firms about why they make the travel or work choices they do.

Identifying areas for expansion

A survey also opens up the possibility for addressing this question more thoroughly. Workers who neither carpool nor telecommute may be the most important people to survey, to determine why. Is it that they are concerned about getting home in an emergency? Do they trip-chain (combine the work trip with several other errands), or drive to complete errands over lunch? Do their employers allow or encourage them to work from home or require them to work on site? TDM programs can be refined based on this feedback to minimize the barriers (for instance, through the program that some employers offer to guarantee their workers rides home). For some employees, there may not be feasible alternatives to driving alone.

Census and ACS tables are too rigid to provide substantial insight into the question of who does not carpool. PUMS data would be a better basis for understanding the characteristics of people who drive alone rather than carpool. Are they more likely to have high incomes and professional or managerial occupations? Is carpooling more likely in one-car households? Do choices differ by age cohort, holding other characteristics equal? How likely is it that parents with children at home will carpool compared with parents with no children at home? Does the propensity for carpooling increase for parents with school-aged versus pre-school-aged children? What impacts do income, occupation, and industry have on the likelihood someone will work at home? The more detailed and flexible analysis that PUMS enables would be an excellent basis for investigating these questions. More carefully targeted campaigns, and a clearer sense of the precise barriers to expanding carpooling and telecommuting could be based on this sort of analysis. Additional questions remain about employers' attitudes to telecommuting and the relationship between telecommuting and productivity; these would require more narrowly targeted surveys or access to administrative data. Unfortunately, the standard employment related datasets discussed in chapter 6 do not gather information on telecommuting practices.

Incorporating administrative data

Most of the cases discussed so far have included administrative data along with census and ACS data. Administrative data provides much more specific information than the census can on topics essential for program design and evaluation. Information about crime rates, participation in free and reduced price lunch programs, and health status is not gathered in the ACS, for instance. Concerns with government intrusiveness and difficult conceptual issues about how to frame questions about experiences of crime or ill-health make it unlikely they would be added to the survey. However, administrative data sources provide these and other important quality of life measures. Table 8.1 summarizes the variety of administrative data included in databases maintained by the National Neighborhood Indicator Partners (NNIP), an initiative of the Urban Institute.

Several arguments support expanding the role of administrative data. Sharing information can improve decision making for the agencies that gather it. Typically, agencies do not have the resources to analyze trends in service demand or delivery in the context of related information generated by other agencies. Investigating the relationship between vacant boarded-up properties and some types of crime, for instance, may suggest

how housing code enforcement and crime prevention agencies could work together more effectively.

Because administrative data is entered in real time, it is usually more current than census and ACS data. It is also usually tied to a specific individual, household, or address, providing far greater potential for spatial specificity. Of course, this also raises important questions about protecting confidentiality. Political concern about confidentiality has been growing, and the tremendous potential administrative data offers may be foreclosed if legitimate concerns about privacy are ignored. For instance, although the precise location of some criminal incidents (such as mugging) is valuable information because it allows people to protect themselves, address-level data about domestic violence would violate privacy. Most address-level personal information should never be publicly accessible. Confidentiality agreements should bind entities that aggregate geocoded data, specifying the appropriate spatial scales at which it may be released. When events or characteristics tracked are infrequent or rare (such as some causes of death, employment in specialized industries, or some sorts of families), the appropriate geographic scale for reporting annual data might be substantially larger than a census tract, if confidentiality is to be preserved. Careful review is needed by the administrative agencies responsible for releasing the data (Coulton 2008).

Another challenge is the inconsistency of administrative databases across places. Data related to federal programs is usually fairly consistent, but local programs and agencies have different structures and technical capacities that result in different qualities and formats of data across states and even sometimes cities. Claudia Coulton (2008) discusses the reasons for the unevenness of quality control across agencies. Although substantial

Table 8.1   Spatial aggregation of administrative data used by NNIP partners

	Partners Using Item	Address or Parcel	School	Block Group	Census Tract	ZIP Code	Other Small Area	City County
Births and deaths								
Births	25	12	0	0	3	4	4	2
Births by prenatal care level	21	10	0	0	3	3	3	2
Births by birth weight	24	11	0	0	3	4	4	2
Deaths by cause	17	7	0	0	1	3	1	5
Education								
Student enrollment	26	7	15	0	1	0	2	1
Student proficiency	26	7	15	0	2	0	2	0
Student absences	21	7	11	0	2	0	1	0
Free/reduced price lunch	24	7	13	0	2	0	1	1
Special education	20	7	9	0	2	0	2	0
Kindergarten readiness assessment	8	3	4	0	1	0	0	0
Head Start enrollment	9	2	3	0	1	0	1	2
Other pre-school enrollment	8	3	2	0	0	1	1	1
Health								
Communicable diseases	7	0	0	0	0	2	1	4
Asthma hospitalizations	10	2	0	0	1	4	1	2
Child blood-lead level	10	3	0	0	1	2	2	2
Sexually transmitted diseases	13	1	0	0	0	2	3	7
Hospital admissions by cause	11	2	0	0	0	4	0	5
Immunizations	13	1	1	0	0	2	0	8
Public assistance								
TANF	15	3	0	0	4	3	2	2
Food stamps	16	3	0	0	3	4	1	4
Medicaid	11	2	0	0	1	4	1	2
S-Chip	8	1	0	0	0	2	0	4
WIC	8	3	0	0	0	2	0	2
Foster care	7	1	0	0	0	4	0	2
Subsidized child care	5	2	0	0	0	1	0	2
Housing assistance								
Public housing units	16	8	0	0	2	0	1	5
Housing choice vouchers	11	7	0	0	0	0	1	3
Other subsidized housing	11	5	0	0	1	0	2	3

	Partners Using Item	Address or Parcel	School	Block Group	Census Tract	ZIP Code	Other Small Area	City County
Crime								
Reported crime (Part I)	22	13	0	1	1	1	4	2
Reported crime (Part II)	18	9	0	1	1	1	3	3
Child abuse/neglect	17	5	0	0	2	3	1	6
Arrests	15	8	0	0	1	1	1	3
Arrests (juvenile)	12	6	0	0	1	1	1	2
Emergency (911) calls	6	5	0	0	0	0	0	1
Prisoner reentry								
Ex-offenders returning from prison	12	9	0	0	1	1	0	0
Ex-offenders returning from jail	8	5	0	0	1	1	0	0
Persons on probation/parole	12	8	0	0	1	0	0	2
Business/economy								
ES-202 Employment/ establishments	13	2	0	1	1	3	0	5
Business inventory (other)	12	6	0	0	1	3	1	0
Business licenses	5	5	0	0	0	0	0	0
Liquor licenses/stores	12	12	0	0	0	0	0	0
Property transactions/characteristics								
Building permits	20	14	0	0	0	0	2	4
Housing code violations	12	11	0	0	0	0	1	0
Demolitions	15	12	0	0	1	0	1	1
Lead paint abatements	3	2	0	0	1	0	0	0
Property sales (volumes, prices)	23	18	0	0	2	1	1	1
Property characteristics	19	16	1	0	1	0	0	0
Vacant parcels	17	14	0	1	0	0	1	0
Property tax assessments	20	19	0	0	0	0	0	0
Tax delinquencies	11	9	0	0	0	0	1	0
Foreclosures	20	12	0	1	2	0	2	2
Water shut-offs	2	2	0	0	0	0	0	0
Electric shut-offs	1	1	0	0	0	0	0	0
Water usage	4	2	0	0	0	0	0	1
Voting								
Voting records	18	7	0	0	0	0	10	1

Source: Guernsey and Pettit 2007, table A2

effort may be devoted to ensuring the accuracy of the data items the agency cares about (for instance, a public housing agency may have accurate records related to a household's eligibility for rental assistance), the agency may not have as strong an incentive to ensure the accuracy of peripheral data (such as education levels).

Administrative data is driven by several imperatives that may bias what is measured (Coulton 2008). The most notorious examples are often drawn from crime statistics; a mayor's announcement of a blitz on graffiti, for instance, may inflate arrests for the offense, producing a temporary spike in trend data. Epidemiological data may be reported inconsistently over time: at what point, for example, does flu get redefined as swine flu? In many communities, households are given priority on housing assistance waiting lists if their current place of residence is a homeless shelter. Can we assume that those housing agency reports of homelessness are equivalent to those in communities where this is not the case?

Although much administrative data is spatially precise, this precision may be misleading. Lower-income households are more likely to move often, and agencies are typically concerned with keeping addresses up to date. Health and other personal history records may not accurately reflect where someone was living when an event occurred. This might be a particular problem in tracking the spatial concentration of people with environmental health problems, such as asthma or cancer clusters, or where links are being investigated between the environment and behavior (for instance, whether access to public transit reduces the incidence of obesity). These challenges do not undermine the potential of combining administrative data with census and ACS, but they do highlight the need for careful critical scrutiny, both by the agencies releasing the administrative data and by data users.

Conclusions

The U.S. Census is a work in progress. Each decade its rationale, scope, and form are renegotiated: How much continuity will there be with previous censuses? Which new concepts will we measure? How much accuracy are we willing to pay for? How much government intrusion into individual privacy is justified? On one side of the negotiation are the advocates of change: special interest groups and researchers concerned with topics such as Asian American rights, same-sex partner rights, and veterans' rights. On the other side are the forces of inertia: bureaucracies, politicians, and others concerned with preserving continuity and limiting pressures to expand topics. Outside this debate are those concerned with limiting government intrusion into individual privacy, who argue for rolling back rather than expanding data gathering. Debates are structured around the themes of continuity versus change, cost versus accuracy, and privacy versus spatial detail. These battles are fought in the public policy arena, and are solved slightly differently each decade.

Replacing the census long form with the ACS is a dramatic restructuring. Advocates of the ACS aimed to find a new way to meet demands for timely comprehensive information and simultaneously manage both costs and intrusion. The move to continuous measurement was not inevitable; it was a reasonable solution to multiple constraints. Trading off spatial precision for timeliness was a practical way to solve these constraints, but it poses several challenges for spatial analysts. In many cases, the legislation that justifies specific census questions assumes more spatial precision than the ACS can provide, given a sample size of 3 million addresses. The improved timeliness the ACS offers over the decennial census is not a substitute for spatial detail. Policy is still made and evaluated in and for particular places. Thus the first challenge is how analysts can use less precise spatial data to provide spatially detailed assessments of need, trends, and impact to inform policymakers.

Creative solutions are emerging, and spatial analysis will be central to making these solutions work. Instead of relying heavily on statistical projection and forecasting methods to update aged decennial census data, attention has shifted to developing spatial disaggregation methods to refine data reported for larger areas. Paying attention to confidence intervals around small-area estimates, using time series to construct comparable midpoint estimates for communities of different sizes, and developing proportional breakdowns offer different approaches to spatial disaggregation.

Data-focused strategies have demonstrated the potential to supplement ACS estimates with local administrative data sources. A much wider range of information is gathered and held electronically compared to the 1990 or even 2000 census cycles, and much of it is address-based. Although confidentiality concerns do (and should) limit free access to some address-based data (people are concerned about identity theft, intrusive neighbors, and intrusive government agencies), we could answer many questions about estimating need, assessing outcomes, and modeling change if we were to integrate local administrative data with annual ACS releases. Data quality is less even across jurisdictions and across variables than census sources are, but again nothing about

this is inevitable: it reflects public priorities and resource distribution. Local policymakers could improve the quality of local administrative data sources if they were convinced of its value.

Synthesizing local information based on a combination of surveys, administrative data, and statistical techniques, offers another promising path. We are still in the early stages of assessing the value of synthetic data for policymaking, but projects such as Local Employment Dynamics (discussed in chapter 6) and the Longitudinal Employer-Household Dynamics program (discussed in chapter 7) demonstrate the potential. Synthetic data undermines the traditional view of the census as an activity of measuring and counting, but it may offer a more defensible approach to small-area estimation than simplistic disaggregation methods. It also resolves concerns about confidentiality quite effectively by providing spatially detailed statistical constructs rather than real information about real people. If we think carefully about the construction of traditional census data and its inevitable limitations, synthetic data may not be as bad or as different an alternative. More explicit debate about estimation methods, spatial aggregation, and temporal smoothing may be preferable to clumsy attempts to make a round ACS fit into square reporting holes. GIS technology will play a central role in constructing these new estimates from disparate data sources.

In this book, we have tried to clarify the connections among several interrelated issues and discuss how these do (and should) affect spatial analysis. Census data has a special status as the official source of information about communities and people. This claim to legitimacy, combined with its continuity, spatial comparability, and easy access, provides the foundation of an information infrastructure that is essential to many public policy debates and decisions. But while ACS data is necessary for most social or economic analyses, it is probably not enough on its own. Other more detailed official surveys, administrative records, and special-purpose local surveys were essential complements in the studies we outlined in this chapter. This has made spatial information systems a far more important component of policy analysis; spatial analytic tools provide the methodological bridge to blend census, ACS, and many other data sources in ways that are meaningful for decision makers at all levels. We hope this book provides a guide to meeting the challenges of making spatial analysis accessible, clear, and relevant for as diverse an audience as possible. Information plays a powerful role in framing public questions and shaping policy; better quality spatial analyses can advance democratic debate.

References

Abowd, John M., and Julia Lane. 2004. "New Approaches to Confidentiality Protection: Synthetic Data, Remote Access, and Research Data Centers." In *Privacy in Statistical Databases*, 518. Heidelberg and Berlin: Springer-Verlag.

Alexander, Charles H. 2001. "Still Rolling: Leslie Kish's 'Rolling Samples' and the American Community Survey." *Proceedings of Statistics Canada Symposium 2001, Achieving Data Quality in a Statistical Agency*. Ottawa, ON: Statistics Canada.

Alexander, Charles H. 2002. "A discussion of the quality of the estimates from the American Community Survey for small population groups." Washington, DC: U.S. Census Bureau. http://www.census.gov/acs/www/Downloads/library/2002/THEQUALITYOF.pdf

American Public Transportation Association (APTA). 2005. "The Benefits of Public Transportation: Relieving Traffic Congestion." http://www.publictransportation.org/pdf/reports/congestion.pdf.

Anderson, Margo J. 1988. *The American Census: A Social History* New Haven, CT: Yale University Press.

Anderson, Margo J., and Stephen E. Feinberg. 1999. *Who Counts? The Politics of Census-Taking in Contemporary America*. New York: Russell Sage Foundation.

Andersson, Frederik, Harry Holzer, and Julia Lane. 2002. "The Interactions of Workers and Firms in the Low-Wage Labor Market." Washington, DC: The Urban Institute. http://www.urban.org/publications/410608.html.

Batten, David F., and David E. Boyce. 1987. "Spatial Interaction, Transportation, and Interregional Commodity Flow Models." In *Handbook of Regional and Urban Economics*, edited by Peter Nijkamp, 357–406. New York: Elsevier Science.

Bennett, Claudette E., and Deborah H. Griffin. 2002. "Race and Hispanic Origin Data: A Comparison of Results from the Census 2000 Supplementary Survey and Census 2000." In *2002 Proceedings of the American Statistical Association*. Alexandria, VA: American Statistical Association.

Blake, Kevin S., Rebecca L. Kellerson, and Aleksandra Simic. 2007. *Measuring Overcrowding in Housing*. Washington, DC: U.S. Department of Housing and Urban Development.

Boarnet, Marlon, and Randall Crane. 2001. "The Influence of Land Use on Travel Behaviour: Specification and Estimation Strategies." *Transportation Research Part A: Policy and Practice* 35, no. 9: 823–45.

Bonnette, Robert. 2003. "Housing Costs of Homeowners: 2000." C2KBR–27. Census 2000 Brief. Washington, DC: U.S. Department of Commerce. http://www.census.gov/prod/2003pubs/c2kbr-27.pdf.

Brewer, Cynthia A. 2005. *Designing Better Maps: A Guide for GIS Users.* Redlands, CA: Esri Press.

Brown, Michael, and Larry Knopp 2006. "Places or Polygons? Governmentality, Scale, and the Census." *The Gay and Lesbian Atlas: Population, Space and Place* 12: 223–42.

Cambridge Systematics, NuStats, Nancy McGuckin, and Earl Ruiter. 2007. *A Guidebook for Using American Community Survey Data for Transportation Planning.* NCHRP Report 588. Washington, DC: Transportation Research Board.

Cambridge Systematics, Stephen E. Fienberg, and Tanzy M. T. P. Love. 2009. *Disclosure Avoidance Techniques to Improve ACS Data Availability for Transportation Planners.* Prepared for American Association of State and Highway Transportation Officials, Standing Committee on Planning (May). http://onlinepubs.trb.org/onlinepubs/archive/NotesDocs/NCHRP08-36(71)_FR.pdf.

Cantwell, Patrick J., Howard Hogan, and Kathleen M. Styles. 2003. *The Use of Statistical Methods in the U.S. Census: Utah vs. Evans.* Research Report Series #2003-05. Washington, DC: U.S. Census Bureau, Statistical Research Division.

Card, David, and Alan B. Krueger. 2000. "Minimum Wages and Employment: A Case Study of the Fast Food Industry in New Jersey and Pennsylvania." *The American Economic Review* 90, no. 5: 1397–420.

Cauthen, Nancy K., and Sarah Fass. 2007. "Measuring Income and Poverty in the United States." Fact Sheet. New York: National Center for Children in Poverty. http://www.nccp.org/publications/pdf/text_707.pdf.

Concas, Sisinno, and Philip L. Winters. 2007. "Impact of Carpooling on Trip-Chaining Behaviour and Emission Reductions." *Transportation Research Record* 2010: 83–91.

Coulton, Claudia J. 2007. "Catalog of Administrative Data Sources for Neighborhood Indicators." Washington, DC: The Urban Institute.

Congressional Budget Office. 2009. "An Analysis of Health Insurance Premiums under the Patient Protection and Affordable Care Act" (November 30). http://www.cbo.gov/ftpdocs/107xx/doc10781/11-30-Premiums.pdf.

Crane, Randall. 2007. "Is There a Quiet Revolution in Women's Travel? Revisiting the Gender Gap in Commuting." *Journal of the American Planning Association* 73, no. 3: 298–316.

de la Puenta, Manuel. 1995. "Using Ethnography to Explain Why People Are Missed or Erroneously Included by the Census: Evidence from Small Area Ethnographic Studies." *Proceedings of the Section on Survey Research Methods.* Alexandria, VA: American Statistical Association. http://www.census.gov/srd/papers/pdf/mdp9501.pdf.

Diffendahl, Gregg, Rita Petroni, and Andre L. Williams. 2004. "Comparison of the American Community Survey's Three-Year Averages and the Census Sample for a Sample of Counties and Tracts." Washington, DC: U.S. Census Bureau.

Downs, Anthony. 2004. *Still Stuck in Traffic: Coping with Peak-Hour Traffic Congestion.* Washington, DC: Brookings Institute Press.

Engel, Mary. 2010. "The Real Unemployment Rate? 16.6%." MSN Money, June 4, 2010. http://articles.moneycentral.msn.com/learn-how-to-invest/The-real-unemployment-rate.aspx.

Federal Financial Institutions Examination Council. 2010a. Home Mortgage Disclosure Act. http://www.ffiec.gov/hmda/.

Federal Housing Finance Agency. 2010b. "Public Use Database for Fannie Mae and Freddie Mac." http://www.fhfa.gov/Default.aspx?Page=137.

Fisher, Gordon M. 1997. "The Development of the Orshansky Poverty Thresholds and Their Subsequent History as the Official U.S. Poverty Measure." Poverty Measurement Working Paper. Washington, DC: U.S. Census Bureau. http://www.census.gov/hhes/www/povmeas/papers/orshansky.html.

Florida, Richard. 2002. *The Rise of the Creative Class: And How It's Transforming Work, Leisure, Community and Everyday Life.* New York: Basic Books.

Gage, Linda. 2004. "Comparison of Census 2000 and American Community Survey 1999–2001 Estimates: San Francisco and Tulare Counties, California." Sacramento: California Department of Finance.

Gaines, Leonard M.. 2009. *A Compass for Understanding and Using American Community Survey Data: What PUMS Data Users Need to Know.* Washington, DC: U.S. Census Bureau.

Garrett, Mark, and Martin Wachs. 1998. *Transportation Planning on Trial: The Clean Air Act and Traffic Forecasting.* Thousand Oaks, CA: Sage Publications.

Genz, Richard. 2001. "Why Advocates Need to Rethink Manufactured Housing." *Housing Policy Debate* 12, no. 2: 393–414.

Giuliano, Genevieve, and Dhiraj Narayan. 2003. "Another Look at Travel Patterns and Urban Form: The US and Great Britain." *Urban Studies* 40, no. 11: 2295–312.

Guernsey, Elizabeth H., and Kathryn L. S. Pettit. 2007. *NNIP Data Inventory 2007: A Picture of Local Data Collection across the Country.* Washington, DC: The Urban Institute.

Hewings, Geoffrey J., Yasuhide Okuyama, and Michael Sonis. 2001. "Economic Interdependence within the Chicago Metropolitan Area: A Miyazawa Analysis." *Journal of Regional Science* 41, no. 2: 195–217.

Hough, George C., and David A. Swanson. 2004. "The 1999–2001 American Community Survey and the 2000 Census Data Quality and Data Comparisons: Multnomah County, Oregon." Portland, Oregon: Population Research Center, Portland State University.

Ihlanfeldt, Keith R., and David L. Sjoquist. 1998. "The Spatial Mismatch Hypothesis: A Review of Recent Studies and Their Implications for Welfare Reform." *Housing Policy Debate* 9, no. 4: 849–92.

Immergluck, Dan. 2009. "Intrametropolitan Patterns of Foreclosed Homes: ZIP-Code Level Distributions of Real-Estate-Owned (REO) Properties during the U.S. Mortgage Crisis." *Community Affairs* Discussion Paper No. 01-09. Atlanta: Federal Reserve Bank of Atlanta. http://www.frbatlanta.org/filelegacydocs/dp _ 0109.pdf.

Innes, Judith E. 1990. *Knowledge and Public Policy: The Search for Meaningful Indicators.* New Brunswick, NJ: Transaction Publishers.

Isserman, Andrew M. 1993. "The Right People, The Right Rates." *Journal of the American Planning Association* 59, no. 1: 45–64.

Jacobs, David E., Robert P. Clickner, Joey Y. Zhou, Susan M. Viet, David A. Marker, John W. Rogers, Darryl C. Zeldin, Pamela Broene, and Warren Friedman. 2002. "The Prevalence of Lead-Based Paint Hazards in U.S. Homes." *Environmental Health Perspectives* 110, no. 10: 599–606.

Kaiser Family Foundation. 2010. "Side-by-Side Comparison of Major Health Care Reform Proposals." http://www.kff.org/healthreform/sidebyside.cfm?utm _ source= kffweekly&utm _ medium=email&utm _ campaign=nl101609

Kane, Thomas. 2004. "National Household Travel Survey Add-On Use in the Des Moines, Iowa, Metropolitan Area." Presentation to Transportation Research Board's National Household Travel Survey Conference. http://onlinepubs.trb.org/onlinepubs/archive/conferences/nhts/Kane. pdf.

Kingsley, G. Thomas, and Kathryn L. S. Petit. 2008. *Data and Decisions: Parcel-Level Information Changing the Way Business Gets Done.* Washington, DC: Brookings Institute Press.

Klosterman, Richard E. 1990. *Community Analysis and Planning Techniques.* Laurel, MD: Rowman & Littlefield.

Kwan, Mei-Po. 1999. "Gender, the Home-Work Link, and Space-Time Patterns of Nonemployment Activities." *Economic Geography* 75, no. 4: 370–94.

Lavin, Michael R. 1996. *Understanding the Census: A Guide for Marketers, Planners, Grant Writers and Other Users.* Kenmore, NY: Epoch Books.

Lee, Barrett A., R. S. Orepesa, and James W. Kanan. 1994. "Neighborhood Context and Residential Mobility." *Demography* 31, no. 2: 249–70.

Li, Wei, and Keith S. Ernst. 2006. *The Best Value in the Subprime Market: State Predatory Lending Reforms.* Washington, DC: Center for Responsible Lending.

Lipton, Eric. 2004. "Panel Says Census Move on Arab-Americans Recalls World War II Internments." *New York Times,* November 10, 2004, A19.

Lugaila, Terry, and Julia Overturf 2004. *Children and the Households They Live In: 2000.* CENSR-14. Washington, DC: U.S. Census Bureau.

MacDonald, Heather. 2006. "The American Community Survey: Warmer (More Current), but Fuzzier (Less Precise) than the Decennial Census" *Journal of the American Planning Association* 72, no. 4: 491–503.

———. 2008. "City Planning and the U.S. Census, 1910 to 1960." *Journal of Planning History* 7, no. 4: 263–94.

McDonald, Noreen C. 2008. "Critical Factors for Active Transportation to School among Low-Income and Minority Students." *American Journal of Preventive Medicine* 34, no. 4: 341–44.

McElroy, Tucker. 2007. "Coherent Trends, Turning Points, and Forecasts for ACS Data." Paper presented at the Federal Committee on Statistical Methodology Research Conference, Washington, DC (November 5, 2007). http://www.fcsm.gov/07papers/McElroy.II-B.pdf.

Megbolugbe, Isaac F., and Peter D. Linneman. 1993. "Home Ownership." *Urban Studies* 30, no. 4/5: 659–82.

Meyer, Michael D. 1999. "Demand Management as an Element of Transportation Policy: Using Carrots and Sticks to Influence Travel Behaviour." *Transportation Research Record Part A: Policy and Practice* 33, no. 7–8: 575–99.

Monmonier, Mark. 1996. *How to Lie with Maps*, 2nd ed. Chicago: University of Chicago Press.

Murakama, Elaine. 2007. "Longitudinal Employer-Household Dynamics." Washington, DC: U.S. Department of Transportation, Federal Highway Administration. http://www.fhwa.dot.gov/planning/census/lehd07april.htm.

Murazaki, Kazuyo, and Peter G. M. Hess. 2006. "How Does Climate Change Contribute to Surface Ozone Change over the United States?" *Journal of Geophysical Research* 111: DO5301. doi:10.1029/2005JD005873.

Nagel, Joanne. 1994. "Constructing Ethnicity: Creating and Recreating Ethnic Identity and Culture." *Social Problems* 41, no. 1: 152–76.

Nathan, Richard P. 1987. "The Politics of Printouts: The Use of Official Numbers to Allocate Federal Grants-in-Aid." In *The Politics of Numbers*, edited by William Alonso and Paul Starr, 331–42. New York: Russell Sage Foundation.

de Nazelle, Audrey, and Daniel A. Rodriguez. 2009. "Tradeoffs in Incremental Changes towards Pedestrian-Friendly Environments: Physical Activity and Pollution Exposure." *Transportation Research Part D: Transport and Environment* 14, no. 4: 255–63. doi:10.1016/j.trd.2009.02.002.

Neufeld, Maurice F. 1938. "Shall Mr. Crockett Enter Planning?" *The Planners' Journal* 4, no. 5 (September-October): 125–28.

Newman, Mark. 2008. "Maps of the 2008 U.S. Presidential Election Race." http://www-personal.umich.edu/~mejn/election/2008.

Northwest Research Group. 2005. *Idaho Transportation Department Traveler Opinion and Perception (TOP) Survey*. Boise, ID: Northwest Research Group. http://www.compassidaho.org/documents/planning/studies/TOPreport.pdf.

Office for National Statistics. 2006. "The One Number Census—An Estimate of the Whole Population." http://www.statistics.gov.uk/census2001/onc.asp.

ORC Macro. 2002. *The American Community Survey: Challenges and Opportunities for HUD*. Washington, DC: U.S. Department of Housing and Urban Development.

Orwell, George. 1946. "Politics and the English Language." *Horizon* 13, no. 76 (April): 252–65.

Pacific Institute. 2009. "Liquor Stores and Community Health." Oakland, CA: Pacific Institute. http://www.pacinst.org/reports/measuring_what_matters/issues/liquor_store.pdf.

Parkany, Emily. 2004. "Seasonality of Transportation Data." Washington, DC: U.S. Department of Transportation, Federal Highway Administration. http://www.fhwa.dot.gov/planning/census/seatrand.htm.

Petersen, William. 1987. "Politics and the Measurement of Ethnicity." In *The Politics of Numbers*, edited by William Alonso and Paul Starr, 187–234. New York: Russell Sage Foundation.

Prewitt, Kenneth. 2003. *Politics and Science in Census Taking.* New York: Russell Sage Foundation.

———. 2004. "What If We Give a Census and No-One Comes?" *Science* 304, no. 4 (June): 1452–453.

Proscio, Tony. 2006. *Food Markets and Healthy Communities.* New York: Local Initiatives Support Corporation. http://www.lisc.org/content/publications/detail/1388

Raphael, Steven, and Lorien Rice. 2002. "Car Ownership, Employment, and Earnings." *Journal of Urban Economics* 52, no. 1: 109–30.

Robinson, J. Gregory. 2001. "ESCAP II: Demographic Analysis Results." Report No. 1. Washington, DC: U.S. Census Bureau.

Robinson, J. Gregory, and Arjun Adlakha. 2002. "Comparison of ACE Revision II Results with Demographic Analysis." DSSD ACE Revision II Estimates Memorandum Series #PP-41. Washington, DC: U.S. Government Printing Office. http://www.census.gov/dmd/www/pdf/pp-41r.pdf.

Rosenbloom, Sandra. 2007. "Transportation Patterns and Problems of People with Disabilities." In *The Future of Disability in America*, edited by Mary Jane Field and Alan M. Jette, 519–60. Washington, DC: National Academies Press.

Salvo, Joseph J., A. Peter Lobo, and Timothy Calabrese. 2004. *Small Area Data Quality: A Comparison of Estimates from the 2000 Census and the 1999-2001 ACS Bronx New York Test Site.* New York: Population Division, New York City Department of City Planning.

Salvo, Joseph J., A. Peter Lobo, Adam L. Willett, and Joel A. Alvarez. 2007. *An Evaluation of the Quality and Utility of ACS Five Year Estimates for Bronx Census Tracts and Neighborhoods.* New York: Population Division, New York City Department of City Planning.

Sanchez, Thomas W. 1999. "The Connection between Public Transit and Employment: The Cases of Portland and Atlanta." *Journal of the American Planning Association* 65, no. 3: 284–96.

Schmitz, Adrienne, and Deborah L. Brett. 2001. *Real Estate Market Analysis: A Case Study Approach.* Washington, DC: Urban Land Institute.

Schnare, Ann B. 2001. "The Impact of Changes in Multifamily Housing Finance in Older Urban Areas." Discussion paper prepared for the Brookings Institute and Harvard Joint Center for Housing Studies. Washington, DC: Brookings Institute. http://www.brookings.edu/es/urban/schnarefinal.pdf.

Schnore, Leo F. 1963. "A Planner's Guide to the 1960 Census of Population." *Journal of the American Institute of Planners* 29, no. 1 (February): 29–39.

Schuetz, Jenny, Vicki Been, and Ingrid G. Ellen. 2008. "Neighborhood Effects of Concentrated Mortgage Foreclosures." *Journal of Housing Economics* 17, no. 4: 306–19.

Schwanen, Timothy, and Martin Dijst. 2002. "Travel-Time Ratios for Visits to the Workplace: The Relationship between Commuting Time and Work Duration." *Transportation Research Part A: Policy and Practice* 36, no. 7: 573–92.

Skerry, Peter. 2000. *Counting on the Census? Race, Group Identity, and the Evasion of the Census.* Washington, DC: Brookings Institute Press.

Slack, Tim. 2010. "Working Poverty across the Metro-Non-Metro Divide: A Quarter Century in Perspective, 1979–2003." *Rural Sociology* 75, no. 3: 363–87.

Small Business Administration. 2004. "Evaluating Veteran Business Owner Data." Advocacy Research Report No. 244. Washington, DC: Office of Advocacy. http://www.sba.gov/advo/research/rs244tot.pdf.

Starr, Paul. 1987. "The Sociology of Official Statistics." In *The Politics of Numbers*, edited by William Alonso and Paul Starr. New York: Russell Sage Foundation.

Stern, Sharon. 2003. "Counting People with Disabilities: A Comparison of Estimates in Census 2000 and the Census 2000 Supplementary Survey." Washington, DC: U.S. Census Bureau.

Transportation for America. 2010. "Smart Mobility for a 21st Century America." Washington, DC: Intelligent Transportation Society of America. http://www.itsa.org/itsa/files/pdf/ITS-White-Paper-100710-FINAL.pdf.

Transportation Capacity-Building Peer Exchange Program (TCBPEP). 2007. *Using ACS Data in Transportation Planning Applications.* Washington, DC: U.S. Department of Transportation, Federal Highway Administration, Federal Transit Administration. http://planning.dot.gov/Peer/Daytona/daytona _ 2007.pdf.

Turner, Eugene. 1977. "Life in Los Angeles." http://www.csun.edu/~hfgeg005/eturner/gallery/lifeinla.GIF.

Turner, Tracey, and Debbie Niemeier. 1997. "Travel to Work and Household Responsibility: New Evidence." *Transportation* 24, no. 4: 397–419.

U.S. Census Bureau. 1990. "Building Permits." http://censtats.census.gov/bldg/bldgprmt.shtml.

———. 2000. "United States Census 2000." Washington, DC: U.S. Government Printing Office. http://www.census.gov/dmd/www/pdf/d02p.pdf.

———. 2007b. "2007 Economic Census." Washington, DC: U.S. Government Printing Office. http://www.census.gov/econ/census07.

———. 2002a. "2002 Economic Census." Washington, DC: U.S. Government Printing Office. http://www.census.gov/econ.

———. 2002b. *Meeting 21st Century Data Needs—Implementing the American Community Survey. Report 2: Demonstrating Survey Quality.* Washington, DC: U.S. Government Printing Office.

———. 2003a. *Census of Population and Housing, Public Use Microdata Sample: Technical Documentation.* Washington, DC: U.S. Government Printing Office.

———. 2003b. *Technical Assessment of ACE Revision II.* Washington, DC: U.S. Government Printing Office. http://www.census.gov/dmd/www/pdf/ACETechAssess.pdf.

———. 2003c. "Using Census Data to Help Local Communities: Census Information Centers at Work." CLO/03-CIC. Washington, DC: U.S. Government Printing Office.

———. 2003d. Census 2000 Public Use Microdata Area (PUMA) Maps. Washington, DC: U.S. Government Printing Office. http://www.census.gov/geo/www/maps/puma5pct.htm

———. 2004. *Meeting 21st Century Data Needs—Implementing the American Community Survey. Report 7: Comparing Quality Measures: Comparing the American Community Survey's Three-Year Averages and Census 2000's Long Form Sample Estimates.* Washington, DC: U.S. Government Printing Office.

———. 2006. *American Community Survey: Design and Methodology.* Technical Paper 67. Washington, DC: U.S. Government Printing Office.

———. 2007a. *Summary File 3, 2000 Census of Population and Housing: Technical Documentation.* Washington, DC: U.S. Government Printing Office.

———. 2008. "Questions Planned for the 2010 Census and American Community Survey." http://www.census.gov/acs/www/Downloads/operations_admin/Questions_Planned_for_the_2010_Census_and_American_Community_Survey.pdf.

———. 2009a. "American Community Survey and Puerto Rico Community Survey 2009 Subject Definitions." http://www.census.gov/acs/www/Downloads/data_documentation/SubjectDefinitions/2009_ACSSubjectDefinitions.pdf.

———. 2009b. "Public Use Microdata Samples (PUMS) files: Subjects in the PUMS." http://www.census.gov/acs/www/Products/PUMS/PUMS3.htm.

———. 2009c. "NAICS Concordances." http://www.census.gov/eos/www/naics/concordances/concordances.html.

———. 2010a. "Census Bureau Reports Nearly 6 in 10 Advanced Degree Holders Age 25–29 Are Women." CB 10-55. http://www.census.gov/newsroom/releases/archives/education/cb10-55.html.

———. 2010b. "2008 ACS Accuracy of the Data (US)." http://www.census.gov/acs/www/Downloads/data_documentation/Accuracy/accuracy2008.pdf.

———. 2010c. "Methodology for the State and County Total Resident Population Estimates (Vintage 2008): April 1, 2000 to July 1, 2008." http://www.census.gov/popest/topics/methodology/2008-st-co-meth.pdf.

———. 2010d. "Special Processing Procedures for the Areas Affected by Hurricanes Katrina and Rita (Vintage 2009): April 1 2000 to July 1, 2009." http://www.census.gov/popest/topics/methodology/2009-hurr-spcl-meth.pdf.

———. 2010e. "Fact Sheet: Differences between the Income and Poverty Estimates from the American Community Survey and the Annual Social Economic Supplement to the Current Population Survey—August 26, 2008." http://www.census.gov/hhes/www/income/method/guidance/factsheet.html.

———. 2010f. "About Health Insurance." http://www.census.gov/hhes/www/hlthins/about/.

———. 2010g. "Industry and Occupation Crosswalks." http://www.census.gov/hhes/www/ioindex/crosswalks.html.

———. 2010h. "Survey of Construction Microdata Files." http://www.census.gov/const/www/surveyofconstructionmicrodatafile_cust.pdf.

———. 2010i. "County Business Patterns: Coverage and Methodology." http://www.census.gov/econ/cbp/methodology.htm.

U.S. Census Bureau. Geographic Division (GD). 2006a. "2010 Decennial Census Local Update of Census Addresses (LUCA)." http://www.census.gov/geo/www/luca2010/luca.html.

———. 2006b. "2008 Census Dress Rehearsal LUCA Program." http://www.census.gov/geo/www/luca2010/luca_DR2008.html.

———. 2009a. "Reference Resources for Understanding Census Bureau Geography." http://www.census.gov/geo/www/reference.html.

———. 2009b. "American National Standards Institute (ANSI) Codes." http://www.census.gov/geo/www/ansi/ansi.html.

U.S. Census Bureau. Manufacturing, Mining, and Construction Statistics (MMCS). 2006a. "Relationship between Building Permits, Housing Starts, and Housing Completions." http://www.census.gov/const/www/nrcdatarelationships.html.

———. 2006b. "New Residential Construction." http://www.census.gov/const/www/newresconstindex.html.

U.S. Census Bureau and U.S. Department of Housing and Urban Development (Census Bureau and HUD). 2009. "American Housing Survey 2009 National Tables." http://www.census.gov/hhes/www/housing/ahs/ahs09/ahs09.html.

U.S. Congress. House of Representatives. 2004. *American Community Survey: the Challenges of Eliminating the Long Form from the 2010 Census: Hearing Before the Subcommittee on Technology, Information Policy, Intergovernmental Relations and the Census of the Committee on Government Reform.* 108th Congr., 1st sess., May 13, 2003. SN 108–97 (May 13).

U.S. Department of Housing and Urban Development (HUD). 2009. *Valuation Analysis for Single Family One-to-Four Unit Dwellings.* Handbook 4150.2. Washington, DC: Government Printing Office. http://www.hud.gov/offices/adm/hudclips/handbooks/hsgh/4150.2/41502c8HSGH.pdf.

———. 2010. "Affordable Housing." http://www.hud.gov/offices/cpd/affordablehousing/.

———. n.d.a. "Data Sets: Fair Market Rents." http://www.huduser.org/portal/datasets/fmr.html.

———. n.d.b. "Physical Inspection Scores." http://www.huduser.org/portal/datasets/pis.html.

———. n.d.c. "Metropolitan Area Quarterly Residential and Business Vacancy Report." http://www.huduser.org/portal/datasets/usps.html.

U.S. Department of Labor. Bureau of Labor Statistics. 2009a. "How the Government Measures Unemployment." http://www.bls.gov/cps/cps_htgm.htm.

———. 2009b. "Local Area Unemployment Statistics: Estimation Methodology." http://www.bls.gov/lau/laumthd.htm.

———. 2010. "Monthly Employment Situation Report: Guide to Methods and Measurement Issues." http://www.bls.gov/bls/empsitquickguide.htm.

U.S. Department of Transportation, Bureau of Transportation Statistics (Transportation). 2002. *National Transportation Statistics.* BTS 02-08. Washington, DC: U.S. Department of Transportation

————. 2003. *NHTS 2001 Highlights Report.* BTS 03-05. Washington, DC: U.S. Department of Transportation.

U.S. General Accounting Office (GAO). 2000. *Short- and Long-Form Response Rates.* GAO/GGD-00–6. Washington, DC: Government Printing Office.

————. 2003. *Decennial Census: Methods for Collecting and Reporting Data on the Homeless and Others without Conventional Housing Need Refinement.* GAO-03–227. Washington, DC: Government Printing Office.

U.S. Government Accountability Office (GAO). 2004. *2010 Census: Cost and Design Issues Need to Be Addressed Soon.* GAO-04-37. Washington, DC: Government Printing Office.

————. 2009. *Fair Lending: Data Limitations and the Fragmented US Financial Regulatory Structure Challenge Federal Oversight and Enforcement Efforts.* GAO-09–704. Washington, DC: U.S. Government Accountability Office.

Van Auken, Paul M., Roger B. Hammer, Paul R. Voss, and Daniel L. Veroff. 2004. *American Community Survey and Census Comparison Final Analytical Report: Vilas and Oneida Counties, Wisconsin, Flathead and Lake Counties, Montana.* Madison: Applied Population Laboratory, University of Wisconsin.

Virella, Kelly. 2010. "Three Reasons New Yorkers Ignore the Census." *City Limits*, April 20, 2010. http://www.citylimits.org/news/article _ print.cfm?article _ id=3944.

Waite, Preston J., and Burton H. Reist. 2005. "Reengineering the Census of Population and Housing in the United States." *Statistical Journal of the United Nations Economic Commission for Europe* 22, no. 1: 13–23.

Webster, Bruce H., Jr. 2007. "Evaluation of Median Income and Earnings Estimates: A Comparison of the American Community Survey and the Current Population Survey." Washington, DC: U.S. Census Bureau, Housing and Household Economic Statistics Division. http://www.census.gov/acs/www/Downloads/library/2007/Evaluation _ of _ Income _ Estimates31207.pdf.

Westat. 2001. *Survey of Income and Program Participation User's Guide*, 3rd ed. Washington, DC: U.S. Census Bureau. http://www.census.gov/sipp/usrguide/sipp2001.pdf.

Wial, Howard, and Richard Shearer. 2010. "Metro Monitor: Tracking Economic Recession and Recovery in Ameria's 100 Largest Metropolitan Areas." Washington, DC: Brookings Institute Press. http://www.brookings.edu/reports/2010/0615 _ metro _ monitor.aspx.

About the authors

Heather MacDonald is course director for the master's of planning in the School of the Built Environment at the University of Technology, Sydney. Previously she was an associate professor in the graduate program in urban and regional planning at the University of Iowa. She completed her PhD at Rutgers, the State University of New Jersey. Her research has focused on affordable housing policy and finance, the links between employment and commuting, and the use of evidence in planning and policymaking. Currently she is engaged in research on housing discrimination in Australia and on the relationship between planning regulations and housing markets. With Alan Peters, she coauthored *Unlocking the Census with GIS*, published by Esri Press in 2004.

Alan Peters is a professor in the faculty of the built environment at the University of New South Wales. Previously, he held the positions of professor and chair of urban and regional planning at both the University of Iowa and the University of Sydney. Most of his work has concerned planning, economic development, and spatial policy. He has co-authored two books with Peter Fisher on economic development, *Industrial Incentives* and *State Enterprise Zone Programs*, and a book with Heather MacDonald on the census and GIS, *Unlocking the Census with GIS*. His research has been supported by various federal, state, and international organizations. He teaches courses on land economics and GIS.

Index

1930 census, 33–34

2000 Census of Population and Housing: compared to ACS, 3, 5–8, 16, 26–32; disability definition, 63–64; homeless count, 9; imputation rates for housing data, 77; language question wording, 41–44; Supplementary Survey (C2SS), 16; unemployment rates, 106

2010 census: and choice of ACS, 23; demographic measures, 55–58; and homeless count, 142–43; housing data, 29, 72–75, 146; preparation for, 9, 54; revised definition of residence, 54–55

Accuracy and Coverage Evaluations (ACE), 9

ACS. *See* American Community Survey (ACS)

addresses, 4, 8, 9, 17

administrative data, 99, 138, 142, 143, 146, 157–62

Aerometric Information Retrieval System, 136

African American population, undercounting of, 4, 5

age data, 55

AHS (American Housing Survey), 79, 91

Allocations of Low-Income Housing Tax Credits, 72

American Community Survey (ACS): compared to Census 2000, 3, 5–8, 16, 26–32; continuous vs. point-in-time measurement, 16–22; inception of, 5–6; limitations of, 23–26; release schedules for data, 6, 32, 65–66; sample error in, 7–8, 16–23, 32; sample size in, 6, 18, 27; transforming analytic framework, 15–16, 160–62

American Housing Survey (AHS), 79, 91

American National Standards Institute (ANSI) codes, 12

ancestry data, 60–61

Annual Social and Economic Supplement (ASEC), 69, 98–99, 101–2

ANSI (American National Standards Institute) codes, 12

averaging of data, 15–18, 25, 32, 79

banks and other mortgage lenders, 77, 89, 93–95, 112

building permits, 90–91

Bureau of Labor Statistics (BLS), 98, 115

Bureau of Transportation Statistics (BTS), 136, 137

businesses, 77, 111–15

C2SS (Supplementary Survey), 16, 27

caregivers, grandparents as, 60

carpooling, 20, 154–57

cartograms, 35

CBSAs (core-based statistical areas), 12

CDPs (census designated places), 112

cell phones, 81

Census 2000. *See* 2000 Census of Population and Housing

census blocks, 10–11, 129, 131

Census Bureau staff, 8, 17

census data: averaging of, 15–18, 25, 32, 79; data formats, 12–13, 65–67; follow-up to, 17, 27–29, 45, 74; fuzzy data, 23–24; geographic framework, 10–12; limitations of, 38–39; population framework, 10; release schedules for, 6, 32, 65–66; special censuses, 69; use in disasters, 139–40

census designated places (CDPs), 112

census tracts, 11, 20

Census Tracts, Qualified (QCTs), 72, 92–93

Census Transportation Planning Package (CTPP), 13, 122, 129, 130–31, 138

Center for the Study of Complex Systems, 35

CES (Current Employment Statistics), 115–16

CFS (Commodity Flow Survey), 137

childcare facilities planning, 141–45

children, 57

choropleth maps, 49

citizenship, 61–62

class of worker, 111

Clean Air Act, 125, 136, 153–54

Committee on Statistics of the Unemployed, 34

Commodity Flow Survey (CFS), 137

Community Reinvestment Act, 112

commuting: bus ridership trends, 20–23; Clean Air Act, 153–54; forecasting, 131–32; and MSA boundaries, 12; peak work-travel hours, 125, 127; place of work, 106–7; special-purpose surveys, 136–37

confidence intervals: and estimates, 7–8, 12; as overlay in maps, 25; and sample error, 20–23

confidentiality, 12, 39, 67, 138, 157

Congress. *See* U.S. Congress

construction industry: building permits, 90–91; Construction Division of Census Bureau, 90; forecasting housing demand, 72, 81, 92, 146–49; housing starts, 91–92; Survey of Construction (SOC), 91 continuous vs. point-in-time measurement, 16–22

core-based statistical areas (CBSAs), 12

cost of census, 5, 18, 55, 71

counties: boundaries of, 11–12; County Business Patterns, 115, 142; County-to-County Worker Flows, 132–33; differences in ACS data vs. Census 2000, 29–31

CPS (Current Population Survey), 69, 103, 104–5

CTPP (Census Transportation Planning Package), 13, 122, 129, 130–31, 138

Current Business Surveys, 115

Current Employment Statistics (CES), 115–16

Current Population Survey (CPS), 69, 103, 104–5

data precision, 16–18, 23–26, 39. *See also* averaging of data; synthetic data methods

data swapping, 67, 133

daytime populations, 107, 123

DDAs (Difficult Development Areas), 72

Deficit Reduction Act of 2005, 59

demographic analysis, 4

demographic and social measures: age, 55; ancestry and place of birth, 60–61; citizenship, year of entry, and migration, 61–62; disability, 63–64; educational attainment, 62–63; fertility, 59–60; grandparents as caregivers, 60; household and family structure, 55–57; language spoken at home, 61; marital status and history, 59; race and Hispanic origin, 57–58; school enrollment, 63; sex, 55; veteran status and period of military service, 64–65

demographic and social policy research design, 141–45

Department of Housing and Urban Development (HUD), 76, 78, 90–95, 99, 147

Difficult Development Areas (DDAs), 72, 92–93

disability data, 28–29, 63–64

disasters, use of census data in, 139–40

Economic Census, 98, 111–15

economic data: class of worker, 111; County Business Patterns, 115, 142; Current Employment Statistics (CES), 115–16; Economic Census, 98, 111–15; employment and labor force status, 102–6; health insurance, 101–2; income, 98–99; industry and occupation, 107–11; Local Employment Dynamics series, 116–17; place of work, 106–7; poverty status, 99–101; unemployment insurance, 116; work status and experience, 106

economic growth, 111, 115

economic multiplier, 150–52

economic policy research design, 149–53

educational attainment, 62–63

election results, 34–35, 37

employment, 102–6, 107, 111, 115–17

English competence, 45

enumeration vs. sample survey, 4–8

error. *See* nonsample error; sample error

estimating. *See also* forecasting: daytime populations, 107, 123; employment, 106, 116; household spending power, 147–48; income levels, 98–99; migration rates, 61–62, 69, 143; population, 17, 67–69, 92; subprime mortgage locations, 92; undercounts, 4–5, 8; unemployment, 33–34

ethnic groups, 9

evidence-based policymaking, 37–38, 40, 145, 161

export sector industries, 151

family structure, 55–57, 60

Fannie Mae, 94–95

farms, 77

Fatality Analysis Reporting System, 137

Federal Information Processing Standards (FIPS) codes, 12

fertility data, 59–60

FIPS (Federal Information Processing Standards) codes, 12

follow-up on census, 17, 27–29, 45, 74

forecasting: childcare demand, 142–44; economic growth, 111, 115; housing demand, 72, 81, 92, 146–49; impact of future immigration on business starts, 112; travel demand, 20–23, 122–27, 129, 153–60

foreclosed vacant homes, 145–49

Freddie Mac, 94–95

freight movement data, 137

fuzzy data, 23–24

geographic aggregation, 133

geographically uneven data, 25–26

geographic framework, 10–12

GIS systems: and data quality, 31; error margins, 9; historical data comparisons, 11; and housing conditions, 147; improving data access, 2–3, 37, 39

grandparents as caregivers, 60

group quarters, 10, 55

Hawaiian and Pacific Islanders, undercounting of, 5

Healthcare and Education Reconciliation Act of 2010, 101–2

health insurance, 101–2

Healthy Marriage Initiative, 59

Highway Congestion (Urban Mobility) study, 137

Highway Performance Monitoring System, 136–37

Hispanic origin, 57–58

histograms, 51

HMDA (Home Mortgage Disclosure Act), 93–94

home-based work, 77, 155

Homeland Security, 54

homeless population, 9, 142–43

Home Mortgage Disclosure Act (HMDA), 93–94

households, 10, 55–57, 81, 147–48

housing measures: farms vs. businesses and residences, 77; house heating fuel, 83; mortgage status and owner costs, 86–87, 89–90, 92–95; number of rooms and occupancy, 78–79; occupied and vacant units, 73–74; plumbing and kitchen facilities, 79; rents, 75, 83–85, 92; residence, definitions of, 54–55, 73; subsidized housing, 92–93; telephones, 79, 81; tenure, 74–75; units in structure, 73, 75–77; value of structure, 85–86; year householder moved into unit, 81; year structure built, 77–78

housing policy research design, 145–49

housing starts, 91–92

Housing Vacancy and Homeownership Survey (HVS), 91

HUD (Department of Housing and Urban Development), 76, 78, 90–95, 99, 147

HVS (Housing Vacancy and Homeownership Survey), 91

immigration, 61–62, 112

imputation procedures, 9, 45, 77–78, 89–90

income data, 17, 98–99

industry and occupation, 107, 109–11

information economy, 35, 107, 109–10

intelligent transportation systems (ITS), 138

journey-to-work data. *See* travel data

Kaiser Foundation, 101–2
kitchen facilities data, 79

labor force, 102–6, 123, 150–51
language: English competence, 45; groups and classes of languages, 40–41, 44; imputation of, 45; linguistic isolation,
  39–46, 61–62; spoken at home, 61
LAUS (Local Area Unemployment Statistics), 105
LEHD (Longitudinal Employer-Household Dynamics), 135–36
living quarters, 10, 55, 73, 76
local areas, 10–11, 105
Local Area Unemployment Statistics (LAUS), 105
local economic impact analysis, 149–53
Local Employment Dynamics series, 116–17
Local Update of Census Addresses (LUCA), 8, 9
long form, 5, 6
Longitudinal Employer-Household Dynamics (LEHD), 135–36
LUCA (Local Update of Census Addresses), 8

MAF (master address file), 4, 8, 17
maps. *See also* spatial scale: charting businesses, 114; communicating effectively with, 2–3, 46–47, 49; defining intervals
  for, 49, 51; overlays for confidence intervals, 25; supporting
  information, 51–52
marital status and history, 59
master address file (MAF), 4, 8, 17
MCD (Minor Civil Division), 107, 132
Metropolitan Area Quarterly Vacancy Report, 93
metropolitan planning organizations (MPOs), 129, 154
metropolitan statistical areas (MSAs), 12
microdata. *See* public use microdata sample (PUMS)
micropolitan areas, 12
migration, 61–62, 69, 81, 143
military service and veteran status, 64–65
Minor Civil Division (MCD), 107, 132
modal split, 123–24
mortgage lenders, 77, 89, 93–95, 112
Mortgage Reform & Anti-Predatory Lending Act of 2010, 89
mortgages, 86–87, 89–90, 92–95
mother tongue concept, 41
MPOs (metropolitan planning organizations), 129, 154
MSAs (metropolitan statistical areas), 12
multiplier effects, 150–52
multiracial identities, 57–58

NAFTA (North American Free Trade Area), 109
NAICS (North American Industrial Classification System),
  109–10, 112
National Air Quality Database, 136
National Household Travel Survey (NHTS), 125, 134–35
National Neighborhood Indicator Partners, 157
National Transportation Availability and Use Survey, 136
National Transportation Statistics, 137
Native Americans, 5, 8
NHTS (National Household Travel Survey), 125, 134–35
nonresponse, 6, 9, 19, 27–29, 31
nonsample error, 6–8, 18–19, 32, 45
nonwork travel, 127, 133–36
North American Free Trade Area (NAFTA), 109

North American Industrial Classification System (NAICS),
  109–10, 112
number formats in data reporting, 47, 49

occupancy rates, 73–74
occupants per room, 78–79
One Number Census, 5
opposition to census, 54
overcrowding, 78–79
oversampling, 19
ownership of homes, 74–77

Patient Protection and Affordable Care Act, 101–2
peak work-travel hours, 125, 127
place of birth data, 60–61
place of work data, 106–7
plumbing data, 79
point-in-time measurement vs. continuous, 16–22
policymaking. *See* urban policymaking, evidence-based
policy research designs. *See* urban policy research designs
political boundaries, 10, 34–35
population framework, 10
populations: African American, undercounting of, 4, 5; Current
  Population Survey (CPS), 69, 103, 104–5; daytime, 107,
  123; Hawaiian and Pacific Islanders, undercounting of, 5;
  homeless, 9, 142–43; Population Estimates Program, 17,
  67–69; population fluidity, 31
postal delivery of U.S. census, 8–9
postcensus surveys, 4–5
poverty, 19–20, 59, 60, 99–101
property valuation processes, 147
public use microdata sample (PUMS), 13, 44, 66–67, 122, 133
Puerto Rico Community Survey (PRCS), 69
PUMAs (public use microdata areas). *See* PUMS
PUMS (public use microdata sample), 13, 44, 66–67, 122, 133

Qualified Census Tracts (QCTs), 72, 92–93
quality control in census data, 38–39
Quarterly Workforce Indicators, 117

race, 28, 57–58
release schedules for census data, 6, 32, 65–66
rent data, 75, 83–85, 92
residence, definitions of, 54–55, 73
Residential Energy Consumption Survey, 83
retail business outlook, 114
rooms, number and occupants of, 78–79
rural areas, 8, 12, 34–35, 93

SAHIE (Small Area Health Insurance Estimates), 102
SAIPE (Small Area Income and Poverty Estimates), 99, 152
sample error: in ACS, 7–8, 16–23, 32; estimating size of, 6–8; in
  PUMS, 67, 133
sample frame, 8, 31
sample size: in ACS, 6, 18, 27; and Census Bureau staff, 17; and
  CPS data, 69, 105; and nonresponse rates, 31–32; and
  oversampling, 19; and spatial summaries, 12
sample survey vs. enumeration, 4–8
sex and sex ratios, 4, 55
short form, 5, 6
SIC (Standard Industrial Classification) code, 109

SIPP (Survey of Income and Program Participation), 99, 105, 106, 136
Small Area Health Insurance Estimates (SAHIE), 102
Small Area Income and Poverty Estimates (SAIPE), 99, 152
Small Business Administration, 112
SOC (Standard Occupational Classification), 109
SOC (Survey of Construction), 91
spatial analysis: accuracy of measurement, 44–45; factors being measured, 41, 44; improving access to data, 2–3, 37, 39; incorporating into urban policy, 2–3, 37–38, 161; justification for, 23–24; presentation of data, 46–52; spatial disaggregation, 136, 161; spatial summaries, 12; types of information required, 39–41
spatial scale: and charting overcrowding, 79; in choosing data parameters, 16; and confidentiality, 39, 67, 157; and data averaging, 39; in Economic Census data, 114; and errors in projections, 143; and home-based work, 155; in housing surveys, 91, 135, 147; in maps, 51; in population surveys, 69
special censuses, 69
Standard Industrial Classification (SIC) code, 109
Standard Occupational Classification (SOC), 109
statistical boundaries, 10–12
subprime mortgages, 92
subsidized housing, 92–93
summary files, 13
Super-PUMAS, 67
Supplementary Survey (C2SS), 16, 27
surveillance, criticism of census as, 54
Survey of Construction (SOC), 91
Survey of Income and Program Participation (SIPP), 99, 105, 106, 136
synthetic data methods, 105, 117, 132, 136, 138, 161

TANF (Temporary Assistance to Needy Families), 59, 60
TDM. See travel demand management
telephones, 79, 81
Temporary Assistance to Needy Families (TANF), 59, 60
time-series analysis, 25–26, 109, 111
Title 13, U.S. Code, 5, 12, 13
top-coding, 67, 133
traffic analysis zones (TAZs), 13, 129, 131
transit planning: and commuting, 20–23, 121–22; public transit and the labor market, 123; special-purpose work travel surveys, 136; and transportation analysis data, 129, 131–33, 137
transportation infrastructure, 136–37
transportation policy research design, 153–60
travel data: nonwork travel, 127, 133–37; number of persons in vehicle, 125; place of work, 123; time of departure for work, 125; usual means of transportation, 122–24; usual travel time to work, 127; vehicles available, 127
travel data reporting formats, 129, 131–37
travel demand management (TDM): evaluation of, 153–60; and traffic congestion, 122, 125, 127, 137
Traveler Opinion and Perception Survey, 136
trend filter model, 25–26

U.K. census, 5
U.S. Code, Title 13, 5, 12, 13

U.S. Congress: and census costs, 5, 18, 55, 71; census reporting, 65; congressional apportionments, 5; congressional districts and area boundaries, 10; and health insurance, 101; and housing data, 90; and mortgage industry, 94; and passing ACS, 21, 23
U.S. Postal Service, 8–9, 93
U.S. voters currently nonresidents, 10
undercounting: African American population, 4, 5; Hawaiian and Pacific Islanders, 5; of nonresident U.S. voters, 10; and urban policy, 4–5, 8; vacant housing units, 29, 73–74, 93
undocumented noncitizens, 61
unemployment, 33–34, 103–5, 116
units in structure, 73, 75–77
universe, 8, 54
urban policy and undercounting, 4–5, 8
urban policymaking, evidence-based, 37–38, 40, 145, 161
urban policy research designs: childcare facilities planning, 141–45; evaluation of TDM programs, 153–60; foreclosed vacant homes, 145–49; local economic impact analysis, 149–53
urban-rural distinction, 12, 34–35

vacant housing units, 29, 73–74, 91, 93, 145–49
vehicles, 125, 127
Veterans Administration, 64–65
voters, 10, 34–35, 37

work status, 16, 106

year householder moved into unit, 81
year of entry, 61–62

Related titles from Esri Press

GIS for the Urban Environment

ISBN: 978-1-58948-082-7

GIS for the Urban Environment is a tool for all students and practitioners who want to learn more about how they might apply GIS to urban planning, public health, urban environmental assessment, hazard and emergency management, geographic analysis, or sustainable community development. The exercises and case studies in the book present clear illustrations of GIS usage in contemporary cities and urban regions through examples of real-life applications.

Mapping Global Cities: GIS Methods in Urban Analysis

ISBN: 978-1-58948-143-5

Mapping Global Cities: GIS Methods in Urban Analysis illustrates how GIS technology can be applied to urban planning and policy challenges to enhance our efforts in providing solutions. This book is a valuable resource for urban studies and planning students, international development professionals, human settlement experts in the developing world, as well as urban planning practitioners.

Unlocking the Census with GIS

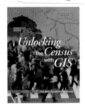

ISBN: 978-1-58948-113-8

Unlocking the Census with GIS describes how GIS can be used to better access, understand, manage, and analyze census data and census-related information and present it in a spatial format. Numerous maps, tables, sidebars, and other in-depth examples and explanations are provided to guide readers to an understanding of the census and its value to those using powerful GIS software tools.

Esri Press publishes books about the science, application, and technology of GIS.
Ask for these titles at your local bookstore or order by calling 1-800-447-9778.
You can also read book descriptions, read reviews, and shop online at www.esri.com/esripress.
Outside the United States, visit our Web site at www.esri.com/esripressorders
for a full list of book distributors and their territories.